Information for
Collective Action

Information for Collective Action

A Microanalytic View of Plural Decision-Making

Stephen S. Skjei

University of Virginia

Lexington Books
D.C. Heath and Company
Lexington, Massachusetts
Toronto   London

Library of Congress Cataloging in Publication Data

Skjei, Stephen S
    Information for collective action.

    1. Decision-making. 2. Public administration. 3. Political participation.
4. Schools–Decentralization. 5. New York (City)–Public schools. I. Title.
JF1525.D4S55   350   73–1562
ISBN 0-669-85399-2

Published simultaneously in Canada

Printed in the United States of America

International Standard Book Number: 0-669-85399-2

Library of Congress Catalog Card Number: 73-1562

1793144

To Ann Priscilla,
Ann Louise, and Stephen Daniel

Contents

List of Figures and Tables   ix

Acknowledgments   xi

Chapter 1 **Introduction**   1
           Analytical Dimensions of the Study   2
           Plan of the Study   4

Chapter 2 **Information**   9
           Facts and Values   9
           Types of Information   10
           The Production of Information   16
           The Value of Information   20
           Control and Planning   26
           Three Consequences of Planning   27
           How Much Information   32

Chapter 3 **Public Decision Systems**   47
           Decision Centers   50
           Planning Fields   53
           Subsystem Interaction   64
           An Example   69

Chapter 4 **The Control of Collective Action**   71
           Conflicting Objectives   73
           Mutually Consistent Objectives   82
           Inconsistent Objectives   91
           Information in a Public Decision System   101
           Conclusions   111

Chapter 5 **An Empirical Investigation of Plural Decision Making** 115
           The Proposal Developed by the Mayor's Panel   117
           The Mayor's Plan   121
           The Teachers' Union Proposals   123
           Plans Prepared by the Demonstration School Districts   125
           Plans Developed by the Board of Education   127
           Information Developed by Other Participants   130

The Legislature 136
Useful Information 139
Assessment 150
Alternative Interpretations 153

Chapter 6 **The Provision of Adequate Control Capability** 161
Two Possible Approaches 161
Assessment 167

Notes 169

Index 187

About the Author 189

List of Figures and Tables

Figures

2.1	Contribution of Alternative Solutions to Relevant Objectives and Representation as an Array	15
2.2	Minimizing the Costs of Information for Purposes of Maximal Control	37
3.1	An Organizational Chart for Local Government	48
4.1	Information Produced by a Benefit Conscious Participant Given Increasing Expectations About the Value of Information	78
4.2	Alternative Benefit, Social Cost and Resource Expenditure Changes Revealed by Planning	100

Tables

2.1	The Ideal Planning Process and the Production of Information	17
4.1	Framework for Analysis of Plural Decision Making	73

Acknowledgments

A number of persons have contributed their time in reviewing and commenting on this study. To Dr. Maynard M. Hufschmidt, Dr. George C. Hemmens, Dr. Michael Brooks, Dr. Richard C. Bolan, and Dr. Lynn A. Pollnow the author would like to express his deep gratitude and thanks. Also the author owes the deepest debt of gratitude to his wife without whose help this study could never have been completed.

Chapter One
Introduction

Citizen participation. Government by the people. Involvement. Community control. Decentralization. These are the watchwords of a reaction to decades of governmental reform which has succeeded all too well in placing the delivery of governmental services in the hands of large bureaucracies and in centralizing the formal power and authority to decide. Decisions are made downtown, not in the neighborhoods. Programs are designed and implemented by the authority or special purpose district or a hired bureaucrat, not the people. In some cases the result is equal treatment of all, which is unsatisfactory to some. Thus the rules and regulations of an educational bureaucracy may insure that equipment, supplies and instructional programs are similar throughout a city. Such uniformity ignores the varying needs of children from different socio-economic backgrounds, and therefore for some communities the educational program is unsatisfactory. In other cases there is unequal treatment of citizens, which is satisfactory to some. Urban renewal and urban highway construction are illustrative. They have promoted the interests of the affluent at the expense of the poor. Thus the reaction.

American society may now be entering the participatory era on a broad scale. Yet little direct evidence exists to suggest what might be expected from such change. Will it be good or bad? It is difficult to say, for the answer depends on the perspective taken. Participatory decision making may be an important means by which the individual can overcome his alienation and identify himself with the collectivity. Involvement may generate a feeling of belonging, a sense of significance. In addition, it may bring about the realization of a traditional goal, government of, by, and for the people. Equally as important, in a plural society, i.e., a society fractured into numerous relatively independent organizations and interest groups, participation in public decision making may improve the likelihood that public programs and policy contribute effectively to ends. A number of authors have asserted that participatory decision making may produce outcomes superior to those generated by a highly centralized choice process. Banfield suggests that "the more complicated the problem, the stronger the case" for a participatory process.[1] Etzioni observes that "the less restricted the *participation* [in public decision making] , the more effective will be the knowledge *supply*; and the . . . more effective will be the societal course followed."[2] In a seminal contribution to the literature of professional planning Davidoff reached similar conclusions.[3] Lastly, Lindblom asserts that a multiplicity of decision makers, each participating in some aspect of a public choice process, is "a great strength" for it "copes with the inevitability of omission and other errors in complex problem solving."[4]

The present study attempts to amplify these conclusions. Based on the premise advanced by Wiener that "to live effectively is to live with adequate information,"[5] it asks the following question: can the actions of a society or collectivity be effectively controlled, that is, effectively directed to ends, using the information voluntarily produced by those members who participate in the public decision making process? This question is somewhat complex, and the answer to it is dependent on a number of factors. For example, the perspective participants in a plural decision making process take toward a problem, whether it be parochial or altruistic, influences the data they produce and their comprehension of the problem situation. Similarly the structure of power or influence among participants will affect the extent of their individual involvement, the time and other resources they will expend in analyzing a problem and the potential solutions to it, and thus the ability of decision makers depending on them for information to determine the best course of action to take. Given the complexity that surrounds the question of control, knowing that in general participatory choice mechanisms are superior to centralized ones leaves many unanswered questions. It does not, in particular, establish the effectiveness or desirability of participatory mechanisms; they as well as centralized mechanisms may be inadequate.

In sum, this is a microanalytic study of the potential within a society for control of the actions that its members undertake as a collectivity.[6] It explores the behavior of participants in the public arena. What are their contributions to the society's ability to attain its objectives? What factors limit the contributions they might make? In the aggregate or individually, do their plans and proposals provide an adequate basis for controlling collective action?

Analytical Dimensions of the Study

In looking at the operation of participatory processes three analytical dimensions may be distinguished. First there is the decision to collect data. How much information should be generated in any problem situation? Without any information a problem cannot be defined, there is no ability to choose and thus no question of control capability. On the other hand, with complete or perfect information uncertainty about the precise nature of a problem or the best means for eliminating it is at a minimum or nonexistent. With complete information a decision maker knows which of his goals are relevant criteria for the evaluation of alternatives and he knows their priorities. He possesses the most precise estimates and assessments of both environmental conditions and the potential consequences of any course of action. Here control capability is at a maximum and any doubt that may exist about the appropriate response to a problem cannot be reduced or eliminated by further efforts to acquire information.

Between these two extremes of no information and complete information lie the problem situations which usually confront decision makers. The uncertainty that characterizes these problem situations is, of course, not incapacitating. Decisions can be made and action can be taken in the face of it. However confidence in the decisions made will not be complete. Whether the right problem has been solved will be in doubt. Uncertainty which could have been reduced by the acquisition of more information will exist about the actual consequences of action. With better information about environmental conditions or the consequences of any alternative a different decision might have been made. Accordingly, in responding to a problem resources may be misallocated. The "wrong" problem may be solved; an unnecessary or an unsatisfactory alternative may be implemented; unexpected environmental conditions may change the nature of the problem or the consequences of action from what was anticipated.

By acquiring information the probability of such a resource misallocation can be reduced and control capability can be increased. Prior to action the more information available and the more precise it is the less uncertain are the consequences of action and the more likely is achievement of desired goals. Yet information is not a sufficient condition for control. The very notion of action indicates that the concept has another aspect, that of power or authority to allocate resources. Without this an actor will not be able to direct means to ends no matter how precise and well analyzed his plans may be. But power alone is also not a sufficient condition for control. In the absence of adequate planning means will not achieve ends. The two aspects of control are interrelated; each is necessary, and together both may be sufficient for the existence of control.

Power is the second analytical dimension of this study, especially as it affects participatory activity. In some problem situations one or a few participants will be able to determine the course of action to be taken. Through the exercise of power or influence they can insure that their viewpoints dominate the decision-making process. In other problem situations several participants may exercise some power but no participant possesses the ability to insure that his viewpoint dominates. In still other problem situations participants may not possess any power except that of their ideas, plans, and proposals. No participant has any reason to expect that his viewpoint is more likely than that of other participants to dominate. In this study the use of power by participants to obtain a public decision favorable to their interests is not directly examined since this particular aspect of control has been explored in depth by political scientists.[7] Instead the possession or lack of power is explored from the standpoint of its effect on a participant's planning activities. Whose views dominate is not as important here as is the effect of power on a participant's expenditure of time and other resources for the development of information which might be used by a decision maker to determine the best response to a problem.

The third analytical dimension is the motivation of participants. What induces them to become involved? Do they seek to advance parochial objectives or do they pursue broader concerns and thus in some sense further the public interest through their involvement? These questions do not have a single answer, and so participants are assumed to be motivated by a variety of interests, ranging from pure self-interest to altruism. The implications of each of these for control in plural decision making are examined.

Although the objectives of participants may be uncertain, their general behavior in pursuit of these objectives is assumed not to be. For the purposes of this study the production and exchange of information are the essential characteristics of participation in public debate. Negotiation, bargaining, criticism, and the proposing of alternatives involve the exchange of information and require the collection or analysis of data. Participants cannot determine what they seek from involvement, what their objectives should be or how these objectives should be obtained without producing data themselves. The question is how adequate a guide for collective action is the information participants produce? What are the characteristics of the data participants produce vis-à-vis the information needed to control collective action? The answers to these questions, which reflect the first analytical dimension of this study, are evolved in terms of the other two analytical dimensions. The decision to collect information, participant motivations, and the possession or lack of power are combined in an analysis of the inherent capability of plural decision-making processes to determine or discover those public programs and policies which will constitute the most effective response to a problem.

Plan of the Study

Each of the three analytical dimensions of this study is discussed separately and then combined with the others in an analysis of plural decision making. This conceptual analysis is followed by an empirical investigation of the New York City school decentralization debate of 1967-69.[8] The debate casts light on certain unavoidable ambiguities of the conceptual analysis and indicates how well it reflects reality.

A minimum of assumptions is employed in the analysis. Wherever possible an effort has been made to encompass complexity rather than exclude it by means of an appropriate assumption. Nevertheless, abstraction does enter the analysis, particularly in the central discussion of information produced by participants. That discussion proceeds by establishing an ideal model of the decision to produce information. This model neither asserts the objectives that participants seek to obtain nor the objectives which should be relevant for collective action. In particular it does not demand that a broad concept of the public interest be served by the collective action taken in response to a problem nor does it require that participants recognize such a concept. Instead a degree of verisimilitude is obtained in the model by recognizing that in the design and evaluation of public programs and public policy the interests of all individuals, groups, and organizations that might be affected are often not considered and that participants may take a variety of perspectives and attitudes toward their involvement in the public decision making process. The model also does not set complete or perfect information as a standard. An economic criterion which requires that the costs of any unit of information be justified by its expected benefits is used to establish how much data should be developed in any problem situation. Using this relative standard, conclusions about the control capability inherent in plural decision making are obtained.

Several assumptions are implicit in the model. First and most important, participants are assumed to determine the amount of information they should produce consciously and efficiently. As will become apparent, even if this assumption is relaxed the conclusions are not necessarily endangered; in fact they may be strengthened. Second, participants are assumed to communicate what data they do produce completely, and it is assumed to be received without distortion. Again relaxing this assumption would appear primarily to strengthen, not weaken the results. Third, it is assumed that the greater the number of people affected by a public decision the more valuable is information pertinent to that decision likely to be. This assumption appears self-evident.

In sum, the conceptual analysis attempts to derive implications about plural decision making from a small number of assumptions about participant behavior and the production of information. Yet abstraction does enter into the analysis, and in order to judge some of its effects an empirical study of the 1967-69 school decentralization debate in New York City is included.

The School System Debate: Background

With an enrollment of more than 1,100,000 students, the New York City school system has a service population which exceeds the resident population of all but the six largest cities in the United States. The value of the resources used in operating this urban service system, over 1.2 billion dollars in 1968, was double the total local governmental expenditures of the city of Baltimore in 1968-69. In addition the human resources available in the city schools, approximately 55,000 teachers in 1967, exceeded by 18,000 the total number of full- and part-time employees of that city. Appropriately the debate about the future of this immense service system involved a large number of participants. A broad spectrum of established interest groups from across the city participated, and new groups such as the Teachers for Community Control emerged primarily to articulate the viewpoints of their members. Both because so many participants were involved and because so much apparently could be gained or lost by redesigning the school system, the debate about its future affords a significant basis for assessing the control capability of plural decision making. While this case study does not illustrate the complete range of conclusions that emerge from the conceptual analysis, it does cast light on a number of important issues and the degree to which abstraction in that analysis distorts the conclusions about reality obtained from it.

The impetus for decentralization dates back at least to a 1940 study by Cillié,[9] who compared community schools in the centralized city system with those in decentralized systems elsewhere in the state. Cillié concluded that neither complete centralization nor complete decentralization but some combination of the two was needed "before the ultimate goal of educational adaptation" could be achieved.[10] From 1940 to 1967 a number of additional studies were undertaken. In 1947 Westby recognized the potential contributions that community involvement could make to control.[11] He suggested that administrators who worked with community residents would more quickly recognize school short-comings and more readily solve problems. In 1948 Beach came to similar conclusions.[12] The functioning of local schools could be significantly improved by community involvement. Better information about problems and alternatives would be available for guiding decisions. In a decentralized system not only parents but also teachers would be encouraged to report shortcomings in physical plant and educational programs and to suggest alternative solutions.[13]

In 1966 a commission on city finances found that four major problems plagued the school system: insufficient municipal involvement, slow response to change, inadequate funds, and budgets which provided no means of control.[14, 15] The commission recommended that the school system be decentralized. In addition to opening the system up to parents and making it more manageable, decentralization might qualify the city schools for increased state educational subsidies. Since state aid was computed on the total assessed valuation of property in a city, in New York the very high valuation of property in Manhattan had the effect of obscuring the relatively low value of property in the other four boroughs. Computing state aid on a borough rather than on a citywide basis would yield substantial additional revenues.[16]

This official call for school decentralization was soon supplemented by demands in several communities for local control of schools. A group called the Peoples' Board of Education in East Harlem sought greater community involvement and a "suitable 'black image' for pupils" after it recognized that a new intermediate school, I.S. 201, would not be integrated.[17] Peoples' boards were also formed in other communities to pursue similar ends.

In early 1967 the mayor made his annual pilgrimage to Albany seeking more state educational aid. Acting perhaps in accordance with the findings of the Temporary Commission on City Finances, he suggested that the city school system be treated as five separate borough systems. The legislature's response was a bill, passed on April 24, 1967, requiring the mayor to prepare a plan for greater community participation in educational decision making by December 1, 1967.[18] Additional aid would require a school system which actually was decentralized.

Tension between the city Board of Education and the mayor over the issue of school decentralization existed almost from the time of the mayor's request for additional aid.[19] Concurrent with legislative debate over the mayor's proposal, the board moved to implement its own decentralization proposal. A plan, prepared in early February and revised after public hearings in March,[20] was approved by the board on April 19, 1967. As part of the proposal the board announced its intention to experiment on a limited basis with various forms of community involvement. In July 1967 three experimental school decentralization districts were created, one in Ocean Hill-Brownsville (Brooklyn), one in Harlem, and one in the lower East Side of Manhattan.[21] The first of these was to have a major role in bringing about the teachers strikes of 1968.

In late April 1967, Mayor Lindsay appointed a panel of educational and welfare experts, headed by the president of the Ford Foundation, McGeorge Bundy, to prepare a plan for the decentralization of the city school system. By early November 1967 the panel had completed its plan and the debate was about to begin in earnest. Few issues have had the impact on the citizenry of New York City that school decentralization did. By 1969, when the New York state legislature acted to enable "a community school district system in the city of New York,"[22] the debate had raged over such issues as the appropriate goals of a decentralized system, the amount of power to be invested in community school boards, the protection of teachers' rights, the method of allocating resources, and the procedure for electing representatives to local school boards. During the two years when the fate of the school system was in doubt many groups voiced opinions, prepared plans, and testified at hearings held by legislative committees, the Board of Education and the New York City Human Rights Commission. The school system debate was plural decision making on a large scale over a significant and substantial urban service system. It would seem, therefore, to be an appropriate basis from which to assess the conceptual arguments of this study.

Chapter Two
Information

Facts and Values

Any discussion of information and its role in decision making probably must begin with the distinction that can be made between facts and values.[1] In concept both are a form of information. Values indicate what should be or what is thought appropriate. For example, profit maximization is an objective of the firm; it is something the firm should accomplish. Similarly clean air, integration, and equal opportunity are objectives of American society. They should be obtained; public and private action should be structured so that contributions are made to these objectives, i.e., progress is made toward them. Strictly interpreted "facts" indicate what is, but when uncertainty is present facts can only indicate what is likely to be. Thus it is a fact that the New York City school system budget in 1972 was 1.6 billion dollars and that this represented an expenditure of approximately $1,400 per student. On the other hand it may be true that the interstate highway system will be completed in 1975 or that the academic achievement of public school students does not vary with class size. These three statements contain "facts" in that their truth or falsity can be established by empirical investigation. This is not the case with respect to values, which do not carry a dimension of truth or falsity. Values, objectives, and goals may appear in statements about what is desired and these statements conceivably could be examined for their truth or falsity. But the values, objectives, and goals cannot.

From a decision-making perspective facts are meaningless without values. The often repeated observation that two individuals in the possession of the same facts can disagree reflects this.[2] While disagreement over the truth or falsity of factual statements can be resolved by empirical observation, lasting disagreement may exist over the interpretation of these statements because this depends upon the values the individuals hold. Only if one of the two individuals adopts the values of the other can their difference of opinion be eliminated. Only then will their interpretations of the facts be the same and only then will they reach the same conclusions about what should be done in view of the facts.

Frequently the claim is made that facts cannot be distinguished from values.[3] To a degree this is misleading. The interpretation or significance of any fact depends implicitly upon a value or a set of values which may be difficult to distinguish. But facts alone carry no normative or evaluative significance. Knowing the 1972 school budget is of little significance to an elected official not concerned with the objective of governmental efficiency (what was obtained for such an expenditure), the objective of reducing taxes, or some set of educational objectives. Facts can exist and factual statements can be made without an implied or attached value element. Moreover, values can be discussed without an appeal to facts. As the analysis of the school decentralization debate will illustrate, those who become involved in public decision making are often advocates for a cause. As such they are in the position of reaffirming values and they do so frequently without any recourse to facts.

Just as facts without values lack significance, values without facts are useless for decision-making purposes. They may also be confusing. Real contributions cannot be made to objectives without some understanding of the material world. Facts are needed to design, direct, and evaluate alternative courses of action which might achieve ends. In addition, facts are useful in distinguishing among ends and determining their relative priority. By revealing what is possible in any problem situation they cast light on what is desirable. Without them a decision maker is left with an overwhelming array of goals among which he may not be able to differentiate. Thus facts and values are interrelated; one without the other is of marginal or no value.

Rational Decision Making

Establishing which objectives are relevant in any problem situation and how they may be obtained is not a costless process. The production of information consumes resources which have alternative uses. For this reason the concept of a rational decision must be distinguished from the process of rational decision making. A decision is rational (or optimal) with respect to a set of objectives. Thus an entrepreneur acts rationally with respect to the objective of profit maximization when he undertakes the course of action which will make the greatest contribution to that objective. Similarly an elected official may exercise a form of political rationality when his position on an issue reflects that of his financial backers or a majority of the electorate.[4] A rational decision thus depends upon a determination of appropriate objectives (for the entrepreneur profit maximization and for the official reelection) to guide choice and implies the selection of a course of action which will make the greatest contributions to those objectives.[5]

Rational decision making, on the other hand, recognizes that the costs of reaching a rational decision may exceed the benefits. Information which will eliminate uncertainty about appropriate objectives or the range of alternatives is, like any other commodity, not costless. Unless its costs are exceeded by the gains expected from solving the right (as opposed to the wrong) problem or finding a less expensive alternative, it should not be acquired. Because decisions can and should be made in the face of uncertainty, the objective of rational decision making is not a rational decision. It is the efficient use of resources in the decision-making process to acquire control, the ability to direct means to ends.

Types of Information

What Is Information?

Some problem situations occur so frequently that a standardized set of procedures may be developed for responding to them. Civil service regulations and the rules by which government contracts are granted provide good examples. The former are applied daily in decisions about who shall be employed in the public sector and how, as employees, they shall be treated. The latter are used just as regularly to determine from whom the government will purchase goods and services. Zoning laws, traffic codes, and the institutions for their enforcement function, from a decision-making perspective, in much the same way. They provide a uniform response mechanism to problems that reoccur with great frequency. Rules and regulations such as these are used not only to insure fairness and equal treatment but also to eliminate uncertainty. They establish the objectives and criteria which are relevant in each individual instance of a problem situation which reappears repeatedly and they specify the alternative courses of action which may constitute an appropriate response.[6] They thus may be viewed as eliminating uncertainty and the need to acquire information in these problem situations.

Standardized procedures for dealing with recurrent problems may be evolved in a number of ways. They may emerge from a process of trial and error. The frequent reappearance of a problem provides the opportunity for learning by experience how to respond to it successfully. Rules and regulations then become a codification of this experience which is intended to insure a successful response to individual instances of the problem. At the other extreme a set of standardized procedures may be consciously and deliberately created. Appropriate rules and regulations then become the product of an investigation or investigations to determine to what ends they should be directed and what their structure and content should be.

Not all problem situations appear with enough frequency to permit or justify the development of a routine response mechanism. Even though previous experience with similar or related problem situations may provide some guidance, significant uncertainty about how to respond in any problem situation may still exist. Rational decision making may suggest that some information be developed. When it is used in decision making, information takes on its significance and relevance from the uncertainty it is intended to eliminate. If it does not clarify the ambiguity that surrounds a problem situation and does not increase the likelihood that the decision made will contribute to desired ends, information is of little value. It is noise and it may heighten uncertainty by diverting attention from what is relevant. For example, the relative inability of many children in public schools to read and write can rarely be understood in terms of expenditures per child or student-teacher ratios. More than a decade of research indicates that over a wide range of variation student-teacher ratios have little effect on educational quality,[7] and one of the largest social science investigations ever undertaken suggests that variations in expenditures per child are related only slightly to variation in achievement.[8] Poor school performance cannot be understood in terms of these factors. Instead they speciously redirect concern for that problem to the question of teacher work conditions, upon which they do reflect. Accordingly in responding to the problem of poor student educational achievement they may either be viewed as noise or as expanding the scope of the problem and thus the total amount of uncertainty surrounding the solution to it.

Three categories of information can be distinguished as relevant in any problem situation. First, problem data defines the problem. It clarifies or articulates the needs that must be met, the objectives against which any alternative solution should be evaluated, and the relative priority of different needs and objectives. Second, problem environment information reveals the constraints (for example, legal, technological, social, political) that restrict the range of possible solutions and the general environmental conditions which will affect the contributions any potential solution will make to the various objectives. To be of any actual value, these two types of information must be supplemented by a third, information about the alternative means of solving a problem, which indicates the nature, characteristics and consequences of the actions or programs that can be implemented. Each of these types of information reduces and may eliminate a different type of uncertainty, and each will be needed only if the type of uncertainty which it eliminates is present in a problem situation. Thus the type of uncertainty that exists in a problem situation determines the type and the nature of the information that will be relevant.[9] Whether that information should be collected, however, depends on economic factors. The question of concern, then, is will the cost of information expected to lead to a better decision be justified or will the errors that inevitably result from acting in the face of uncertainty be so minor that the costs of acquiring information will exceed in value the benefits expected from reaching a better decision?

Problem Information

The initiation of a decision-making procedure or a commitment to action is usually motivated by an objective which may loosely be described as that of "solving the problem." To determine exactly what the problem is, however, requires two types of information. First, the factual nature of a problem, its physical, social, economic, legal, and other dimensions, must be specified. The failure of central city schools, for example, can be understood in terms of a number of different dimensions, some of which can be expressed quantitatively (reading scores) and some of which cannot (socialization of students).[10] Moreover, effective action cannot be undertaken without knowing who cannot read or who cannot cope with modern society, the numbers of students who fall short and by how much or in what ways, and how these problems develop over time.[11] Rarely is the initial perception of any problem this detailed. Accordingly time and other resources must usually be spent in collecting data to refine the original description of the nature and extent of a problem before effective action can be directed against it.

Second, the normative criteria to be used in evaluating any potential response to a problem must be established. The alternative ways of responding to any problem can often be distinguished by the different degrees to which they contribute to objectives other than that of solving the problem. A decision must be made about which of these objectives may or should be ignored and about the relative priority or ranking of those which are to guide the design and evaluation of a solution. Should efforts to solve the problem of school system failure also be efficient, i.e., should the benefits expected from the last unit of resources committed to solving the problem equal the value of those resources in alternative uses? Should community participation be another objective? What is the relative importance of this objective with respect to the efficiency objective?

Uncertainty about appropriate objectives or their relative priority can frequently be reduced by an appreciation of the alternative means of achieving these objectives. An analysis of alternatives will provide evidence about the degree to which various objectives may be achieved and the consequences of using any objective to guide action. It not only provides a basis for determining the relative priority of objectives but will also reveal previously unrecognized conflicts among objectives and will suggest additional objectives to be considered in responding to the problem. For example, a reading skills improvement program can be designed to contribute to the goal of parental involvement and still be efficient. At some point, however, contributions to one of these objectives will require that contributions to the other be reduced, resulting in increasing degrees of parental involvement being obtained only at the expense of the efficiency objective and vice versa. After looking at the alternative programs, conflict between the efficiency objective and the previously unrecognized objective of teacher job security may also become apparent. To reconcile these conflicts and yet permit all objectives to influence the final decision, the relative importance of contributions to each objective must be determined. Once the relative priority of the three objectives has been established the ranking of one alone cannot usually be changed; the three objectives are now an interdependent set; even a marginal change in the ranking of one may require that the relative importance of the others be reconsidered.

Problem Environment Information

The solution to a problem cannot be designed or evaluated without some knowledge of the economic, demographic, social, political, legal, and physical environment within which it will function. Problem environment information indicates those factors and conditions which will affect the consequences of action but which in any problem situation cannot be controlled by the decision maker. Economic and demographic projections are obvious examples. They reveal future conditions which will affect the performance of any alternative but whose character and nature is autonomously determined. In a similar way other environmental conditions must often be taken as a given. These conditions will affect the degree to which any course of action advances ends and so must be recognized in designing the response to a problem.

Frequently absolute certainty about environmental conditions cannot be established. No expenditure of resources, however great, can completely eliminate uncertainty about the magnitude of future residential development or the level of future commercial activity. Nor can uncertainty about conditions in the physical environment, such as the timing and magnitude of a flood or thermal inversion, be reduced beyond the probability distributions which describe the likelihoods of their occurrence at various scales. Some time after action has been taken the accuracy of estimates of these environmental conditions can be judged. But at the time a decision is made, uncertainty about them and thus the consequences of action affected by them will of necessity exist.

Although uncertainty about the problem environment in many cases cannot be eliminated, the same is not necessarily true for uncertainty about the nature of the problem or uncertainty about the range of alternatives. These uncertainties reflect ignorance and can in concept be eliminated by additional analysis and investigation. In this respect they differ from the uncertainties which exist about environmental conditions, but they have the same implications for the control of action.

Alternatives Information

Information about alternatives reduces or eliminates uncertainty about the range of solutions to a problem, about the attributes of any course of action, and about the consequences of implementing any course of action. To some extent determining the range of alternatives is a creative act, and to some extent it is a matter of surveying and cataloguing known solutions. Normally information about the attributes of any alternative (for example, the vehicular capacity of a bridge) is combined with information about the problem environment in an analysis, which often may be quite costly, to obtain information about the consequences of action (for example, the degree of racial integration resulting from new school district boundaries). Although it does include assessments of the consequences of implementing any course of action, information about alternatives does not include the evaluation or ranking of different solutions to a problem. Information is, of course, produced when alternatives are ranked because uncertainty about the best response to a problem is reduced, but this type of information depends upon and summarizes the problem, problem environment and alternatives data that has been collected. Information about alternatives merely reveals the range of alternatives and the attributes and consequences of any course of action. It answers three questions: what can be done, what are the characteristics of relevant alternatives, and what contribution to a given objective will be made by a given alternative?

The evaluation of alternatives is ultimately the reason why problem, problem environment, and alternatives information is acquired. Normally the process of evaluation requires that problem environment and alternatives information be analyzed in terms of problem information, but this need not always be the case. To illustrate, suppose that the only objective considered relevant in a problem situation is that of solving a problem which has only one dimension. Then alternatives can be ranked directly by the degree to which they appear likely, given environmental conditions, to solve the problem. That alternative which promises

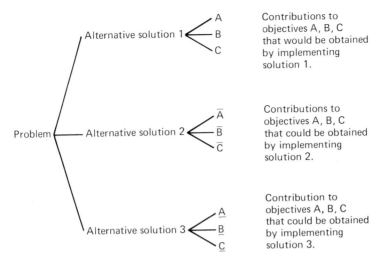

Figure 2-1. Contribution of Alternative Solutions to Relevant Objectives and Representation as an Array.

to reduce the problem to the greatest degree will be implemented. On the other hand, suppose that several objectives are considered relevant in a problem situation and that a set of alternatives exists, each of whose members appears likely to make contributions to each of these objectives. After the needed problem environment and alternatives data has been collected, each of the alternative responses to the problem may be represented by an array of elements which indicates the contribution to each objective an alternative is expected to make. Evaluation of the set of alternatives can then be undertaken in terms of these arrays. If one array is clearly and unambiguously superior to the rest, then the alternative which it represents should be implemented because it makes the greatest contributions to all objectives. Often, however, no alternative will be unambiguously superior. Some alternatives will make outstanding contributions to some objectives and inferior contributions to others. To evaluate the set of alternatives, the elements of each array must be combined to form a single index of relative merit. This can be done with the problem information that establishes the relative importance of contributions to each objective. By multiplying each element of an array by the weight or trade-off ratio indicating its relative importance and summing the products for all elements in an array, an index for each alternative can be obtained. Ranking these indices ranks the alternatives. Thus evaluation depends upon and to a great degree simply summarizes problem, problem environment, and alternatives data.

Feedback

Whenever a decision is based on less than complete information, its consequences are not certain. After action is taken inadequacies in the initial solution will appear because objectives were not completely understood and alternatives not thoroughly investigated. Unanticipated consequences will arise, because expectations about the problem environment were incorrect and also because knowledge of the attributes of the alternative implemented was deficient. Post-decision data or feedback can be developed to remedy these shortcomings. Three types of feedback may be used: problem, problem environment, and alternatives. They are analogous to the pre-decision data of each type and serve the same general purpose, to reduce uncertainty. From a decision making perspective reliance on feedback to determine the best response to a problem may be desirable. Rational decision making may dictate the use of feedback rather than pre-decision data where (a) the benefits lost from doing so appear to be limited, (b) the resources committed initially to a solution are limited, and (c) the costs of correcting deficiencies in an original decision are expected to be low. If in these situations the difficultues and costs involved in collecting pre-decision data are great, action in the face of great uncertainty, that is with little pre-decision data, may be the best response. Post-decision efforts to correct deficiencies can be made in view of the information gained from the passage of time and the lessons of experience and may ultimately provide a better and cheaper solution to the problem. For example, the timing of a directional traffic light at a busy intersection may be accomplished most expediently by trial and error. Elaborate analysis may not be justified if observations on the effectiveness of various timing strategies can easily be made and corrective action can readily be taken when deficiencies become apparent.

The Production of Information

In any problem situation control over the quantity of information available for a decision can be exercised through the choice of a planning process, the set of procedures in accordance with which information is produced. By varying these procedures from the very intuitive to the very rigorous, alternative planning processes are obtained which will yield alternative quantities of information.[12] Corresponding to the types of information needed for decision making, four general stages of an ideal planning process, each composed of different planning tasks, may be distinguished. Associated with information about the nature of the problem are the following tasks: analysis of needs, determination of objectives, operational definition of objectives, and specification of standards and criteria. Comprising stage I, these tasks indicate those actions which can and often must be taken to define the problem. The three tasks of stage II, basic studies, construction of projections, and development of an analytical model, relate to the development of information about the problem environment. Corresponding to information about the alternatives are the two tasks of stage III, systems synthesis and systems assessment. Stage IV, feedback and review of both the results of previous planning stages and the effectiveness of collective action, is associated with the production of feedback. Table 2-1 gives a paradigm of these associations.

**Table 2-1. The Ideal Planning Process and the
Production of Information**

Type of Information	Stage and Tasks of the Ideal Planning Process
Nature of problem	(I) Analysis of needs Determination of objectives Operational definition of objectives Specification of standards and criteria
Problem environment	(II) Basic studies: resource potentials and needs Projections Analytical model
Type and consequences of alternatives	(III) Systems synthesis Systems assessment
Feedback	(IV) Feedback-review

The four tasks in stage I of the ideal planning process contribute to the identification of the problem. Analysis of needs and determination of objectives can be viewed as establishing respectively the factual and the normative nature of the problem. Operational definition of objectives and specification of standards and criteria rigorously indicate what is meant by objectives. An operational definition states the operations that must be undertaken to measure objective attainment. Standards and criteria such as the time horizon, the relative weights to be accorded various objectives, and acceptable levels of output or system performance are related to or derived from objectives. The three tasks in stage II of the ideal planning process identify various aspects of the problem environment. Basic studies reveal natural and human resource quantities and qualities and identify other attributes of the problem environment such as the values of important environmental parameters. Projections specify levels of future needs primarily through analysis of future demographic factors, rates of resource utilization, and related environmental factors affecting success of the implemented solution. Development of analytical models combines projections, parameter estimates, and other environmental studies into a coherent whole for the purpose of designing and evaluating alternative solutions. Stage III of the ideal planning process employs information developed in the preceding stages to define the range and attributes of appropriate alternatives (systems synthesis) and their consequences (systems assessment). Stage IV, feedback-review, provides information about the results of completed tasks in any previous stage and about the success of the implemented solution. Reviewing the results of the systems assessment task in stage III, for example, may suggest new objectives, new alternatives, new consequences, or the need for more data about the problem environment. Feedback-review after implementation produces information about the adopted solution which can be used to revise it.

In the ideal model a planning agency is assumed to be responsible for the completion of all tasks and operations within each of the four stages. Through its selection of procedures for completing each task the planning agency determines the amount of problem, problem environment, and alternatives data available prior to a decision and the amount of feedback available after action has been taken. However, in the ideal model the work of the planning agency is reviewed by elected officials, who may suggest additional analyses or studies and who must aid it in the analysis of needs and the determination of objectives (stage I). In addition, the evaluation of alternatives is prepared by the planning agency for the review and approval of these officials. The ideal model thus distinguishes clearly between decision making and information acquisition; the latter function is the province of civil servants, whereas the former is seen as the domain of elected officials. The separation of these two functions cannot be complete, however. Information must guide decision making, but the purposes of any decision can *only* be established by elected officials. The technicians who provide the facts must be guided and directed by those responsible for establishing the purpose of collective action and responsible, therefore, for the bases for interpreting those facts. In this way the ideal model assures (in concept at least) that facts will be relevant and that technicians do not unilaterally impose their values on the electroate.[13]

Types of Planning Processes

Using the outlined ideal planning process, alternative processes may be obtained in three ways. First, various tasks or combinations of tasks in any stage of the ideal process may be omitted completely. Second, while any given process may contain all tasks in each stage of the ideal process, unlike the ideal it may place differential weight or emphasis on one or more stages. Third, planning processes may be formed by omitting some tasks and stages and placing differential emphasis on others. In professional planning practice this last approach seems to be a common way to generate a process. Planning agencies frequently form processes from the ideal by omitting or underemphasizing one or both tasks in stage III (systems synthesis and systems assessment) and internally applying stage IV (feedback-review). For example, the process by which comprehensive end-state master plans are produced often underemphasizes the two tasks of stage III. These plans rarely contain alternatives; and if their single proposals are evaluated, the analysis is usually intuitive and truncated.[14] To compensate, the process by which they are generated may emphasize stage IV. Through sequential review an initial idea may be modified at the conclusion of stages I, II, and III, and a number of alternatives may in fact be generated. However, emphasizing stage IV and neglecting stage III creates a process in which the information produced may not be as comprehensive as that obtained from the ideal process and may not eliminate uncertainty to the extent that the ideal process would. Although successive end-state master plans usually become more detailed, they will be analyzed sequentially and possibly in terms of different sets of objectives. As a consequence, substantial uncertainty may remain about which set of objectives is appropriate and, therefore, about which alternative is superior. Nevertheless, in some situations a planning process with this output may be entirely acceptable.

Other examples of planning processes obtained by modifying the ideal model may be cited. In some problem situations the Critical Path Method (CPM) and Program Evaluation Review Technique (PERT) may represent variants of the ideal model which contain its four stages but accord differential weight to systems assessment and problem environment analysis.[15] In developing a public works project schedule through CPM and PERT, the vast number of separate tasks which must be completed are ordered so as to minimize the construction period. After detailed analysis of the problem environment, the range, and the consequences of alternative schedules, the sequence of individual tasks which will implement the project in the minimum time period is selected. In this problem situation there is little need for detailed analysis of objectives. The single objective, minimization of the implementation period or costs, is usually known and its operational definition is implicit. A feedback-review stage after action would be of heuristic value to the analyst.[16]

Given appropriate problem situations the planning process might consist primarily of needs analysis and objectives determination or basic studies. In allocating the annual budget elected officials might desire only information about problems and needs and their relative importance. Stages II and III of the ideal process would be unnecessary under these circumstances; but stage IV (feedback-review) might yield valuable information after stage I had been completed. On the other hand, in marketing a bond issue officials might rely predominantly on problem environment information: the foreseeable rate of inflation, possible changes in interest rates, and the timing of other bond issues. In this problem situation the objective, to minimize cost, and the alternatives, to market or not to market the bonds, need no analysis. Only problem environment information is important. Thus the appropriate planning process would consist only of stage II of the ideal model.

Techniques and Tools

Implied by the choice of any planning process is a selection of procedures, or techniques and tools of analysis. Even though several processes may have the same stages, those employing different techniques and tools will be distinct. Population forecasts, for example, may be made in a variety of ways, some of which yield better estimates than others.[17] Land use–transportation plans may be analyzed with or without the aid of a computer and/or urban development model. A planning process requiring the relatively sophisticated cohort survival technique of population projection should ceteris paribus produce more precise data and be more expensive than one employing simple linear trend projection. In the same manner two otherwise similar processes will be distinct if one employs a computerized simulation model and the other a verbal or intuitive approximation of land use–transportation interaction.

The distinction that can be drawn between the quantity of information and its quality corresponds roughly to the distinction between the planning process and the tools and techniques employed within it. Quality and quantity are interrelated attributes of information that can be measured by the same information theoretic concept.[18] But as used here the terms refer to different characteristics of the information available for a decision. Quantity refers to the number of different types of data available and quality refers to its precision. Thus the quantity of problem environment information available is measured by the number of environmental parameters analyzed, the number of environmental studies undertaken. The quality of this data is measured by the certainty with which statements about the problem environment may be made. In this respect the choice of a planning process determines the quantity of each type of information to be produced and the extent to which feedback is to be the basis for solving a problem. The quality of that information is determined by the actual tools and techniques used to generate it.

The Value of Information

The alternative planning processes constitute an extensive set of alternative means of transforming limited resources, time, human effort, and capital into given quantities and qualities of problem, problem environment, and alternatives data. Choice of any process from this set should depend on two factors: available resources and information needs. Simply stated, resources spent on one type of information are not available for producing other types, and small, unimportant increments of one type of information should not be obtained at the expense of large, relatively important increments of other types. A planning process which uses expensive, sophisticated computer models to make marginal improvements in the information available about alternatives should not be selected when objectives are uncertain or planning resources are limited. Expensive surveys should not be conducted to obtain the value of an environmental parameter when the actual decision does not appear to be sensitive to it. Nor should sophisticated analytical procedures be employed to eliminate relatively small or unimportant amounts of uncertainty. Such data would have relatively little value and might be prohibitively expensive in terms of the opportunity cost of other types of information which are foregone.

The information generated by any planning process provides the expectation of an improved action. It is acquired for decision-making purposes when action is anticipated or a tentative commitment to action has been made. If no intention to act exists, information has no decision-making value and will not be sought. In general information prevents resources from being wasted and opportunities for advancing ends from being lost. In a technologically advanced, institutionally complex, and numerically populous society the value of information can be substantial. Any action will affect large numbers of citizens, and the opportunity loss associated with not attaining ends because a decision was based on inadequate data may be quite large. The resource costs of any action will also be great so that failure to obtain desired ends imposes not only a large opportunity loss but also substantially reduces the capability of achieving other ends. Better data may lead to better use of resources and greater ability to achieve ends. Inadequate data may prevent recognition and solution of problems and may lead to acceptance of the status quo. The following discussion attempts to demonstrate how the value of problem, problem environment, and alternatives data is dependent on its usefulness in controlling the consequences of action, in reducing the probability that ends are not attained.

Problem Information

Problem information may reveal that the original assessment of the factual dimensions of a problem was incorrect. Information about the magnitude of a problem may reveal that more people will make use of a service or will require aid than was originally recognized and that the commitment of greater resources to the solution of the problem will be justified. On the other hand, needs analysis may reveal that the first estimates of the demand for a transportation link or a new product were high and that resources with alternative uses will be wasted in providing the service or good at the scale initially envisioned.[19] Predicting the precise magnitude of a problem will frequently be impossible. Nevertheless given the Scylla and Charybdis nature of a response which is inadequate or excessive, the acquisition of substantial information about its dimensions may be justified.[20]

Problem information may also reveal which objectives should or should not be considered as relevant in determining how a problem should be solved. It will thus suggest benefits to be achieved or costs to be avoided other than those which arise from direct concern with solving the problem. The initial conception of a problem may be too parochial in that it does not recognize a number of values which will be affected by any action taken. Expanding the problem to recognize these values may increase the benefits obtained from action or permit conscious efforts to limit the adverse impacts on or costs to objectives initially neglected. On the other hand, as first defined the statement of a problem may be too broad. Achievement of any one objective may be improved by reducing the number of other objectives to which contributions are sought. Consider, for example, the problem of increasing the recreational opportunities in a city. As originally conceived the problem might be defined as the need to provide more recreational space subject to the efficiency objective. Pre-decision analysis might also reveal that two other social objectives can be influenced by the provision of such space: environmental quality and income redistribution. Public recreation has a redistributive impact to the extent that taxpayers finance real goods and services for those too poor to pay through their taxes for what they consume. In practice this may mean that the proposed recreational space must be accessible to the poor. Environmental quality can be improved by providing recreational space in a number of ways, but suppose that the primary effect in this instance is an aesthetic one. Additional recreational space will improve the beauty of the city. By considering these new objectives in the design and analysis of the additional recreational space, the total benefits obtained from action may be increased. Ignoring these objectives will waste opportunities to advance important societal goals. Alternatively the set of four objectives might be too broad and conflicting. Aesthetic goals might require one type of recreational space and redistributional goals another. And the efficiency objective might be incompatible with both. A careful analysis of the normative nature of the problem to determine which combination of objectives produces the most desired set of results might be justified.

Problem Environment Information

Environmental conditions are, in any problem situation, givens, factors which cannot be changed to improve the effectiveness of action. Problem environment data reveals the nature and character of these factors and is used to design the most effective course of action possible in the face of them and consistent with all objectives. Ignorance of environmental conditions may hinder or frustrate attempts to alter reality. For example, underestimation of the magnitude of population growth can foil a school building program designed to accommodate enrollment increases in an orderly fashion. Similarly, overestimation can lead to vacant classrooms. In the latter case public resources are needlessly wasted while in the former the costs of miscalculation are imposed on the students, who may only be inconvenienced or who may suffer some decrement in the level of their educational attainment. Yet even if a precise estimate of population growth were attainable, its costs might not be justified. Given a relatively small number of students who would suffer only slightly and/or an ability to respond quickly to overcrowding, the value of a precise estimate might be less than its costs. In a different problem situation where a different set of ends was involved and thus different costs were associated with underestimation or overestimation, the value placed on a precise estimate might be higher or lower and the expenditure on any estimate thus would be correspondingly greater or smaller.

Problem environment data also reveals the political, social, legal, physical, and other restrictions that confront any attempt to act. In concept, information of this type may be invaluable—the success of any action taken may depend completely upon it. Where these restrictions are binding, successful action may be impossible and decisions will fail if made in ignorance of them. Where they are not binding, however, resources may be expended to determine how best to avoid them. Uncertainty about this may be extensive and the value of information which eliminates it high.

Alternatives Information

Information about alternatives reduces the likelihood that resources will be wasted because an unnecessarily expensive course of action is chosen or that opportunities will be lost because the alternative implemented does not solve the problem to the degree anticipated. A catalogue of compensatory educational programs which omits several effective alternatives may restrict the scholastic attainment of students or require more expensive remedial programs in the future. Similarly a compensatory educational program which promises to increase reading scores but does not do so wastes opportunities as well as resources. By revealing the consequences of any action alternatives data also reduces the likelihood that a new problem will arise because action taken has unanticipated results. From alternatives data it should be possible to determine, for example, whether a decentralized system of city school districts has the flexibility to accommodate shifts in the spatial distribution of school children and at what cost. Otherwise unexpected problems which will be unnecessarily costly to remedy may ultimately occur.

The search for alternative responses to a complex problem and the assessment of their consequences may never be complete. In some cases either or both may be impossible to complete; in others rational decision making may suggest that either be terminated well short of being complete. The search for alternative technological responses to a problem may not appear rewarding enough to justify its costs. The investigation of the consequences of any course of action may be abandoned before all have been identified because those remaining appear to be insignificant in scale, of no concern given the ends of action, or unlikely to occur. Like other types of information, alternatives data should not be acquired if its expected benefits do not justify its costs.

Feedback

Feedback can be used once action has been taken to improve the degree to which means contribute to ends. In many problem situations the difficulty and costs of collecting pre-decision data may compel decisions in the face of substantial uncertainty, while in others complete use of pre-decision data may be an unnecessarily expensive way to obtain control. Reliance on feedback to correct the errors and shortcomings of decisions made with incomplete pre-decision data is, however, not without its disadvantages. Opportunities to make contributions to objectives may be temporarily or irretrievably lost. Resources may be wasted and written off as sunk costs which can never be recovered. Finally, the costs of correcting an error normally will exceed the costs of having avoided it initially. Inadequate capacity on a new bridge, the result of underestimation of potential traffic use, will create a problem which will be costly and difficult to correct. Similarly, though an instructional program which does not improve scholastic attainment may be replaced, resources will have been wasted on equipment which may have no alternative use and opportunities will have been irretrievably lost.

Yet once an error has been made, the decision to correct it depends upon the benefits and costs associated with action. At times the costs of correcting an inadequate solution to a problem may be prohibitive and the gains minimal.

23 INFORMATION

Excess highway capacity cannot be reclaimed; it must be accepted. Similarly the use of an inferior incineration technology to solve a solid waste disposal problem may never be rectified. In other cases the benefits to be obtained may justify a response. Inadequate highway capacity can be expanded and the operating costs of excess capacity can be saved or reduced by permitting deterioration. Unused rooms in a school or hospital can be closed, saving operating costs, even though the resources used in constructing them will have been wasted.

The Value of Information: An Example

In the late 1960s the town in which a major university was located was confronted with a decision that illustrates the importance of information in decision making. Though small, around 15,000 total population, the town had a discouraging unemployment problem centered primarily among its non-white population. And it had pockets of povery and slum housing conditions which would rival those of a much larger city. The university, a major employer of the town's unskilled non-whites, paid them an average weekly salary of $70. For this reason alone the proposal of a firm offering to train between 1,400 and 2,500 unskilled workers and pay them average weekly wages of about $110 was an important community issue. The proposal made by the firm was to construct a manufacturing plant on a large tract of land approximately two miles outside city limits in the county. The firm promised to control its liquid effluents, which would be discharged into a stream, to the maximum extent that economic and technological factors permitted. Downstream from the proposed plant site lay an area used by university researchers for biological and ecological research, and further downstream were dumped the wastes from a relatively large city.

Controversy arose immediately about the impacts of the firm's proposal. Of major concern was the potential for water pollution. State water quality control regulations would eventually require all users of the stream to provide 95 percent treatment of their wastes. The firm had in operation elsewhere a plant that provided on the average 98 percent treatment, and it was widely recognized as one of the most environmentally conscious firms in its industry. Moreover, it claimed to recycle more than 50 percent of the water it used and was supporting research to improve its abilities. University professors were convinced, however, that, located where proposed, the firm's plant would destroy the value of the stream for research purposes. They asserted that to conduct their research after the plant was in operation would require the use of another stream which was over an hour's drive away, clearly an intolerable cost to impose on them and their graduate students.

Another issue of major consequence was that of jobs. Just how many would be provided, who would get them, whether the firm would in fact train the area's unskilled workers, and how many people outside the area would be attracted as commuters or new residents by this job source were unknowns of some concern. In addition, some residents of the community felt that the presence of such a large manufacturing plant so close by would destroy the aesthetic qualities of their town. They would have preferred area growth spurred by white-collar employment, research and development facilities, corporate headquarters, and certain types of services. The regional planner commented that the main issue in the controversy surrounding the firm's proposal was the future development of the area. Would the location of the plant on its proposed site precipitate undesirable residential and commercial expansion in contiguous areas? More importantly, since the area would probably develop anyway, would the plant induce additional industrial development which might not be as environmentally benign or which in the aggregate might destroy aesthetic qualities? County officials were of the opinion that existing zoning, particularly that in the area drained by the stream, would preclude this.

Some residents suggested that the firm choose an alternate site. But from the firm's perspective the land it owned was the only feasible location in the county. This land had an adequate water supply but more importantly it was near the university and thus the technical staff at the plant could have ready access to the knowledge and expertise of university personnel.

The controversy about the firm's proposal was to be short. Within three months of the firm's public announcement, county officials were to act upon its request for a zoning change permitting plant construction on its site. Outside of taking the issue into the courts, this would be the only certain opportunity the public had to exercise its influence. Several days before the county officials were to act a public meeting was held in the town hall. Much of the information that had been gathered was presented there. When county officials met, they voted to delay a decision. A few weeks later the firm's management withdrew its proposal, announcing that its objectives could not be achieved if it entered the county under such controversial conditions. Several weeks after that the mayor of the town was talking about the need for public housing.

The manufacturing plant controversy illustrates each of the three types of uncertainty, problem, problem environment, and alternatives. First, the importance that should be attached to environmental quality and aesthetic objectives versus human objectives was never clearly established. The community was at the time generally known as a liberal one. Its university community was decidedly liberal. Earlier in the year a university service employees strike had received both moral and financial support from other university members. Yet the decision about whether contributions to the objectives of human development and elimination of poverty were more or less important than environmental or aesthetic objectives could not be clearly made. Discussion of them was vague and imprecise and impeded by a lack of the other two types of data. Without knowing how many unskilled workers would be trained or the extent to which the firm's plant would induce other types of industrial development, the relative priority of objectives could not be established. Some loss in aesthetic quality might be accepted if contributions to human development objectives were fairly certain to result. But the relatively simple data on which such a decision could be based were not available. The present and predicted labor force in the area and region was unknown, preventing predictions of the extent to which the company would have to train and use local labor. Similarly the extent to which labor and other factors would limit additional industrial growth was unknown. While the area itself might be expected to grow, the extent to which the plant would induce further industrial and thus further commercial and residential development was unknown. Moreover, the question of whether reductions in regional unemployment might not justify whatever local costs of environmental and aesthetic degradation might occur was neither asked nor answered.

Lastly, there was uncertainty about the water quality effects of the plant. Its effluent could have been pumped past the downstream area of interest to university researchers, but the cost of this was unknown. The precise impact its effluent might have was also unknown. Would the entire community be offended by the extent to which the quality of the stream would be degraded? Or would university professors and their graduate students be those primarily affected? Equally as unknown were the likelihood that that plant's treatment facilities would fail and the consequences of failure. Could the stream recover or would the plant have the capacity to contain the results of such failure?

The industrial plant issue illustrates the value of information in eliminating uncertainty. The information needed was not available, and it was likely that substantial benefits could be lost if an incorrect decision was made. Members of the community recognized this and sought to delay the decision of county officials. They were adamant; a date had been set for action and a decision would be made on that date. The results were unfortunate; debate was terminated prematurely and a conclusion was forced before sufficient information for a decision had been developed.

Control and Planning

Except in trivial cases a commitment to action raises the question of control and therefore of the need to select a planning process or means of producing information. Prior to the selection of a planning process the expected value of action may be zero or negative because a proposed expenditure of resources cannot be accompanied by an assurance that appropriate ends will be obtained. Planning or the development of information will be expected to increase the value of action by improving the likelihood that means will achieve ends. Preplanning assessments of the possible response to a problem nevertheless serve several purposes. First, they may reveal one or more alternative courses of action and indicate in a rough manner relevant environmental conditions and objectives. Thus, in 1967, when the New York state legislature instructed Mayor Lindsay to prepare a plan for school decentralization several courses of action had already been advanced. The mayor himself had proposed breaking the city system down into five borough systems. A year earlier the Temporary Commission on City Finances had advanced three additional ways to decentralize the school system:

1. increase the power of existing local school boards
2. develop educational parks
3. create fifteen fairly independent school districts.[21]

In addition the state legislature had required that any plan should

> afford members of the community an opportunity to take a more active
> and meaningful role in the development of educational policy closely
> related to the diverse needs and aspirations of the community.[22]

And it had asserted that

> increased community awareness and participation in the educational
> process [would be] essential to the furtherance of educational innovation
> and excellence in the public school system within the city of New
> York.[23]

Thus before any planning had actually occurred two goals of any plan, quality education and greater community involvement in educational decision making, had been established and several possible responses had been suggested. In addition, all participants in the school decentralization debate who possessed a working knowledge of the city school system had a general idea of the environmental conditions under which it labored.

Second, preplanning assessments of the possible response to a problem will provide an initial estimate of the quality and quantity of information that should be developed about the nature of the problem, problem environment, and alternatives. Initial specifications of objectives suggest uncertainties about their relative importance and their operational definitions. Initial proposals for responding to a problem raise questions not only about appropriate objectives but also about the impact of environmental factors and the consequences of action. Thus before planning ever begins a range of uncertainties may surround the response to a problem, and this suggests the types of information that might be needed in the development of final plans and proposals.

Preplanning assessments do not exactly or uniquely establish the amount of information needed for control purposes. Once planning begins new uncertainties about the factual and normative nature of the problem, the problem environment and alternatives may be revealed. It is not unlikely that the original estimate of what was needed to determine the best response to a problem will be modified and that different planning processes will be employed as planning proceeds. The decision to produce information may in effect be a sequence of decisions, each modifying its successor, each clarifying the nature and extent of uncertainty and each improving control capability.

Three Consequences of Planning

Given an initial commitment to action and an initial preplanning estimate of the best response to a problem and hence an initial assessment of the value of action, the production of information may have three conclusions. First, information may show that the benefits of action can be increased and the costs reduced. This may be called the case of positive conclusions. In the second case, that of mixed conclusions, information reveals that while benefits may be less or costs may be greater than preplanning estimates suggested the net benefits of action will be greater than originally expected. In the third case, that of negative conclusions, information reveals that the benefits of action may be smaller and the costs may be greater than originally foreseen.

To discuss these three conclusions further a distinction must be drawn between action, in the sense of implementing a decision, and a course of action, in the sense of a particular response. The three conclusions of a planning process will appear in terms of distinct courses of action. To illustrate, suppose that prior to planning three courses of action appear to be possible responses to a problem but that, given the range of uncertainties about environmental conditions, the consequences of any alternative, and appropriate objectives, the first is expected to yield the greatest net benefits if implemented.[24] The *expected value of the decision or of action* is the magnitude of net benefits expected from implementing the first alternative. After planning, however, the second alternative may appear superior. Then the expected value of a decision and of action will have been increased by information which indicates a different course of action from that originally contemplated. This does not imply the elimination of all the preplanning uncertainties surrounding the response to the problem. Uncertainty about environmental conditions, the consequences of any alternative, and the factual and normative nature of the problem may still exist after planning is terminated. A decision must then be based on the benefits expected from any course of action; that promising the greatest net benefits will be the one for which the expected value of action is greatest. Planning may, of course, reduce uncertainty to such a degree that it is an insignificant factor. And in some cases great expenditures on information may be justified to reduce uncertainty to a point where it is inconsequential. Such expenditures will increase control capability to its maximum feasible level. But in many problem situations this may not be physically possible; even substantial expenditures prior to a decision may not increase control capability so that the consequences and value of action are certain.

The Positive Case

In the positive case planning reveals that expected benefits will be greater than or at least equal in magnitude to original estimates and that costs will be less than or equal to original estimates. If BP and CP are the preplanning estimates of expected benefits and costs, then in the positive case planning indicates that

$$B \geqslant BP \quad \text{and} \quad C \leqslant CP.$$

After planning benefits B are expected to be larger and costs C are expected to be smaller than originally estimated, but neither of the expected gains occurs at the expense of the other. That is, in the positive case expected benefit increases are obtained without cost increases and anticipated cost decreases are achieved without corresponding decreases in benefits. Both may occur concurrently as a result of planning and the production of information.

In the positive case information about the normative and factual aspects of a problem may permit the selection of alternatives focused more directly on ends. As a consequence the expected benefits of action may rise and the costs may decline. Prior to planning uncertainty about the normative aspects of a problem may mean that alternatives which promise to make moderate contributions to several objectives are selected over those which promise larger contributions to a smaller set of objectives. Eliminating this uncertainty may increase the total benefits expected from action and, by allowing means to be focused more efficiently on ends, may reduce costs. The preplanning uncertainties surrounding the physical nature of a problem may induce the selection of alternatives which respond equally to several vaguely perceived dimensions of it. Information may reveal that several aspects of the problem are more important than others and permit thereby the implementation of more efficient alternatives directed more precisely to resolving the "true" problem.

Problem environment and alternatives data might provide similar insights into the best response to a problem. Clarification of the problem environment could show that it would adversely effect the consequences of some courses of action more than others and thus that resource expenditures initially thought necessary to insure success in the face of extreme conditions were needed to a lesser degree or not at all. Alternatives information might establish the superiority of one course of action by assuring that its more favorable rather than its less favorable consequences were likely to occur. Such information might also reveal the effectiveness of a new technology or a novel design, thereby permitting reductions in the operating and capital costs of a response at the same time that it allowed increased benefits. More simply, planning might disclose that initial estimates of what needed to be done to attain objectives could be improved upon by implementation of a course of action discovered in the search for alternatives (systems synthesis). By responding appropriately to both problem environment and alternatives data the benefits of action could be increased and the costs could be decreased.

The Mixed Case

The number of real world problem situations which fall into the positive category may be small. A far greater number may fall into the mixed category, which has two conditions, expressed symbolically as

$$B > BP \quad \text{and} \quad C > CP$$

and

$$B < BP \quad \text{and} \quad C < CP.$$

According to the first condition planning shows that the expected benefits of action can be increased but only by committing greater resources to the solution of the problem. Under the second condition planning would indicate that decreases in the costs of action would be accompanied by reductions in the level of benefits achieved. However, benefit increases are always expected to exceed associated cost increases, and cost decreases are expected to exceed associated benefit decreases. In other words, the net expected value of action is increased by the acquisition of data.

In the mixed case planning could have some of the following conclusions. Increased factual information about the nature of the problem might indicate that, contrary to many preplanning estimates, the problem was quite substantial. Responding to the true problem would increase the resource costs of and the net benefits expected from action. Planning could reveal, for example, that the true demand for recreational space was the largest original estimate, an estimate which was at first considered least likely to be correct. The action initially contemplated would be inadequate to solve the problem; more space should be provided, and while its provision would increase resource costs it would also be expected to generate a large increment in benefits. Normative information about the problem might reveal that the total benefits from action could be increased by considering previously unrecognized objectives. For example, in responding to the problem of school system failure the objective of increased community involvement in educational decision making might appear relevant after an analysis of alternatives and the problem environment. Detailed examination of this objective would probably suggest, however, that it could not be advanced without increasing the costs of action. Thus planning might reveal that net benefits from action could be increased by attempting to direct a response to the problem of school system failure toward a previously unrecognized end.

Information which clarified preplanning uncertainties about environmental conditions and the consequences of any course of action might have similar results. Problem environment information might reveal that adverse conditions were more likely than favorable ones and that, to achieve ends fully, expenditures for limiting environmental impacts would be required. The result should be contributions to benefits in excess of costs; otherwise the expenditures would not be incurred. On the other hand, improved alternatives data might demonstrate that a more expensive course of action would provide higher quality contributions to ends. The expected costs of action would increase, but benefits would rise by a greater amount.

When planning would indicate that the costs of action could or should be reduced, problem information might reveal that most initial estimates of the demand for a good or service were high and that more would be spent providing the last unit than would be received in benefits by its consumer. By providing fewer units, resources could be saved which, in most circumstances, would exceed the value of the benefits lost. Alternatives information, on the other hand, might reveal that most initial estimates of what could be accomplished by any course of action were low. Without reducing achievement at all or by reducing it only marginally, significant resources could be saved by implementing a course of action that originally appeared inadequate. In the extreme, alternatives data might disclose that contributions to objectives could not be made under any circumstances. This information would save resources, but expectations of the benefits from action would decline to zero. Inaction might be the best decision. Situations like this are aspects of the negative case.

The Negative Case

In the negative case planning will terminate in a decision not to act or will substantially diminish expectations about the net benefits to be obtained from action. Thus planning might reveal that while the initial estimates of benefits were optimistic there were few if any errors in preplanning cost estimates. Symbolically this may be represented as

$$B < BP \quad \text{and} \quad C \leqslant CP.$$

Planning might equally indicate the reverse—relatively few errors in benefit estimates, substantial errors in cost estimates. Symbolically this may be represented as

$$B \geqslant BP \quad \text{and} \quad C > CP.$$

Both of these conditions indicate that after planning the expected net benefits of action will be smaller than preplanning anticipations and may be negative. Finally the negative case includes the situation of

$$B < BP \quad \text{and} \quad C > CP$$

that is, benefits less and costs greater than first anticipated. Here planning reveals that preplanning expectations of the benefits of action were inflated and that initially costs were underestimated. Consequently in the negative case planning casts doubt on the initial assumption that action is desirable. It may signal that action should not be taken and that resources should be saved for other uses which promise to yield benefits in excess of costs. Or it may suggest that though the preplanning estimates of the net benefits of action were optimistic the net expected benefits of action were still greater than zero.

Once planning has revealed excessive optimism in preplanning appraisals, the question of whether more information should be collected arises. If the conclusions that emerge from an initial round of planning indicate that the expected value of action is negative, no further information may be acquired. On the other hand, if these conclusions suggest that, although smaller than initially perceived, the expected value of action is still positive, further information may be sought. The conclusions obtained from it may fall into the positive, mixed, or negative categories. If they fall into the first and second categories they will suggest courses of action expected to increase the net benefits obtained from a decision. If they fit into the third category they may suggest inaction.

How Much Information?

Exactly what conclusions a planning process will yield about the *expected value of action* cannot be known in advance without eliminating the need to plan. Given an initial or preplanning set of uncertainties about the best response to a problem, any planning process may be expected to generate a range of findings about appropriate objectives, consequences of any course of action, and environmental conditions.[25] Each possible set of these findings may dictate a different course of action and therefore a different conclusion about the expected value of action. If this is not true to some degree, there is no need to plan. When all possible sets of findings from planning are expected to dictate the same course of action, the result of planning is known. While the expected value of action is in doubt, the best or most appropriate response to the problem is not.

For analytical purposes two sets of expectations about the value or usefulness of planning may be distinguished. In the first, which may be called positive expectations, planning is expected to indicate that the benefits of action could be increased and/or the costs decreased from what was originally anticipated. Prior to the initiation of a planning process uncertainty exists about which of several alternative courses of action will constitute the best response to a problem, i.e., which will yield the greatest increase in net benefits. A decision could, of course, be made on the basis of a preplanning appraisal of the problem and the best solution to it, but an assessment of the value of additional information might suggest that planning was both justified and desirable. When this assessment yields positive expectations, on the average planning is expected both to improve the benefits and to decrease the costs of action. This does not imply, however, that each of the possible sets of findings that might be obtained from the implementation of any planning process would be expected to yield positive conclusions about the value of action. Some findings might yield mixed conclusions about the value of action, and others might yield negative conclusions. But, given all conceivable sets of findings, under positive expectations about the value of information planning is expected to increase the benefits and decrease the costs of action. Planning is necessary, of course, to determine which of the possible sets of findings and which of the several alternative conclusions will actually emerge from the acquisition of data. With the second set of expectations, which may be called mixed, planning would be expected to indicate that the benefits of action could be increased if greater resource expenditures than initially foreseen were undertaken or that costs could be reduced, though as a result the benefits initially anticipated from action would decrease. Under mixed expectations the possible sets of findings which might be obtained from planning will also yield positive, mixed, or negative conclusions about the value of action. But, given all possible sets of findings, under mixed expectations about the value of information planning is expected to show either that greater resource expenditures than originally anticipated are justified or fewer resource expenditures should be contemplated. In either case planning and the acquisition of information are expected to increase the net benefits of action. Otherwise they would not be undertaken.

For analytical and expositional convenience the subsequent analysis of plural decision making assumes that surprises do not emerge from the implementation of a planning process. The acquisition of information under positive expectations about its value yields positive conclusions; up to the point at which the expected marginal benefits of information become zero or negative each additional unit of information reveals means of increasing benefits and reducing costs. Likewise the acquisition of information under mixed expectations about its value yields mixed conclusions; up to the point at which the expected marginal benefits of information become zero or negative each additional unit of information indicates that greater resource expenditures are justified or that fewer resource expenditures should be contemplated.

This assumption is not as artificial as it may seem. Once planning is initiated on the basis of a preplanning assessment of the problem and an appraisal of the expected value of additional information, it may become apparent that instead of yielding positive conclusions, for example, planning is more likely to yield mixed or negative conclusions. However, after such errors become obvious the results of the current planning activity may become the basis for new analyses and investigations which will be expected to improve the net benefits of action. The uncertainties still surrounding the best response to a problem may be interpreted as the preplanning basis for these new analyses and investigations, which will be undertaken with mixed, rather than positive, expectations about the value of information.

Both types of expectations are analyzed subsequently, and thus the consequences of a transition from one category of expectation to another for the control of plural decision making can in a general way be evaluated. The following analysis of plural decision making compares the quality and quantity of information a participant would produce with the amount that is socially desirable in any problem situation, using as an initial point of departure that participant's preplanning estimate of the best response to a problem. When planning is initiated from this point of departure, a participant voluntarily provides society with the control capability it needs if he bases his plans and proposals on socially desirable amounts of information. Now if, once planning begins, expectations about the value of information change from positive to mixed or vice versa, this affects the analysis only for those participants who, because they do not produce socially desirable quantities of information, do not perceive this. But it follows automatically that the plans of such participants would be based on inadequate information and would propose socially undesirable courses of action. The control capability provided by all participants who do produce sufficient information to perceive a transition in expectations can be analyzed under the assumption of correct expectations about the value of information. The fact that a change may occur in expectations does not affect the analysis of the control capability such participants would provide. Thus because of the comparative nature of the analysis the assumption of correct expectations appears not to influence it to any substantial degree. Conclusions can still be obtained for situations in which the assumption is not tenable.

Maximal Control

The question of how much information should be collected in any problem situation arises from a concern for rational decision making. Conceptually too little information is to be deplored as much as is excessive information, for both will waste resources which have alternative uses. From an economist's perspective the answer to the question is that information should be acquired to the point at which the cost of one additional unit equals the benefit expected from that unit. For the analytical purposes of this study this response has some merit. It provides a standard for assessing the performance of participatory decision making which is neither arbitrary nor absolute but which is derived from and varies with the extent and significance of uncertainty and the costs of eliminating it in any problem situation. If the standard could be applied it would insure that information in any problem situation was neither underproduced nor overproduced.

Two models of the decision to acquire information will be developed. Each treats information development from the standpoint of rational decision making. The first model deals with problem situations in which all uncertainty that can be eliminated will be by some combination of pre- and post-decision information. This is a model of maximal control. The second model is one of imperfect control. It analyzes those problem situations in which the costs of information development prevent the elimination of all uncertainty. This model is used in the analysis of plural decision making.

As defined here, maximal control results in the greatest feasible reduction in uncertainty. If maximal control is sought prior to action, there will be no intention of or provision for collecting feedback; action will be guided solely by pre-decision data. When issues are contentious or divisive, this approach to uncertainty may be appropriate. On the other hand, maximal control may be obtained through some combination of pre- and post-decision data. This approach to uncertainty may be desirable where issues can be considered more than once without political costs and where the resource costs of correcting errors are small.

To develop the maximal control model let

$$NB(x) = B(x) - C(x)$$

represent the net benefits expected from a decision based on x units of pre-decision data. The quantity $B(x)$ represents the benefits expected from and $C(x)$ the expected costs of a decision based on x units of data. Whether positive expectations or mixed expectations about the value of information are assumed, $NB(x)$ is a measure of expected value which increases with x. The variable x may represent an amount of pre-decision data about the problem, problem environment, or alternatives. The units in which x is defined are assumed to be standard quantities, each of which eliminates the same amount of uncertainty. For purposes of simplicity assume that one standard unit of information eliminates one standard unit of uncertainty.

The net benefits $NB(x)$ anticipated from any quantity of data x require that expenditures, which may be represented by $D(x)$, be made for that information.

These costs of information may also be expected to increase with the magnitude of x.

Now let X represent the total amount of uncertainty that can be eliminated and thus the total amount of pre-decision information that can be produced in the problem situation. Then X is a constant and

$$NB(X) = B(X) - C(X)$$

represents the net expected benefits of action when maximal control is provided solely by pre-decision information. The difference

$$NB(X) - NB(x) \qquad\qquad \textbf{1793144} \qquad\qquad (2.1)$$

symbolically indicates the loss in net benefits expected from using x units of pre-decision information rather than the maximal number X. This difference also establishes an upper limit on the value and the number of units of feedback that could be collected to increase net benefits after a course of action had been implemented. Since the total amount of information that can be produced is X, the difference between this and x, or $(X - x)$, is the amount of feedback that can be generated. Likewise since $NB(X)$ represents the total net benefits that would be expected with perfect pre-decision information the difference in (2.1) establishes an upper limit on the value of $(X - x)$ units of feedback.

The actual value of any amount of feedback may be less than the difference indicated by (2.1). Using feedback to correct the deficiencies of a decision will not be costless. It will require additional resource expenditures and will be accompanied by the permanent loss of substantial benefits which would have been obtained from a decision based on better information. For example, additional space for an existing educational facility usually requires the commitment of more real resources than the same amount of space would have required if provided when the structure was first built. Similarly the benefits lost while an additional span is added to a new and heavily used bridge may be substantial. In general, in public decision making the larger the number of potential beneficiaries from any action the more substantial in magnitude are the benefits lost likely to be because means, chosen on the basis of inadequate data, failed to achieve ends. Opportunity losses will be even greater when deficiencies may not be corrected. In this case society must accept the discrepancy between means and ends and forego the benefits lost because of such a discrepancy for the life of the program or project.

To account for these considerations let

$$K(X - x) = \bar{K}(x)$$

represent the costs of producing $(X - x)$ units of feedback and the expected opportunity and resource costs of using this amount of feedback to obtain maximal control. In general these costs may be expected to vary inversely with x. An extra unit of pre-decision data will decrease the expected total cost of developing and using feedback. A fairly well-designed system constructed after the acquisition of substantial quantities of pre-decision data should be less expensive to modify than a poorly designed system because its imperfections are fewer. In addition, the opportunity costs or benefits foregone should be lower. Selection of the wrong technological alternative, for example, (say highways instead of mass transit) may be more likely to occur with inferior pre-decision data. Better pre-decision data will reduce the probability of such a decision and thus the expected opportunity costs associated with and the resource costs of correcting an initial action to obtain the best solution to a problem. Better pre-decision data will also reduce the amount of feedback needed and thus expenditures for it. Additional units of both pre- and post-decision data will become successively more expensive, but where maximal control is sought each additional unit of pre-decision data collected reduces by one the number of units of feedback needed, and the total expenditures for the latter decline with the amount of the former acquired.

Consequently when maximal information will be developed from some combination of pre- and post-decision data, the expected net benefits of action are

$$NB(X) - D(x) - \bar{K}(x).$$

That is, they are equal in quantity to the maximal benefits of action $NB(X)$ minus the costs $D(x)$ incurred in producing x units of pre-decision data and minus the expected costs $\bar{K}(x)$ of using feedback to remedy any deficiencies of a decision based on only x units of information. This quantity is greatest when the sum of these two costs is at a minimum. Such a minimum occurs when the decrease in the expected cost of developing and using feedback, which results because another unit of pre-decision information is acquired, equals the costs of that unit of pre-decision data. For an illustration of this, see figure 2-2.

The functions D_x and $\bar{K}_x$ indicate respectively the costs of producing any unit of x and the expected decrease in the cost of developing and using feedback which arises from having one more unit of x. The two curves intersect at x_0, and this is the quantity of pre-decision information which minimizes the sum of $D(x)$ and $\bar{K}(x)$. For quantities of information smaller than x_0, such as x_1, reductions in the cost of using feedback exceed increases in the costs of producing another unit of pre-decision data. Thus by moving to the right or producing more pre-decision information, the sum of the two costs can be decreased. Similarly, for quantities of information larger than x_0, such as x_2, the costs of an additional unit of pre-decision data exceed in value the reductions in the costs of using feedback. By moving to the left or producing less pre-decision information, the sum of the two costs can be decreased.

Consequently where maximal control is sought the amount of pre-decision information to be produced is determined by the point at which the cost of an additional unit of that information equals the gain from reducing the expected costs of relying on feedback. This is the equivalent of the economist's dictum to generate information to the point at which its marginal benefits are equal to its marginal costs. Here the marginal benefits of information are $\bar{K}_x$, the decrement in the expected cost of producing and using feedback associated with one more unit of pre-decision data (and one less unit of feedback). The marginal costs are D_x, the cost of one additional unit of pre-decision data. The quantity of information

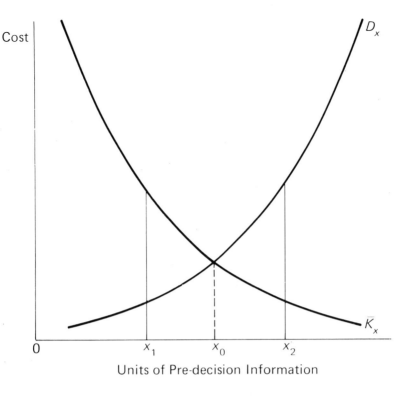

Figure 2-2. Minimizing the Costs of Information for Purposes of Maximal Control.

determined by this condition will minimize the costs of producing pre-decision data plus the expected costs of producing and using feedback. And it will maximize the expected net benefits from action after the costs of decision making have been considered.

Imperfect Control

In many problem situations attempts to acquire maximal control may be irrational. When, for example, the costs of correcting errors, of converting from one technology to another, or of eliminating redundant capacity exceed the benefits, maximal control should not be sought. In this section the conditions which characterize the production of information which gives only imperfect control capability are presented. These conditions, which will be used later in the analysis of plural decision making, require that the development of pre- and post-decision data proceed to the point where the marginal benefits of each type of information equal its marginal costs.

Let x and h represent amounts of pre- and post-decision data of any type such that together they do not sum to more than the total amount of uncertainty that can be eliminated. They can, of course, sum to less. Then

$$NB(x,h) = B(x,h) - R(x,h)$$

represents the expected net benefits from a decision based on x units of pre-decision data and h units of feedback. The quantity $B(x, h)$ is the expected benefits of a decision based on x units of pre-decision data and h units of feedback, and the quantity $R(x, h)$ represents the total resource costs of a decision based on these amounts of information. Then

$$NB_x = B_x - R_x$$

and

$$NB_h = B_h - R_h$$

represent the expected net benefits from a given unit of pre-decision data and a given unit of feedback. The quantities B_x and B_h indicate the change expected in the benefits from action, and R_x and R_h reflect the expected change in the resource costs of action when a decision is based on one more unit of each type of information. In addition to representing resource expenditure changes, R_h indicates the resource costs of using a unit of feedback. If expectations about the value of information are positive, a unit of pre-decision data is expected to increase the benefits foreseen from action by an amount given by B_x or B_h and decrease the resource costs by an amount given by $-R_x$ and $-R_h$. Since decrements in resource costs are negative, the quantity $-R_x$ is positive, and $-R_h$ may be positive if the resource savings enabled by a unit of feedback exceed the resource costs of using that unit of data. If expectations about the value of information are mixed, a unit of information is expected to reveal that the benefits anticipated from action can be increased if resource expenditures are increased or that anticipated resource expenditures can be decreased if some expected benefits are foregone. In the former case B_x and B_h indicate the amounts by which the benefits foreseen from action are expected to increase and R_x and R_h, which are both positive, represent the estimated additional resource expenditures. In the latter case $-R_x$ indicates the amount by which resource expenditures can be reduced and B_x, a negative quantity, represents the magnitude of benefits expected to be foregone. The benefit losses indicated by a unit of feedback are given by B_h, a negative quantity, and $-R_h$ represents the difference between resource expenditures to use that unit of feedback and the resource savings it is expected to enable. In both cases of mixed expectations the marginal benefits foreseen from information NB_x and NB_h are positive.

The net benefits foreseen from feedback NB_h decline with the quantity of pre-decision data collected. The change in the benefits of action B_h vary inversely with x; the more pre-decision data collected, the smaller are the benefit increases expected from any unit of feedback because the action taken is less likely to have shortcomings. The expected benefits of the first unit of feedback will be greater, for example, if only one unit of pre-decision data has been developed than if twenty units have been. The uncertainty eliminated by the second unit of information or first unit of feedback is much more important than is the uncertainty eliminated by the twenty-first unit of information or first unit of feedback. Similarly the change in resource expenditures R_h varies inversely with the amount of pre-decision information. As x increases the action taken is less likely to have shortcomings and R_h is likely to be smaller. Changes in the technology, scale, or management system of an implemented decision will be smaller in magnitude and yield smaller resource savings if twenty units rather than one unit of pre-decision data are developed.

Whether expectations are positive or mixed, the marginal benefits of pre- and post-decision data are assumed to decline with the quantity of each type of information collected. As a plan becomes more refined and more precise, the consequences of uncertainty diminish and the gain from an additional unit of data reducing it becomes smaller. As h increases the costs of using feedback rise and $-R_h$ is more likely to be negative even where a unit of feedback permits the resource costs of action to be reduced.

The total costs of information for the model of imperfect control may be represented by

$$D(x, h)$$

and the costs of an additional unit of pre- and post-decision data by

$$D_x \quad \text{and} \quad D_h.$$

The relationship between these is such that if x and h represent the same unit of information, but collected at different points in time, D_x exceeds D_h. Less effort is needed to appreciate "what should have been done" once action has been taken than before. The passage of time, the implementation of an initial solution and observance of the results may clarify objectives and reduce uncertainty about the problem environment and the consequences of action. The costs of a unit of either type of information are assumed, however, to rise with the amount developed. Movement from a state of little or no knowledge may be relatively easy, but raising the precision of an analysis by a unit of information becomes ever more difficult and expensive the more precise that analysis is, that is, the greater the amount of data collected. For example, uncertainty about which of several sets of objectives is relevant in a problem situation will be less costly to eliminate than will uncertainty about the priorities among or relative importance of objectives in any set. For this reason the marginal costs D_x and D_h of pre- and post-decision data increase with the amount of each type of information collected. In addition, D_h increases with x. The first unit of feedback is the post-decision equivalent of an additional unit of pre-decision data. If the marginal costs of pre-decision data D_x increase with x, then so do the marginal costs of feedback D_h. Thus the greater the quantity x of pre-decision data, the more expensive is the first unit of feedback.

Using these expressions, the economist's advice to collect data to the point at which the marginal benefits equal the costs can be formalized in two conditions

$$B_x - R_x = D_x$$

and

$$B_h - R_h = D_h.$$

These conditions require that the net benefits anticipated from an additional unit of information $B_x - R_x$ or $B_h - R_h$ equal the costs D_x or D_h of that unit. In other words, for rational decision making, marginal benefits must equal marginal costs. If they do not, total net expected benefits may be expanded by producing an additional unit of information when expected marginal benefits exceed marginal costs or by producing one less unit of information when the reverse is true.

Together these two conditions constitute an ideal model of the decision to collect data. This model provides a basis for asking whether plural decision making is likely to provide the control capability society needs to direct means to ends. Like the model of maximal control, this model makes no assumptions about the ends of action. Unlike that model it does not require that all feasible uncertainty be eliminated by some combination of pre- and post-decision data. Instead the model of imperfect control requires that the quantity of each type of information be determined in accordance with its expected marginal benefits and marginal costs, a criterion which may not lead to the elimination of all uncertainty. As a consequence it somewhat better reflects reality and provides greater insight into the control capabilities of plural decision making.

Time and Other Abstractions

A number of factors affecting the decision to acquire information have been excluded from the model of imperfect control. Among the most important of these is time, often a critical element in decision making. Crises are an extreme example. Created both by human (strikes, riots) and natural (floods, droughts) causes, they require immediate action. A decision cannot be delayed for the collection and analysis of data. On the other hand, some problems require a decision within a given time period. Budgetary priorities must be established in some fashion before the beginning of a new fiscal year. Still other problems just worsen over time, and the earlier action can be taken the better. Eutrophication, which results from the discharge by cities of poorly treated wastes into streams and lakes, is an example. Lastly political pressure from the electorate may establish a time horizon within which action must be taken. Public concern over crime in the streets may demand action within a legislative session, not after the problem has been thoroughly analyzed.

The less time available for its collection and analysis, the more expensive any quantity of data will be. Ten thousand man-hours expended over the period of a year are not likely to be as productive if expended over the period of a month. Fifteen thousand man-hours, an increase of 50 percent, might accomplish in a month what could have been achieved in a year with ten thousand man-hours. The very passage of time may generate data, and the longer period will permit more reasoned analysis and investigation. Time may affect the production of problem, problem environment, and alternatives data differently. Through the increased application of human and financial resources, time restrictions may be avoided in the development of the last two types of data. But in the assessment of the normative aspects of a problem this may not be the case. Assessment of objectives requires contemplation and investigation of their implications in terms of alternative courses of action. To the degree that elected officials, generally a nonexpandable resource, must be involved in this, the restrictions that lack of time imposes are less easily evaded. Time-imposed difficulties in developing problem data may adversely affect the development of problem environment and alternatives data and will clearly decrease the benefits expected from these types of information. Imprecision about the factual and normative nature of the problem creates uncertainty about the types of alternatives and environmental conditions that should be analyzed and, therefore, decreases the benefits foreseen from these types of information.

Nevertheless time can be excluded from the model of imperfect control. That model will be used as a basis for comparing the information that is needed for social control with that produced by participants in plural decision-making processes. The components of the model, the benefit and resource expenditure changes indicated by any unit of data and the costs of that unit, can be interpreted in terms of any time frame that might apply to a problem situation. Thus the conclusions obtained from the analysis can be interpreted in a similar manner, and for this reason explicit consideration of time is unnecessary.

Several other factors which influence the value of information are assumed away or are not considered in great detail. The clarity, communicability, and validity of information produced by participants are not questioned. Participants are assumed to employ the results of their studies and analyses to develop plans and proposals. In doing this they are assumed to interpret their information correctly and accurately. In particular they do not ignore the implications of any information in preparing their plans. Participants are also assumed to have adequate resources to undertake the development of information to the extent indicated by their net benefits from it. Thus they are not impeded in their planning by a lack of technical skills, financial resources, and other capabilities needed to develop information. These assumptions may not be tenable. They are made in order to clarify the analysis of main concern and because, when they are not tenable, the problem of control is clearly worsened.

Overload, too much disparate information from too many sources, is also not considered. When it occurs in any problem situation decision makers may overcome it in several ways. They may arbitrarily ignore or reject the proposals of some participants. When it is technically possible they may refer an issue and the proposals for solving it generated by some or all participants to an investigative staff such as a planning department to prepare a synthesizing viewpoint. [26] Moreover, overload may not be a problem in every instance of plural decision making. Although, when it occurs, it does restrict the potentials of participatory decision making, overload is a problem treated best outside the model of imperfect control.

Lastly, the memory function in society is not evaluated here. Records, histories, previous analyses, and other data that are stored are assumed to be available to participants. But the question of what data are stored and the decision to store them are not analyzed here.

Alternative Approaches

The model of imperfect control advanced here is but one of a number of descriptions of the decision to acquire information. Incrementalism,[27] satisficing,[28] rational planning,[29] and mixed scanning [30] offer different interpretations. Of these, the first three are narrowly prescriptive—they maintain that the same general approach be applied in all problem situations. Incrementalism is a feedback dependent approach to decision making which requires a series of small, exploratory, somewhat uncoordinated changes to solve a problem. In terms of the ideal planning process presented earlier, incrementalism suggests that only limited amounts of information be generated in stages I–IV prior to action but that feedback and repeated iterations of the process be employed to determine a policy or program. An incremental planning process produces very little data about objectives (stage I) and alternatives (stage III). It relies on feedback to suggest new alternatives and rectify the consequences of inadequate pre-decision data. From a societal perspective the shortcomings of incrementalism on the part of any decision maker are rectified by an environment of other incremental decision makers who will, through a process of "partisan mutual adjustment," defend objectives that he has ignored in his plans and proposals and suggest environmental conditions and consequences of action that he may have overlooked.

Partisan mutual adjustment is a characteristic of a democracy whose decision-making institutions are open and permeable. In a democracy the self-interest of many distinct public officials will induce development of the information needed to guide public action. Any public official will develop data (through an incremental planning process) to protect his own interests or those of his constituents. Through the processes of partisan mutual adjustment—bargaining, negotiation, manipulation [31]—this information will be aggregated to provide control capability. Thus the response to any problem situation which affects more than one segment of society will be determined within an informational framework indicative of the interests of all represented segments. Moreover, the existence of a system of decision makers insures that when one incrementalist errs others will correct by their own incremental decisions the shortcomings of his action, if he does not do so himself.

In sum, incremental decision makers within a context of partisan mutual adjustment act or propose action with limited information and depend on the positive or negative reaction of others to suggest improvements in their decisions. Little evidence, either logical or empirical, exists, however, to suggest that incrementalism within the context of partisan mutual adjustment provides adequate control capability. On the contrary, the presence of many malfunctioning programs at all levels of government suggests that the flexibility and adaptability needed for partisan mutual adjustment to succeed does not exist. Some errors are irreversible.

This study directly questions the main supposition of partisan mutual adjustment, that a multiplicity of participants will provide adequate control capability. It does not assume, as partisan mutual adjustment does, that all participants have decision-making authority. Moreover it does not postulate a prescriptive approach to the decision by any participant to develop information. In concept it permits participants to recognize that the value of information will be different in different problem situations and to adjust the amount of information they develop accordingly. This is both a more flexible and a more analytically tractable position. In any case this study would question partisan mutual adjustment even without the associated concept of incrementalism.

Like the incremental model, satisficing acknowledges the costliness of information, man's difficulties in analyzing and evaluating (which make those activities expensive), and the general problems involved in defining a problem. A satisficing process specifies acceptable levels of goals achievement but does not define the problem in final form. Through the concept of bounded rationality, an integral part of the satisficing model, the importance of complex, rigorous assessments of the problem environment and alternatives is dismissed. Choice is assumed to be made always with respect to a limited, simplified model of the real situation. Feedback is recognized as useful in adjusting imperfect decisions and in improving those that can easily be modified to make greater contributions to objectives. Satisficing implies a learning-by-doing strategy of decision making and requires a capability to reconsider an action a number of times.

In two respects the satisficing model is similar to the model of imperfect control developed earlier. Four types of information, corresponding roughly to problem, problem environment, and alternatives data, are specified as guiding action.[32] With respect to satisfactory objectives and goals, the search for and analysis of alternatives may be rationally designed.[33] The preferred design is a sequential process which deals with a limited range of alternatives and a limited range of consequences.[34] As soon as a satisfactory course of action is found, the search terminates. If a satisfactory alternative is not found in the initial set, another small set is searched. If continued search of small sets fails to reveal a satisfactory course of action, objectives and goals are adjusted. On the other hand, if the course of action first chosen easily accomplishes ends, or if after a decision is made an alternative is discovered which promises to improve goals achievement, the satisfactory level at which objectives and goals are set will be readjusted. Direct account of the costs and benefits of information is explicitly excluded from the satisficing model.[35]

For this reason and because it postulates learning by doing, satisficing is not an appropriate model of information acquisition with which to analyze plural decision making. Though concepts of expected costs and benefits may be vague in practice, they provide a stronger frame of reference for the analysis of plural decision making than do concepts of satisfactory levels. By using them greater insights are obtained. Equally important, not all participants may have the ability to profit from the lessons of experience. Most cannot learn by doing; at best they can respond to the results of action taken by public officials. In developing their opinions they will not have the benefit of experience in the implementation of action. Yet this does not necessarily mean nor should it mean that their views about what is right or wrong could not improve control capability. The degree to which means ultimately achieve ends need not depend upon the lessons of experience nor in many situations should it depend as heavily on feedback as learning by doing and satisficing requires.

The third approach to the acquisition of data, rational planning, requires maximal information about goals, environmental factors, and alternatives prior to action. The use of feedback is minimized. In terms of the schematic process presented earlier, rational or synoptic planning consists of stages I to IV with limited provision for the use of post-decision data. Rational planning implies comprehensiveness and a long-range perspective. In the absence of a comprehensive perspective, actions which could be beneficially coordinated will operate at cross-purposes resulting in the loss of benefits from and increased costs of action. If myopia prevails, the groundwork needed for the efficient solution of long-term problems will never be prepared and solutions to them will never be executed at minimum cost.

Rational planning is the antithesis of incrementalism and satisficing. Unlike incrementalism, it does not permit the fragmentation of information development into disjoint tasks accomplished by various participants. In the rational planning model the planning agency alone is responsible for the development of information. Rational planning also requires reliance on pre-decision data and, unlike incrementalism and satisficing, neglects feedback. In this sense it is more restrictive than the model of maximal control developed earlier. For this reason alone it is not useful here. Finally, rational planning is in many ways concerned with the substance of planning (for example, long range plans covering all phases of development) rather than with the planning process and the quality of the informational output. Thus it would provide at best an inflexible, substantively oriented basis for exploring plural decision making.

The incremental, satisficing, and rational planning models, with their restrictive prescriptions for the use of one type of planning process, conceal the range of choices available in the decision to produce information. A single planning process should not be ubiquitously employed; little justification exists for doing so. In the decision to collect information the choice is not between reliance on pre-decision data (rational planning) or reliance on feedback (incrementalism, satisficing). Instead it is among a range of planning processes offering different quantities and qualities of pre- and post-decision data. Feedback may be easier and cheaper to develop as incrementalists and satisficers observe. Similarly, as rational planners note, it may result in high opportunity costs in terms of benefits foregone and in the misallocation of resources. However these two alternatives do not exhaust the set of feasible planning processes or the combinations of pre- and post-decision data that can be developed. Under appropriate circumstances either the rational planning model or the incremental-satisficing models might represent a rational choice, but rational decision making is not consistent with blind acquiescence to a prescription or blind application of a rule of thumb. It is misleading to ask whether information development should be synoptic or incremental. A rational approach requires an assessment of the relative costs and benefits of information and a choice based on these assessments.

The mixed scanning model of information acquisition represents a compromise of sorts between the extremes of rational planning and the satisficing or incremental models. As the middle ground it differentiates between fundamental and item decisions. The former establish the framework within which the latter occur; they are the decisions about broad policy or program issues which result in nonincremental change. Item decisions are incremental and specify the details of fundamental decisions. The planning process used in making these two types of decisions differs. Item decisions can be made using an incremental process because the broad context within which they are made has been established by fundamental decisions. Item decisions can assume certain givens; for example, they can assume the objectives prescribed by fundamental decisions and can neglect courses of action precluded by them. Fundamental decisions require a more comprehensive planning process, a more substantial search for alternatives and investigation of objectives. They may be made, however, on the assumption that item decisions will correct minor deficiencies and dispose of details.

In the mixed scanning model the costs of information are to be used to determine planning process choice. Combined with the distinction between fundamental and item decisions, this requirement prevents the model from being prescriptive of a single approach to information acquisition. However, the way in which costs might affect process choice is not developed in any detail. Instead the need to consider costs is noted and the decision to collect information is elaborated in terms of a set of rules and procedures for the analysis of fundamental and item decisions. Consequently, though the model is more flexible than those it is intended to supplant and though it recognizes a greater range of possible choice in the selection of a planning process, it too is prescriptive. It imposes a set of procedures for the collection and analysis of information. The potential range of planning processes is much broader than foreseen in the model. It does not clearly reflect the range of choice.

Conclusion

Any model is an abstraction; no model faithfully or completely represents reality. Even a description of reality would omit or neglect some of its characteristics. Reality is simply too complex to be captured in words or symbols. This is certainly true with respect to models of the decision to acquire information. And for this reason fault can be found with all the models discussed.

This study requires a model of planning process choice for heuristic purposes, that is, to obtain insights into the control capability inherent in plural decision making. Given this objective, the most useful model is that developed earlier because it does not require that a specific set of procedures be used for information development. Under appropriate circumstances the model of imperfect control can imply the use of an incremental or a satisficing or a mixed scanning or a rational planning process. Conclusions obtained from using it thus encompass cases where any of these processes might be useful. As a heuristic device it would therefore appear to be the most useful of the alternatives.

Chapter Three
Public Decision Systems

Plural decision making does not occur in a vacuum nor in an environment which is always the same. This study uses the concept of a public decision system to examine those environmental factors which significantly affect the control capability of plural decision making. Basically a public decision system consists of the individuals, groups, and organizations that become involved in the public debate over a problem situation. This system has two functionally specialized subsystems consisting of (a) those individuals who legally possess the power and authority to allocate public resources and establish public policy and (b) those individuals, groups, and organizations who attempt to influence these decisions. The former subsystem may be called the decision center and the latter, the planning field. The decision center uses an output of the planning field, information in the form of plans and proposals, to produce its own output, decisions about public policies and programs. It is primarily a decision maker and only derivatively a producer of goods and services. The planning field is comprised of all participants in a public debate who cannot themselves allocate collective resources or determine the public response to a problem situation. Its members participate in two related ways; they produce plans and proposals for members of the decision center to use, and they exercise their influence and power to affect the decision that will be made. Since the direct use of power and influence has been thoroughly explored by sociologists and political scientists, this study will be concerned primarily with the degree to which the ability to influence and the possession of power affect the production of information.

The general concept of a public decision system is not novel. Sayre and Kaufman, using different terminology, describe the sources of decisions in New York City as consisting

> ... of two parts: a "core group" at the center, invested by the rules with the formal authority to legitimize decisions (that is, to promulgate them in the prescribed forms and according to the specified procedures that make them binding under the rules) and a constellation of "satellite groups," seeking to influence the authoritative issuances of the core group.[1]

This describes rather well what is meant here by a public decision system. It is a source of decisions, comprised of components—individuals, groups, and organizations—from a larger environment which are brought together by their interest in a problem and its solution. Components involved in one decision system need not interact on a continuous basis in the larger environment nor in other decision systems. Members of the planning field of one decision system may not participate in

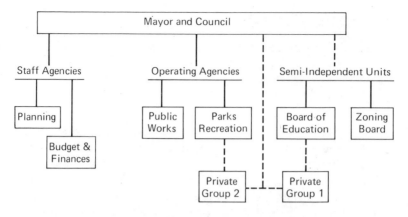

Figure 3-1. An Organizational Chart for Local Government

another or may be members of its decision center.[2] Different problem situations will interest different members of a society and will be the legal jurisdiction of different officials. Thus the concept of a public decision system is situation specific; for different problem situations distinct decision systems, each, however, with the same general form, will emerge to determine the collective action that should be taken.

To illustrate this consider the organizational chart for local government presented in Figure 3-1. For a controversial budgetary issue, every unit on the organizational chart might participate, i.e., the entire chart would reflect the public decision system. Boards, staff agencies, operating agencies, and private groups would comprise the planning field;[3] the mayor and the city council would constitute the decision center. To participate, boards, staff agencies, and operating agencies would present arguments, analyses, opinions, and other data to the mayor and the council in order to influence the budgetary decision. For their part, private groups might attempt to influence the final decision by presenting their views, opinions, and other information directly to the mayor and council, or they might act indirectly, attempting to modify the opinions of the other members of the planning field. Group 2, for example, would attempt to modify the position of the Department of Parks and Recreation so that it would more closely resemble the group's ideas about the appropriate use of public funds. For a less controversial educational issue, on the other hand, the public decision system might consist only of the Board of Education and group 1. The decision center would be the person or persons within the Board of Education who had the legal power to make a decision.[4] The planning field would be composed of group 1 and the educational planners and administrators within the Board of Education who had an interest in the problem situation. Although these two decision systems were composed of some of the same elements from a larger environment, their decision centers and planning fields would be completely different. All participants in the educational decision system, even members of its decision center, could participate only as members of the planning field of the budgetary decision system. Yet the mayor and council, the decision center of this system, might not become involved at all in the educational decision system. In addition, the planning field of the budgetary system would have more members than the planning field of the educational system.

In a democracy any individual, group, or organization may participate in the debate about the public response to a problem. As a result the composition of a public decision system will vary over time as participants initiate and terminate their involvement. Most major variations in the characteristics of a public decision system may be expected to result from changes in the composition of its planning field, but decision center changes may also occur. When they feel their position and demands are legally justified, participants may take an issue into the courts. Alternatively they may attempt to create a new decision center by, for example, taking a local issue to state or federal authorities. For both of these reasons a public decision system may be viewed as an amorphous, transitory entity. In addition, once a solution to a problem has been evolved from the interaction of planning field and decision center members, a decision system may disappear. This does not imply, however, that its component parts will disappear or that they are unstable. They may prevail even in the face of extensive political, social, economic, and physical change in the larger environment of a decision system and they may become involved in different decision systems with the passage of time. Only a decision system, as a distinct subenvironment of a larger environment, may be impermanent. This is not consistent, it should be noted, with the Sayre and Kaufman concept of a decision source, which implies a more permanent configuration of elements from a larger environment.[5] This difference may reflect the different purposes of the two concepts. Sayre and Kaufman sought to summarize a variety of empirical findings, and their concept would of necessity be more general. On the other hand, the details which distinguish different public decision systems are of somewhat greater concern in the present analysis.

The concept of a public decision system provides a framework for analyzing the two aspects of control: power and information. Legally and formally the decision center is the locus of power and the planning field the source of information. Yet the distinction between the functions that the two subsystems perform may be blurred or nonexistent in fact. Members of the decision center are not necessarily independent actors nor are their decisions solely the product of the information produced by members of the planning field. Informal or legally nonbinding relationships may exist between members of the two subsystems to such a degree that the actual power to decide rests with planning field members.[6] Equally, members of the decision center may become involved in the development of plans and proposals. In addition to providing a framework for examining the more prominent modes of interaction between decision center and planning field members, the concept of a public decision system provides an analytically convenient basis for exploring the motivations and expectations of planning field members. What these participants perceive as the potential rewards from involvement will condition their behavior and will ultimately determine the quality and quantity of information they produce for decision center members. In turn this establishes the control capabilities of plural decision making. Thus the concept of a public decision system isolates those factors besides information which may affect the control capability of plural decision making and provides the context for investigating their impact on the plans and proposals participants develop.

Decision Centers

The nature of a decision center, the attributes and authority of its members, may vary substantially among different decision systems. For electoral decisions voters constitute the decision center.[7] Their authority is checked only by a constitution or charter. They may be provided with information about the issues in a referendum or the candidates in a general election by a planning field comprised of interest groups, the candidates themselves, newspapers, and other sources. In comparison with the electorate, most other decision centers in a democracy have limited authority. When they constitute the decision center in a problem situation, the appointed officials and career civil servants of a line bureaucracy or functional authority may find that the factual and normative dimensions of the problem which they can consider and the set of alternatives from which they might select a response are narrowly circumscribed by enabling legislation, political and administrative impediments, and the dictates of tradition. Though their authority is limited, these decision centers may be required to hold public hearings on their plans and proposals and may invite some individuals, interest groups, and organizations to participate to some degree in the development of them.[8] While they may often find themselves opposing already prepared plans, and decisions which in effect have been made, planning field members may be able to suggest feasible alternatives directed toward the attainment of a different ordering of objectives from that considered relevant by a line bureaucracy or functional authority. In these circumstances, however, power or the ability to take an issue to a different decision center may be more important than the information contained in plans and proposals. Thus more because of the vigor of their protest than the rigor of their proposals neighborhood groups may force an urban renewal authority to abandon its plans for clearance and adopt instead a program of code enforcement. Similarly community groups may successfully oppose the plans of the department of public works, although perhaps not without taking the issue to a higher authority such as the mayor or city council.

The most obvious form of decision center is the elected official (mayor, governor) or body of elected officials (city council, state legislature) with broad decision-making authority. Both are invested by society with the responsibility and legal authority to act upon a vast array of issues, and, without their certification of legitimacy, action taken on these issues may not be binding. Formal authority does not necessarily mean real power, however. A mayor may be able to control a city council; individual members of that body may be able to determine the actions it takes; or some planning field members may be able to impose their preferences on it. In general, decision centers consisting of one or more elected officials may obtain substantial information about an issue through public meetings, committee hearings, and direct contact with constituents. While some of this information may be solely expressions of support or opposition, much of it may reflect more concretely on objectives, alternatives, and environmental conditions.[9]

Decision centers convert demands for change into public programs and policies which may have limited or extensive impacts depending on the number of people they affect and the magnitude of the change they engender. The issues with which decision centers are concerned may be routine (e.g., a zoning appeal) or innovative (e.g., school decentralization) and they may affect a relatively small (the residents of a neighborhood) or a relatively large (the majority of a city's inhabitants) number of individuals. The decision made may require the expenditure of public resources for physical facilities, may establish rules and regulations for the use, management, and operation of public programs and facilities, or may directly regulate the behavior of private individuals and public agencies. Decision centers may also try to avoid consideration of controversial issues. Decisions on these issues, for example a civilian review board for police operations, may be delayed by referral to a study group or approached only by the electorate itself in a referendum.

Decision center members may not use the information provided by the planning field. Some decisions may be made purely for the purposes of expanding the political power of the decision maker, for example to permit him to acquire control over a source of patronage or to broaden or contract the authority of an office. Although the means by which political objectives are obtained may affect other nonpolitical objectives, these will not be of concern in the decision to be made. An example is the decision to merge the Chicago and Cook County welfare agencies discussed by Banfield.[10] Efficiencies in the delivery of welfare services were anticipated by some from the merger, but Banfield reports that these consequences and the uncertainty about them were immaterial.[11] The objective of this decision was to associate welfare in the minds of recipients with the Republican party, weakening thereby their allegiance to the Democratic party. This allegiance was fostered, proponents of the decision apparently thought, by the traditional association of the Democrats with welfare.[12] In decisions such as these information about objectives, alternatives, and environmental conditions is not relevant. Clearly defined political objectives are sought, and the costs and benefits to society from action are immaterial.

Not all decisions are made by decision centers with political objectives solely in mind. In the same political milieu of Chicago and Cook County Banfield found the majority of public decisions were made on the basis of social, though still political, concerns. Votes were a primary inducement of this; policies and programs suggested by citizens were implemented when officials felt that they would be favorably evaluated by the general public and thus could become valuable assets in a reelection campaign.[13] Motivated by political concerns, officials nevertheless responded to some of the social needs of the collectivity they governed.

The decision centers Banfield found in Chicago consisted primarily of single individuals, the mayor, and the Cook County chief executive. Both were loathe to offend any segment of the community, preferring to defer a decision in the face of controversy and then to act only on the compromise product of debate. Multimember decision centers may also be sensitive to information produced by members of the planning field. Individual members of these centers may have constituents' views to support or in the extreme a majority of the members may attempt to decide each issue on its merits. In their study of four cities, Williams and Adrian report finding multimember decision centers corresponding to both of these types.[14] They found two cities in which decision centers were "open systems, where government approached being a neutral instrument arbitrating among conflicting claims."[15] In two other cities they found decision centers "much less accessible to all groups in the community,"[16] but nevertheless concerned with the views of those groups they did represent. In both sets of cities decision centers were sensitive to the information generated by planning fields. The decision centers in the cities differed not in their use of information but in their interpretation of it. In the cities where government approximated a neutral instrument, a broader range of objectives was generally considered as relevant for the evaluation of public policy.

Decision centers may thus vary in their sensitivity to and receptivity of information from a planning field. At one extreme elected officials may be adherents of narrow, primitive concepts of political rationality. In this case only that information from a planning field which suggests means of improving contributions to political objectives will be used by them. Participants in public decision making may only achieve their ends through such decision makers if they conceal them behind political objectives. At the other extreme, elected officials may refrain from action until a consensus among debate participants emerges. These officials are substantially dependent on a planning field for ideas, analyses, plans, and proposals. In between are decision centers which do not withdraw so completely from their formal and legal authority to decide. They act in the face of controversy and employ some planning field data in reaching their conclusions about the best response to a problem.

For the purposes of this study none of these uses of information or approaches to decision making is necessarily preferable. What is of interest is the quality and quantity of the information upon which a decision is founded. Politically rational decision making is in general no less likely to be improved with better information than is decision making guided by other objectives. Means still have to be directed to ends and, if uncertainty exists about both or either, rational decision making may dictate the acquisition of data. Given the purpose of this study, to analyze the control capability of plural decision making, politically rational decisions are not of major interest. Of greater concern are those decisions which involve objectives of planning field members and the electorate. Yet the fact that these objectives may be a secondary concern behind political objectives for a decision center, as in Chicago, does not impede the analysis. The question can still be asked: given the broader (though secondary) objectives of these decisions, what is the control capability provided by the information upon which they are based?

Planning Fields

Members

Three general categories of planning field member may be distinguished: individuals, groups, and organizations. Individual citizens usually participate by attending public hearings. They may prepare plans and position papers, undertake surveys and analyses, explore the ironies of a proposed course of action and express sarcastic, bluntly critical, or supportive opinions. Most individuals are, however, nonparticipants. Even the possession of political power does not necessarily induce involvement, as the studies of Banfield,[17] Dahl,[18] and Martin [19] have shown. Individuals, no matter how powerful, usually do not have the time to become involved in problem situations in which they have no interest.

Individuals may participate more effectively as members of a group, which may be defined as a collection of two or more persons created to pursue common interests. Groups are supported primarily by the resources of their individual members, and most members of a group obtain little or no income or employment from it. Thus a large group may employ certain staff personnel from the contributions or dues that a majority of its members make or pay. As a group member an individual shares the costs of participation with others, but he also loses the ability to express his precise opinion.[20] The "paper group" created by a petition reduces the time costs and inconvenience associated with the formulation and expression of an opinion to near zero. But a petition will not normally express the precise opinion of any group member; rather it will reflect some consensus. Not infrequently, parent-teacher associations, supported by the time and other resources of their members, become involved in public debate about the broad issues of public school system policy. But on specific issues parent interests and teacher interests may diverge and participation through their combined association may be satisfactory to neither. If the schism is deep enough, each may form its separate parent or teacher association. The inability to accommodate different emphases within a single group may account, for example, for the many distinct conservation clubs that exist. While all members of these clubs share a general interest in environmental preservation, some are more interested in fish and marine life, others in forest life, others in birds, and some in parks and recreational areas. The members of each group have their own distinct interests which could not be as well served by a larger organization. Still, within these groups individual members may have to compromise their positions on specific issues if a group position is to be obtained.

An organization may be defined as an assemblage of two or more persons created to attain a set of ends from resources provided by the external environment, not necessarily in exchange for services produced.[21] A majority of the members of an organization, as distinct from its clients or customers, look to it as a source of employment and for their income. As elements in the environment external to an organization, customers and clients consume the services it produces. Customers do so in the market place while clients avail themselves of services without incurring any monetary costs. Organizations not dependent on the market place for their resources may obtain them from an endowment or from the public either individually or collectively. If an organization must sell its output to obtain its resources, it is a private firm or a semi-public agency. If it obtains its resources from an endowment or the voluntary contributions of citizens, it is a foundation or charity. Finally, if it does obtain its resources from the public as a collectivity it is some form of public agency supported by taxation. This does not mean that it cannot sell its services; it may do so, but not so much for the purposes of obtaining resources as for the purpose of regulating consumption of them.

Groups may be formed from the members of an organization, from its clients and from individuals interested in the organization's functions. As organizations, public agencies may come to depend on these groups for support when they undertake new programs or become involved in public debate.[22] They may also find, of course, that these groups become adversaries.

In any given public decision system a fourth class of planning field member may also appear. Because they do not have the power or authority to allocate resources and establish public policy, elected officials, who would normally be members of a decision center, may appear in the planning field of a decision system responding to a given problem situation. Thus a mayor may appear before the legislature arguing for a particular response to a problem confronting his city.

Motivation

More important than who participates is why he participates. Involvement in a public debate may be an expensive, time consuming activity which uses resources that could be profitably applied elsewhere. Since participation has an opportunity cost, it seems reasonable to assume that participants expect some return from their activities. Several different types of reward may be sought. Planning field members may seek, for example, relief from some regulatory phase of government or they may oppose completely or seek to modify legislation which would affect them. They may also seek a commitment of public resources to a project or program from which they will benefit directly or obtain some type of satisfaction. Or they may oppose a program or seek to modify it because their interests will suffer from its execution. In each of these cases members of a planning field act as partisans seeking contribution to their objectives from public action. Their primary concern is the private benefits and sanctions that may be associated with the public response to a problem.

The assumption that self-interest motivates participation conceals more than it explains, however. Specifically it does not adequately describe the inducements that lead any of the three participant types to become involved. Consider participation by individuals. Involvement in a decision system may be motivated by the expectation of obtaining either a public or a private good. If the individual seeks the latter, he is trying to obtain from a decision center a good or service which may benefit him alone, for example a zoning variance. If he seeks the former he is requesting that public resources be used to provide a good or service which when made available to him must also be made available to others, for example mosquito control. When an individual participates to obtain a private good, the motivation may be entirely that of personal gain. But when he seeks a public good his purposes are not as precisely defined. As with a request for a private good, personal consumption is an important reason for involvement. But personal satisfaction might also be obtained from the consumption of others. When a public good is sought, self-gain could be only part of the motivation for participation; altruism or a regard for the commonweal could also be involved.

A similar problem arises with the assumption that self-interest motivates groups, because the self-interest of a group is also an ambiguous concept. For some groups the personal consumption or benefit of members may be the inducement for participation. Trade and industrial associations are examples; normally they participate in order to advance the welfare of their members through favorable public policies and programs. For other groups direct gain for their members may be of no consequence. Protection or enhancement of shared interests, which do not necessarily involve direct personal consumption, may constitute the objective of involvement. The reward from participation is, then, whatever satisfaction group members obtain from seeing their common interest, which is the reason for the group's existence, advanced. This does not mean that personal consumption of members may not be advanced. The increased scholastic achievement which may result from changes in educational policy sought by a parent-teacher association will directly benefit some (but not necessarily all) students and their parents. In addition, to the extent that all citizens benefit from the improved academic attainment of some students, that is, to the degree that it is a public good, the welfare of all members of the association will indirectly be advanced. Yet the primary motivation for involvement will not be the direct or indirect personal gains of members but the broader group interest in educational policy. The preservation and enhancement of such an interest may be a much more powerful stimulus to participation than the personal gain of members. In the New York City school decentralization debate a number of groups appeared to participate for this reason. Among them were the National Association for the Advancement of Colored People, the United Bronx Parents, the United Parents Associations, the Public Education Association, the Teachers for Community Control, the Ad-Hoc Committee to Defend the Right to Teach, the Citizens for the Preservation of the Merit System, and the Citizens Committee for Children. In each case the broader interest of the group rather than direct or indirect improvement in members' personal welfare would seem to have been the inducement for involvement.

Self-interest also does not adequately explain the motivation of many organizations. The major objectives of organizational participation may be maintenance and enhancement or survival and expansion of the entity.[23] The question is, however, how are these objectives interpreted? In some cases they can be seen in terms of improving or sustaining the level and quality of services provided to clients. In others they may imply the protection or advancement of the interests of organizational members or groups associated with and affected by what the organization accomplishes. When an attempt is made to consolidate one organization with another, functional survival may be primarily a concern of top management. On the other hand, when an attempt is made to abolish an organization functional survival may be a concern of its members, its clients, and interest groups who place a high priority on the organization's output or services. The members, stockholders, and customers of a firm will benefit if it successfully opposes a legislative threat to its survival, but only certain members of a previously autonomous public agency may benefit if it is not integrated into a larger public organization. Similarly only members and stockholders of a publicly regulated corporation may gain if it succeeds in obtaining permission to raise the prices of its products.

Each of the three categories of participant may attempt to conceal its true motives for participation. Individuals and groups may suggest that satisfaction from improved public programs and policies is the basis of their interest in a public issue when in fact personal gain is the real inducement. Similarly organizations may conceal their maintenance and enhancement goals, which are of concern to members only, behind an appeal to the public interest or the needs of their clients. On the other hand organizations, particularly public agencies, may not pursue maintenance and enhancement activities which would benefit clients to the greatest degree for fear of losing electoral support. In this case the organization may actually be pursuing a strategy designed to obtain the greatest feasible gains for its clients.

Just as the motivations of individuals, groups, and organizations may be difficult to specify with precision, so are those of elected officials who become members of a planning field. These officials will lack the authority to respond to a problem and thus will represent constituents' interests and objectives to a decision center which does have such authority. They will be seeking decisions which will enhance the welfare of their constituents. However whenever they participate as members of a planning field, elected officials may find that the interests of their constituents may conflict and that they must assign priorities to them. In the extreme they may simply ignore the interests of some constituents or they may attempt to find a compromise position among the interests such that some are not sacrificed completely for the advancement of others.

In addition to pursuing a variety of objectives, participants may perceive different levels of contributions to these objectives from collective action. An individual seeking a public good may recognize some but not all of the beneficiaries and thus some but not all of the benefits of that good. A group trying to obtain a private good for its members is quite likely to ignore the benefits other citizens may obtain because it has successfully sought public production of that good. Thus a local association of manufacturers may in name only be concerned about the general benefits to citizens from a widened street or new expressway. Its main and only recognized objective in becoming involved is the benefit to its individual members from being able to ship, deliver, and receive goods more easily. Similarly a hunting club seeking to preserve a forested tract of land may ignore the potential benefits of nonmembers who may picnic, hike, hunt, or fish in that area. Although the club might conceal the private gains to its members behind an appeal to the public interest, it would not necessarily be concerned about or as a participant be influenced by the benefits to nonmembers.

Groups seeking broader ends than the direct welfare of members also might not recognize or as participants acknowledge all the benefits that would be produced if their requests to a decision center were successful. The total statewide gains from a given legislative decision might not be recognized by the parent-teacher association seeking that decision. At most the members of such an association might acknowledge the potential benefits to the students and parents in the school system which they represent. Organizations too may ignore the full range of benefits which might arise if their involvement is successful. When they conceal maintenance and enhancement needs behind the interests of their clients, they may disregard whatever gains are actually obtained by clients. And even when they do take these gains into consideration they may not be aware of the full extent of them. Like a group, an organization may participate in decision systems which will set policy and establish programs for a broader geographical area than that over which it has jurisdiction. Although by its participation it may generate benefits for other organizations and the clients of these organizations, it may not acknowledge these benefits as a participant.

All participants may exhibit some myopia about the potential gains from involvement simply because they are concerned with only one aspect of a large problem. Any public policy or program may have a number of different ends and a number of distinct consequences. Planning field members need not be concerned with all of these, although they can be. To the extent that they are not, they will not be aware of the full range of benefits that might arise. Public agencies, for example, can only undertake those activities and pursue those ends for which they have authorization. When several of them become involved in the same planning field they may each disregard the benefits from a public program which will be obtained by the clients of the others. Thus as participants they will not be motivated by the total potential benefits from a decision.

Motivations and the Production of Information

Participants in plural decision making, especially groups and organizations, may make significant expenditures on information. Banfield found in Chicago, for example, that policies and plans were prepared primarily "within those private organizations having some special stake in the matters involved and by the civic associations."[24] Banfield also observed that these plans and policies were usually carefully prepared. An elected official knows, he suggests,

> . . . that those who come before him have carefully considered the effect upon their organizations (or upon their personal standing if they are "individuals") of taking this or that position. Their presence means that the position they endorse is popular with the membership, or at least that it is not so unpopular as to threaten the maintenance of the organization, and that the leaders think the matter important enough [to participate].[25]

The Chicago model of participatory decision making may, of course, be unique. Yet because they are interested in the distribution of benefits and costs, in the question of who will gain and who will suffer as a consequence of any public action, individuals, groups, and organizations may need to engage in the development of information as a precondition to participation.[26] No participant can effectively influence a decision center unless he determines what his objectives are and how they will be affected by the possible alternatives under foreseeable environmental conditions. Motivated by the expectation that public action will make contributions to their objectives, participants may seek information in order to determine what type of policy or program is most consistent with their interests. Through problem data participants attempt to ascertain the nature and the magnitude of the problem affecting them, the relative priority of their objectives, and the relative value of contributions to them. Through information about the problem environment and alternatives they try to discover the actual contributions to objectives that can be made by the possible courses of action. With this information as the basis for his plans and proposals a participant is more likely to obtain a decision which will prove to be favorable to his interests. These data increase a participant's ability to instruct the decision center about the true nature of his interests and those courses of action which will, in fact, make contributions to them. Without this information participants will not know which courses of action will be of benefit to them and to what extent. They will be uncertain about the degree to which any action they request will in fact achieve their ends. Thus in most cases it is in their interest, whether narrowly or broadly defined, to invest resources in the informational base of their plans and proposals.

The quality and quantity of information that participants produce will be governed, however, by the objectives they perceive to be relevant in any problem situation and the extent to which they recognize the totality of contributions which can be made by a program or policy to these objectives. As noted above, uncertainty exists about the general nature of both of these factors. Since this uncertainty cannot be eliminated, it must be permitted or recognized in the analysis. To accomplish this in an orderly manner three categories of participation are distinguished: altruism, ambivalence, and myopia. These categories differentiate among participants by indicating the degree to which the benefits and costs anticipated from a policy or program influence their production of information.

Altruism

Altruistic involvement means that in his planning a participant recognizes the benefits from a decision based on an extra unit of data which will be obtained by all others sharing his goals. In addition, altruistic participants take into consideration the total resource savings which may be occasioned by better planning. But altruism does not require a participant to take into account when developing plans and proposals the objectives of those who do not share his interests or the contributions that might be made to these objectives by any plan he develops. An altruistic *group* would be one which was motivated to participate not only because of the potential gains to its members but also because of the gains which might be obtained by all other citizens sharing its objectives or interests. Thus a hunting club would participate altruistically if it acknowledged the total expected benefits to all hunters, not only its members, who might use a wildlife area it sought to preserve. In addition, according to the definition, it would recognize all cost savings which might arise because a decision was based on better information. In the same manner a parent-teacher association would act altruistically by letting the benefits to all students and parents and all cost savings guide it in the development of plans and proposals.

Both organizations and groups might be classified as altruistic even when the true purpose of their involvement was the private gain of members. The definition of altruism only requires that participants produce information in accordance with its value to society in the determination of a public program or policy. For example, suppose a welfare agency, concerned primarily about its survival, becomes involved in the planning field of a decision system which is acting on an issue affecting welfare clients in some way. The welfare agency would act altruistically if in its planning it was guided by the potential gains to all welfare clients from a decision based on better information and all cost savings. Because private gains may be obtained simultaneously with public ends, parochial interests may be induced to act altruistically. Note that altruists may be participants with narrow objectives. The definition only requires that they act as if they represented all who share these objectives. Thus an association, comprised of some but not all firms in an industry, could participate altruistically if the potential benefits the entire industry would obtain from a decision based on better information plus all expected resource savings determined the data it would produce. Lastly distinct groups may combine and together act altruistically. Chambers of commerce throughout a state, each representing businessmen in a different locality, may unite to form a group which considers the totality of commercial interests.

The concept of an altruistic participant may be expressed somewhat more rigorously in notational form. Assume a society of M individuals, m of whom can be associated with one set of objectives and interests and the remaining $\bar{m}$ of whom can be associated with another. Let the expected benefits to all individuals in either set from a decision based on any quantity of pre- and post-decision data be specified by

$$B(x,h) \quad \text{or} \quad \bar{B}(x,h).$$

Then the changes in the expected benefits to all individuals in either set which are anticipated from a unit of information may be noted by

$$B_x \quad \text{or} \quad \bar{B}_x$$

for a unit of pre-decision data and

$$B_h \quad \text{or} \quad \bar{B}_h$$

for a unit of feedback.

The expected resource expenditures associated with a decision based on any quantity of pre- and post-decision data may be specified by

$$R(x,h).$$

Then the quantities

$$R_x \quad \text{and} \quad R_h$$

represent the changes in expected resource costs indicated by a unit of pre-decision data or feedback. If a unit of either type of data indicates that resource expenditures can be decreased, then R_x and R_h, the magnitudes of the expected decrement, are negative quantities. An altruistic participant representing either the set of m or $\bar{m}$ individuals evaluates the expected gains from a decision respectively as

$$B(x,h) \quad - \quad R(x,h)$$

or

$$\bar{B}(x,h) \quad - \quad R(x,h).$$

Thus for such a participant the expected value of a unit of pre-decision data is given by

$$B_x \quad - \quad R_x$$

or

$$\bar{B}_x \quad - \quad R_x.$$

An altruistic participant recognizes the total benefits or the total value of the contributions to a set of objectives that might arise from the acquisition of one more unit of pre-decision data or feedback. In addition, such a participant acknowledges the total cost savings promised by the development of that unit of information. Note that while they recognize all potential cost savings, altruistic participants consider the benefits of public action solely to those who share their values.

Ambivalence

Participants in the second category are called ambivalent because they incompletely resemble altruists. They are induced to prepare plans by the total benefits or all contributions to a set of objectives expected from a program or policy or they are motivated by the total resource savings which might be obtained from better data. But they are not motivated by both. Thus an ambivalent participant might recognize the total benefit changes indicated by a unit of information and none or only a small fraction of the potential resource expenditure changes. Alternatively such a participant might consider all the resource changes but none or only a small proportion of the benefit changes revealed by a unit of data. An example of the former type of ambivalent participant might be a public agency. These organizations do not obtain their resources from the sale of services but from the tax revenues collected by the unit of government of which they are a part. Most are responsible only for the expenditure of resources. Thus in their planning they may act altruistically with respect to the total benefits of collective action, but they may find no inducement to do so with respect to the resource costs.

This type of ambivalent participatory behavior may also characterize a group requesting a decision which would aid only its members. In this case no other participants or nonparticipants share the group's objectives, and with respect to contributions to them it may plan altruistically. But the costs of whatever action it seeks may be borne by the entire society, and the group may recognize only a small fraction of the resource expenditure changes disclosed by planning. Such a participant might not recognize any of these changes or it might take into consideration that portion of these changes which it estimated its members might be aware of in, say, the form of reduced or increased taxes. The group's involvement could thus be described as altruistic with respect to the benefits of better data but characterized by self-interest with respect to resource savings.

Notationally this type of ambivalent participatory behavior requires that a group from the set m evaluate a unit of pre- or post-decision data in accordance with

$$B_x - pR_x$$

and

$$B_h - pR_h.$$

The quantities B_x and B_h represent the changes in the expected benefits to all members of m foreseen from a unit of pre- or post-decision data, while R_x and R_h indicate the changes in expected resource expenditures. The fraction p, which is positive, represents the proportion of all resource expenditure changes indicated by a unit of data which are considered by the group in its planning. While it might have a value of zero if the group was only slightly affected by the resource costs of any public policy or program, it would never have a value of one or greater. A value of one would be altruism and a value greater than one would be meaningless.

Notationally the other type of ambivalent participatory behavior requires that a group from the set $\bar{m}$ evaluate a unit of pre- or post-decision data in accordance with

$$p\bar{B}_x - R_x$$

and

$$p\bar{B}_h - R_h.$$

Again $\bar{B}_x$ and $\bar{B}_h$ indicate the changes in expected benefits foreseen from a unit of pre- and post-decision data and R_x and R_h the changes in anticipated resource expenditures. The fraction p is positive and may have a value of zero but not one or greater. While this type of participatory behavior is included here primarily for the purpose of analytical completeness, it may be reflective of the behavior of very fiscally conservative groups and organizations. Thus a taxpayers association might be concerned about the totality of the resource expenditures incurred in responding to a problem but only those benefits of which its members were aware. Here p represents that fraction of the total benefits created by a public program or policy which the members of such an organization might obtain.

Myopia

The last category of planning field member, the myopic participant, may be the most common in practice. These participants recognize only some proportion of the total benefit increases and cost savings expected from planning. A myopic group or organization might recognize only the benefits of better information to its members, although this data would also be expected to increase the benefits a larger group of citizens obtained from a public program or policy. It would also recognize only a proportion of the resource savings that data enabled. Thus when the clients of a number of functionally similar organizations would gain from a public program, any one of these organizatons would act myopically by considering only the benefits of better data which its clients would be expected to receive. The clients of all organizations would benefit from the data any one organization produced, yet in its planning it would be guided only by the gains to its clients. An organization might also act myopically when it pursued maintenance and enhancement goals in the guise, for example, of client objectives. In this case the organization would seek a program or policy ostensibly for the purpose of improving the welfare of its clients but would estimate the value of information about that program not in terms of cliental gains but solely in terms of the maintenance and enhancement gains to its members. In other words, the organization would not prepare plans and proposals in order to improve the gains which society or its clients would obtain from the program but in order to preserve or enhance itself. Because it was concerned in its planning primarily with the development of a proposal which it could promote, the organization might perceive very few actual benefits from the development of information. In most cases its gains from information would be small in comparison to those society or its clients would obtain, for to pursue its ends the organization would not need a refined, well-analyzed, well-designed proposal which would be likely to make the greatest contributions to the objectives of its clients consistent with resource expenditure considerations. In many cases it might be able to satisfy its ends with a proposal which was only a slight improvement over an initial preplanning estimate of the best program. Thus it might act myopically, ignoring most of the expected benefit and resource expenditure changes which any unit of data might reveal. Note, however, that should an organization participate directly in a decision concerned solely with its maintenance or enhancement it might not act myopically. It could act altruistically if it estimated the value of information in terms of the total benefits and costs of this decision.

For similar reasons groups may participate in a myopic manner. When they conceal the direct gains of their members behind an appeal to the public interest, groups may ignore whatever broader benefits might arise from the public action sought. If these broader benefits together with cost savings are neglected by the group when it produces information, it acts myopically. Thus a chamber of commerce might advocate the widening of a street as being in the public interest. But its planning analysis of that proposal might be guided only by the benefit increases and cost savings better data would bring to its members. A group may also act myopically even when as a participant it is not concerned solely with the direct interests of its members. Even though they pursue broad objectives, groups need not evaluate information in light of the net gains that it enables society to obtain. A parent-teacher association may not identify the value of information in terms of the benefits to all those affected by a program it advocates. If a program is expected to have statewide impacts, a parent-teacher association may ignore the beneficiaries outside the school system it represents. On the other hand, even if the impacts of a program are restricted to a single school, a parent-teacher association may not be motivated as a participant by the total benefit increases and cost decreases information would enable. Its satisfaction from successful involvement need not be measured in the same way that it would be if the association were participating in order to aggrandize the private welfare of its members. Here the group probably would evaluate information in terms of the benefit gains and resource savings it was expected to generate for all members. However in pursuing broader objectives than the welfare of members, groups may not evaluate information in an analogous manner. That is, they may not consider the value of information in terms of all that it promises; they may be motivated by and recognize only a portion of the benefit increases and cost savings that all citizens affected by the program would obtain from better data. In this case they will probably underestimate the social value of information which improves the performance of that program.[27]

Notationally myopic participation implies that a group from the set m estimates the expected value of a unit of pre- and post-decision data in terms of

$$qB_x - q'R_x$$
$$qB_h - q'R_h.$$

The fractions q and q' may have the same value. Both are positive and range in value from zero to one but do not take on the value of one.

Motivations: Summary

By categorizing participants as altruistic, ambivalent, or myopic no assumptions have been made about the precise objectives which motivate their involvement. In an analysis of the control capability of plural decision making no such assumption can be made. Public programs and policy can be requested by participants and are in practice designed to make contributions to both relatively narrow private goals and to broader social values. What must be specified in an analysis of plural decision making is the alternative positions participants might take toward the value of information. This is the function of the three categories. Thus whether a trade association acts altruistically, ambivalently, or myopically depends not on the nature of its objectives but on the extent to which it recognizes the total or social value of information used in a public decision which will make contributions to its objectives.

The categories of ambivalent and myopic involvement may be interpreted in part as reflecting the response of participants to what has been called the free rider problem in economics. The benefits obtained by participants from involve-ment—the contributions to objectives, the decreases in resource expenditures—are a public good.[28] Whatever course of action makes these benefits available to a participant also makes them available to all sharing his ends and, in the case of resource expenditure savings, those not sharing his ends. Many potential partici-pants are, therefore, induced to avoid involvement. Such nonparticipants are classical free riders; without bearing any of the expense they obtain the benefits of the participatory activity of others. Actual participants who behave altruistically would take into consideration the benefits these free riders obtain from their involvement, but ambivalent and myopic participants would not. Ambivalent par-ticipants acknowledge only a fraction p of the total benefit or the total resource changes indicated by a unit of data, while myopic participants take into account only a fraction of both. Thus the category of ambivalent or myopic behavior may be viewed as indicating participant neglect of some or all of the gains nonpartici-pants, some of whom may be free riders, obtain from their involvement.

Subsystem Interaction

The power or influence that planning field members may have over the members of a decision center constitutes a second important dimension of partici-patory behavior. Power may be defined as the ability to insure compliance with a request or order through the granting of rewards or the imposition of sanctions. The exercise of power requires that one actor can confer or withhold resources (e.g., votes, money and credit, jobs) valued by another or apply legal restrictions critical to his success. Influence implies an ability which is based on status, friendship, expertise, or persuasive ability to insure compliance with a request or order. Influ-ence can be exercised without the possession of resources that can be conferred or withheld or the threat of applying legal restrictions. For example, the downtown merchants may be able to exercise influence over a city councilman who is also a businessman, while the leader of a political party might be able to exercise power over him. In bargaining the various participants exercise some power over one another to the extent that the cooperation of all is needed for successful action. Power and influence can be issue specific, limited to a narrow range of requests within a given problem situation, and applied discontinuously. Thus while the business community may be able to influence an official in some problem situa-tions, only better government groups might be able to influence or even exercise power (by withholding reelection support) over him in others. Finally, the ability to influence or exercise power may be selectively employed because not all problem situations involve a participant's interests to the same degree. Some may be of no concern, others may be important. Accordingly involvement will vary and with it the exercise of power and influence.

Interaction between the two subsystems of a decision system is characterized by more than the flow of information. Although members of a decision center possess by law the right or authority to determine the policies and programs of a collectivity, they may be subject to the domination of one or more members of the planning field. The communications of these members will be more effective than will be those of planning field members who lack influence or power. Thus the abstract concept of a public decision system will differ from the reality it is intended to represent in a number of ways depending upon the degree to which the decision center is subject to domination by members of the planning field. At the minimum, no participant may be able to influence or exercise power over any member of a decision center, and the abstract concept of a public decision system will describe reality. In such a decision system plural decision making implies participant involvement in an advisory capacity only. At the maximum, one planning field member alone or in coalition with others will be able to determine the action taken by a decision center. Here the decision system may be described as closed because in effect a few members of the planning field are responsible for the choices the decision center makes. But such a decision system can also be described as advisory if the planning field members with power and influence do not have preferences about the response that should be made to a problem and accept the advice of other participants. In such a situation they become the decision center for other members of the planning field for whom participation implies involvement in an advisory capacity. The control of a city council by a strong political leader may result in a closed decision system when the leader imposes his preferences and an advisory decision system when the leader accepts advice from other members of the community.

In between these two extremes are open decision systems in which one or more participants possess some power or influence over some but not a majority of the members of a decision center. Here plural decision making implies that some responsibility for determining the solution to a problem effectively resides with planning field members. This may occur in two ways. Representatives of participants in the planning field may be members of the decision center. A member of a good government group may belong to the decision center (e.g., a city council), while the group itself would belong to the planning field of any decision system. Or planning field members may simply possess power over or influence with some decision center members. In this type of decision system bargaining and negotiation will frequently occur among decision center members who represent participants with conflicting objectives.

Closed Systems

A closed decision system may occur in a number of ways. It may represent a situation-specific example of a monolithic community power structure in which a single cohesive group of individuals or a single individual provides leadership on all community issues. Such a power structure may be depicted by a single pyramid. The group or individual at the top of the pyramid possesses the legal authority to decide for a collectivity or the power and influence needed to determine the choices made by a majority of those who possess this authority. Alternatively a closed decision system may be an individual instance of a polylithic community power structure in which distinct sets of issue areas are governed by different monolithic power structures.[29] Such a community power structure may be represented by a set of pyramids, each with its own cohesive leadership group which possesses the legal authority to decide or the power and influence needed to determine the choices made by a majority of those who possess this authority. In a polylithic community power structure conflicts among leadership groups are resolved by bargaining and negotiation, forms of plural decision making; but closed public decision systems exist in polylithic power structures whenever the decisions of a leadership group are not challenged by other leadership groups. Finally a closed public decision system may occur in a problem situation in which there is little or widely diffused public interest. In this case a planning field member might through a display of acknowledged expertise determine the choice of a decision center. Wilensky contends, for example, that the decision to create the interstate highway system was made in these circumstances. The highway lobby was able to establish itself as the authority on the nation's transportation needs because the general public had vague and inconsistent conceptions of these needs.[30]

Specialization of functions between subsystems does not occur in a closed decision system because it has in effect only one element, the individual or group of individuals who provide leadership. The group that decides is responsible for the informational foundations of decisions. If this group does solicit or use the plans and programs of others, the decision system is no longer closed but is advisory. Consequently in a closed decision system a planning field which has one member develops information for its own use or for use by a decision center whose choices it can determine through the exercise of power or influence. Uncertainty about the effectiveness of involvement and about the value of information does not arise in a closed public decision system because of any inherent characteristics of the participatory process. Participants are assured that their plans and programs will be accepted and are thus assured of a favorable decision. Uncertainty about the consequences of involvement is solely an informational phenomenon in such a decision system.

Open Systems

The main difference between closed and open systems lies in the nature of their planning fields. In an open system planning field members do not form a cohesive group and some, but not necessarily all of them, possess some power or influence though not enough to insure that the decision center will comply with their requests.[31] Specialization of function between subsystems may exist, but it is not pervasive. Decision center members may unite the decision-making and planning activities which occur in open systems by developing their own plans and proposals. For example, the chairman of the Oberlin City Council was, according to Wildavsky, an initiator of policy, engaged in the analysis of public problems and the design of policy alternatives, and he was generally, by virtue of his own efforts, better informed than his opponents.[32] Similarly the two functions are combined in effect when planning field members hold power over or influence with members of the decision center. While they may not be able to dictate what the decision center as a collectivity will do, they can determine the actions of some members, effectively uniting through their power or influence the two functions. In the extreme all members of the decision center might be involved in the development of information, in which case only their divergent interests and objectives would distinguish them from the decision center of a closed system. When the leadership groups of a polylithic community power structure bargain or negotiate they constitute a decision system in which two distinguishable subsystems do not actually exist and in which specialization of function does not in effect occur.[33] Only a diversity of interests differentiates this from a closed decision system; the action upon which all bargaining parties agree affects each differently and is therefore evaluated by each from a different perspective.

Bargaining and negotiation are not necessarily characteristics of an open decision system, however.[34] Not all members of the decision center of such a system may be partisans, committed to the advancement of a definable set of interests and values. Some may be independent of the influence and power of planning field members and may view themselves as arbitrators to be influenced by persuasive argument and discussion with planning field members.[35] Where this is the case, compromise among partisans may not be required before a course of action can be determined. In coalition with the independent members of a decision center, some partisans may be able to obtain a decision which substantially ignores the interests of those partisans with whom they would otherwise have to bargain or negotiate. Through a coalition they could obtain their ends completely whereas a bargain would require that concessions to the interests of other partisans be made. Alternatively the independent members alone may as a group have sufficient authority to decide the response to a problem. Their decision may ignore the interests of all partisans and reflect instead the request or proposal of a planning field member who lacks power or influence. Partisans and independents may also interact in a variety of ways which compromise the interests of the former and the judgments of the latter. Partisans may be forced to modify their requests and proposals to obtain the support of independents. The concessions obtained by independents as a result of this bargaining or negotiation will not necessarily serve their own private objectives but may serve broader social goals or those interests which they are persuaded should not be ignored. The adoption of a housing code in Oberlin as reported by Wildavsky is an example.[36] Championed by a housing committee, the code was opposed by some councilmen until its adverse impacts for different elements of the community had been mitigated. This opposition was not raised entirely because of the power and influence of these community groups but because of a determination that their interests were relevant in the decision to be made about the code.

The nature of the decision-making process impedes the development of information in an open system. Neither the outcome of bargaining and negotiation nor the behavior of independent decision center members can be predicted with certainty. Partisans in the decision center and those members of the planning field who lack power and influence cannot be sure that their plans and proposals will not be neglected nor can they even be sure that a decision will be made. The decision center may not be able either to compromise competing claims or to determine which claims should be advanced over others. Thus the effectiveness of involvement is uncertain because of the inherent nature of the decision-making process. Accordingly the value of information is uncertain for reasons which have little to do with its quality or quantity. Participants who lack power and influence will be more uncertain about the effectiveness of involvement and the potential value of information than those who do not. Similarly a decision center member will be less uncertain about the usefulness of his plans and proposals than a planning field member who lacks power or control. While the inherent uncertainty of an open system affects all participants, it does not do so equally.

Advisory Systems

In advisory decision systems specialization of function is complete. All decision center members are independent of the planning field, and no center member engages in the development or acquisition of data. The planning field is composed of a number of participants, each with distinguishable interests and objectives. While members of the decision center must ultimately arbitrate between these interests, they are at the outset nonpartisan or independent. They possess no initial preferences. An apparent example of this type of decision system is described by Williams and Adrian as follows:

> The typical pattern of policy development was for a group outside the council to take the initiative, with the council reserving judgment until very late in the negotiations that took place between the group and the administration, or between the group and other groups.[37]

And, in effect, Banfield found an advisory system in a number of Chicago issues. He observes that in

> ... the Chicago view, a policy ought to be framed by the interests affected. ... In this view, the affected interests should work out for themselves the "best" solution of the matter (usually a compromise).[38]

In Chicago the political head did not usually initiate policy but responded to plans and proposals upon which there was general agreement. In essence a political head who possessed the power to determine what action the city council took depended on a planning field for the informational bases of his decisions.

Uncertainty about the effectiveness of involvement is greatest for planning field members in an advisory system. All participants have equal reason to expect that a decision will be favorable to their interests, but no participant has any reason to expect that his viewpoint is more likely than those of other participants to prevail. Thus the inherent characteristics of this type of decision system would appear to impede the production of information by all participants to the same degree. By contrast some participants in an open system will have higher expectations than others about the effectiveness of involvement because they have some power or influence.

An Example

The school decentralization debate in New York City, 1967–69, has many of the characteristics of an open decision system. As the decision center, the state legislature had the formal authority to determine the public response to the issue of decentralization. The planning field consisted of many individuals, groups, and organizations who voiced opinions, prepared plans, and testified at hearings held by legislative committees, the New York City Board of Education, and the New York City Human Rights Commission. In addition to the mayor of New York City, the participants included the National Association for the Advancement of Colored People, the New York City Commission on Human Rights, the Council of Supervisory Associations, the High School Principals Association, the United Federation of Teachers (the teachers union), the African-American Teachers Association, the United Bronx Parents, the United Parents Associations, the Public Education Association, the city Board of Examiners, the city Board of Education, the state Board of Regents, the Teachers for Community Control, the Association of Black School Supervisors and Administrators, the Ad-Hoc Committee to Defend the Right to Teach, the Citizens for the Preservation of the Merit System, the Citizens Committee for Children, the Intermediate School 201 and Ocean Hill-Brownsville Demonstration School Districts (which were established formally in the summer of 1967 by the city Board of Education as experiments in school decentralization), numerous private individuals, and many other groups both within and outside the city.

Some of these planning field members possessed decidedly more power and influence with legislators than did others. A few politically powerful participants such as the teachers union and the mayor were readily able to obtain private sessions with individual legislators, while most participants were forced to rely on public hearings to present their viewpoints. The Board of Regents and the city Board of Education, who had recognized expertise in educational issues and lines of communication with individual legislators established over a period of years, clearly wielded greater influence than did the demonstration school districts or the Council Against Poverty. However, while some participants had influence with one or more legislators, no participant had sufficient influence to determine the decision to be made. The debate covered three legislative sessions from 1967 to 1969, and a decision was made only after a number of plans had been proposed and found unacceptable to a majority of the legislators.

Each of the participants in the debate interpreted the factual issues surrounding decentralization from his own perspective and advanced plans and proposals which reflected his values and objectives. Because of the uncertainties inherent in an open system and because of the types of data that are available which reflect on participant behavior, it is impossible to determine whether participants acted altruistically, ambivalently, or myopically. Most participants apparently did not estimate the value of information in accordance with its potential impact on the contributions that could be made to two major objectives of decentralization, improved educational attainment of students and increased citizen involvement in educational decision making.

In sum, the school decentralization debate had the characteristics of an open decision system. The question of concern is, how well did this system perform? When the legislature acted in 1969 to enable the decentralization of a very significant and substantial urban service system, did it possess sufficient information to understand the consequences of its decision or was it in effect experimenting with the scholastic achievement of over one million students in the hope that contributions could be made to the objectives of increased citizen involvement and quality education?

Chapter Four
The Control of Collective Action

Three factors which interact in the public decision-making process, motivations of participants, power, and information, have been discussed. A fourth factor, the ends of collective action, must be examined before the control potential of plural decision making can be analyzed. In most problem situations, if not all, decision centers will not possess either a social welfare function or a concept of the public interest to use in determining the best response to a problem.[1] On the contrary, in most problem situations decision centers must decide what the ends of action are to be and evaluate alternative courses of action in terms of these ends. After exploring the problem and the nature of possible solutions to it, a decision center may determine that the objectives of all segments of society should be served by action or it may decide that the objectives of some are more important than those of others and these alone should be advanced by collective action. From a control perspective the objectives designated as the ends of collective action are important because they affect the value of information and thus the quality and quantity of data that should be collected. For example, if public action is to further commercial but not neighborhood interests, the control capability of plural decision making is determined by and must be judged solely in terms of the former. That substantial neighborhood interests may be sacrificed has little to do with the control of action directed exclusively toward other ends. Participants may investigate the adverse neighborhood impacts in some detail, but their plans and proposals will be of little use in assuring that a decision will contribute to the objectives judged to be the goals of action.

To incorporate this fourth factor into the analysis of plural decision making, three objectives configurations, each representing a different possible specification of the ends of collective action by a decision center, are analyzed. These configurations are characterized by conflict among participant interests, mutuality of interests, and inconsistency of interests. Where participant interests are in conflict, collective action can make contributions to the objectives of only one participant or one homogeneous subset of all participants. The welfare of two or more different participants cannot be improved simultaneously, and the decision center is assumed to choose only one participant's objectives as the ends of collective action. When objectives are consistent, collective action can serve the distinct interests of all or several participants simultaneously; positive contributions to one participant's objectives do not occur at the expense of positive contributions to the objectives of some other participant. Though a decision center does not have to choose among the demands of all participants where objectives are consistent, some choice may nevertheless be involved. The decision center may have to determine which participants' objectives should be, and are consistent enough to be, advanced simultaneously by collective action; accordingly, it may have to determine whether one or more participants' objectives should be ignored. When objectives are inconsistent, collective action cannot advance the ends of all participants simultaneously. Contributions to the objectives of one participant cannot be achieved without the interests of others being sacrificed. In comparison, however, to the case of conflicting objectives and those situations in which some but not all participants' objectives are consistent, the decision center is assumed here to be concerned about some or all of these social costs of action.

Given these three configurations of objectives, the framework within which the analysis of plural decision making will occur has four major components which reflect:

    a.   expectations about the value of information
    b.   motivations of participants
    c.   the distribution of power and influence
    d.   the judgments of a decision center about the appropriate ends of collective action.

These four components and their subcomponents are displayed in table 4-1.

From the four major framework components, fifty-four [2] different combinations of factors, each of which might appear in a problem situation, can be generated. One of these combinations could be

    positive expectations about the value of information
    ambivalent participant motivations
    open decision system
    mutually consistent objectives,

while another might be

    mixed expectations about the value of information
    myopic participant behavior
    open decision system
    mutually consistent objectives.

Not all fifty-four possible combinations are logically possible, however. The decision center of a closed system will not act in problem situations in the manner implied by the categories of mutually consistent or inconsistent objectives for it will always establish only one participant's objectives as the ends of collective action. Thus twelve [3] of the possible combinations can be ignored and only forty-two combinations are relevant to the analysis of plural decision making. These, moreover, are not best examined individually. A more fruitful analysis can be achieved by first exploring participant behavior in relative isolation from decision system characteristics and then using the major conclusions of this analysis to investigate system characteristics.

Underlying the following analysis is the assumption of rational decision making or the rational acquisition of information. As interpreted in the model of

Table 4-1. Framework for Analysis of Plural
Decision Making

Components of Framework	Subcomponents
Expectations about the value of information	Positive expectations Mixed expectations
Participant motivations	Altruism Ambivalence Myopia
Distribution of power and influence	Closed system Open system Advisory system
Configuration of objectives	Conflicting Mutually consistent Inconsistent

imperfect control this assumption does not require that the unproducible be generated or the impossible be developed. That model requires only that different quantities and qualities of data be obtainable through the use of alternative planning processes. In addition it permits the benefits and costs of any quantity or quality of information to vary with such characteristics of the problem situation as the nature of the problem, the number of persons affected by the solution to it, and the time horizon within which a decision must be made. The model, and the assumption of rational decision making therefore, are used only to make comparative assessments, i.e., judgments about the extent to which participants will voluntarily provide the control capability that a collectivity should possess in any problem situation.[4]

The following analysis is in essence quite simple. First an objective configuration is described and its implications for the information a society should acquire in any problem situation are developed. Then the quality and quantity of information which altruistic, ambivalent, and myopic participants would use in preparing their plans and proposals are analyzed. This is compared with the amount of information which would be socially desirable given the conditions of the problem situation and assuming as a starting point for planning a participant's pre-planning appraisal of the problem and the best response to it.

Conflicting Objectives

When the interests of the various segments of a society are in conflict, the objectives of all members cannot be advanced simultaneously. If collective action is to be taken, only one of a competing set of interests may be advanced, quite possibly at the expense of the others. In determining the response to a problem under these conditions, a decision center may consider or ignore these social costs of action. If it decides that they are not to be considered, perhaps because they do not appear to be significant or substantial, collective action will be designed and evaluated solely in terms of its impacts on the objectives of the beneficiaries. Information will not be used to minimize or limit the costs imposed on other segments of society. Consequently the social value of any unit of information is the total resource savings it promises plus the increased benefits to the favored segment.

To illustrate, assume that in the society of M members the interests of the set of m individuals are in conflict with the interests of the $\bar{m}$ individuals and that the decision center concludes that only the interests of the former should be of concern in determining the response to a problem. Then the society should acquire information in accordance with the following conditions:

$$B_x - R_x = D_x$$

$$B_h - R_h = D_h.$$

(4.1)

In (4.1) the subscripts x and h may signify pre- or post-decision data about the problem, problem environment or alternatives. To the left of each equality are the expected marginal benefits (which may be discounted present values to reflect time), and to the right are the marginal costs of each type of data. The quantities D_x and D_h represent the costs of a unit of pre- and post-decision data and increase with the amount of each type of information developed. The more refined and precise a projection or analysis is, the more difficult and expensive is the development of an additional unit of information which further increases the degree of precision. The last unit of pre-decision data should be more expensive than the first unit of feedback to develop, but the costs of that unit of feedback should rise with the amount of pre-decision data developed. As the amount of uncertainty eliminated by pre-decision data increases, the more difficult and expensive are further, albeit post-decision, improvements in precision to obtain. The first unit of feedback will be less expensive if only one unit of pre-decision data has been collected than if twenty have.

The quantities to the left of each equality have somewhat different interpretations depending on whether expectations about the value of information are positive or mixed. First consider the case of positive expectations. Here the quantities B_x and B_h represent the increment in expected benefits to members of the set m from a decision based on an additional unit of pre- and post-decision data; these benefit increases are assumed to decline with the amount of each type of data collected, the first unit of data collected yielding more expected benefit increases than the second and so on. The quantities $-R_x$ and $-R_h$ represent the resource savings foreseen from additional units of each type of information. They are positive because the decreases, R_x and R_h, in resource costs a unit of data is expected to permit are negative quantities. The savings indicated by $-R_h$ are net of any expenditures (other than those for the information itself) needed to obtain them. These resource savings are also assumed to decrease with the total amount of information of each type collected. Thus with positive expectations the marginal benefits of pre-decision data arise from two sources, benefit increases of magnitude B_x and resource savings of magnitude $-R_x$. Both of these quantities are positive, and both decline with the amount of pre-decision data collected. The marginal benefits of feedback arise from two sources, benefit increases B_h and resource savings $-R_h$; each of these quantities is also positive and declines with the amount of feedback collected. Observe that $-R_h$ declines both because resource savings are expected to decrease and because the costs of using feedback are expected to increase with the amount of post-decision data developed. The more feedback that is developed, the more extensive will be the modifications in an original action and the more expensive it will be to use successive units of feedback. Thus while $-R_h$ is positive under positive expectations, it declines more rapidly than would $-R_x$ with additional units of information.

Two categories of mixed expectations must be analyzed. In the first, which may be labeled increasing expectations, a unit of data indicates that by increasing the scale of action or changing its technical characteristics benefit increases B_x may be obtained which exceed the associated increases in resource expenditures R_x. Increasing expectations reflect conservatism in preplanning appraisals. With increasing expectations the marginal benefits of information consist of the benefit increases B_x minus the resource expenditures R_x which must be made to obtain these benefit increases. The marginal benefits $(B_x - R_x)$ decline with the amount of pre-decision data acquired. The benefit increases B_x expected from changing an initial proposal for action to the degree indicated by successive units of information decrease while the resource costs R_x thus incurred increase. More generally, the greater the quantity of data, the less extensive is uncertainty about the appropriate form of action and the less valuable is a unit of data which reduces that uncertainty even further.

The quantities B_h and R_h are interpreted analogously to B_x and R_x. Both are positive; the former declines with the amount of feedback acquired and the latter increases with it. Thus the marginal benefits $(B_h - R_h)$ decline with the amount of feedback acquired.

In the second category, which may be labeled decreasing expectations, a unit of data indicates that by decreasing the scale of action or changing its technical characteristics resource savings $-R_x$ may be obtained which exceed in value the associated benefit losses B_x. Decreasing expectations reflect optimism in initial appraisals. With decreasing expectations the marginal benefits of pre-decision data consist of the resource savings $-R_x$ plus the benefit decreases B_x (which are negative) that arise because the scale of action is contracted. The marginal benefits $(B_x - R_x)$ again decline with the amount of pre-decision data collected. The benefit losses B_x from decreasing the scale of action or changing its technical character to the degree indicated by successive units of information become larger while the expected resource savings $-R_x$ decline. The greater the quantity of data, the less extensive is uncertainty and the less valuable is a unit of data which reduces it even further.

The quantities $-R_h$ and B_h are interpreted analogously to $-R_x$ and B_x. The former is positive, the latter is negative, and the difference, marginal benefits, declines with the amount of feedback acquired.

Given that marginal benefits decline and marginal costs increase with the total amount of information acquired, rational decision making requires that pre- and post-decision data be collected to the point at which the marginal benefits of each equal its marginal costs. Producing more or less information than this results respectively in the costs of the last units exceeding the benefits expected from them or in the benefits anticipated from these units exceeding their costs. In both cases net benefits can be increased, in the former by producing fewer units of data and in the latter by producing more. Under these circumstances the following propositions about participant behavior appear to be valid when decision system characteristics are neglected.

Proposition 1. *No matter what changes planning would reveal as necessary in the preplanning response to a problem, the plans and proposals of altruists will provide an adequate basis for controlling collective action.*

Assume that the decision center determines that the interests of the set of m individuals alone should guide collective action. Then expression (4.1) not only represents the conditions that should guide the collection of pre- and post-decision problem, problem environment and alternatives data for the purposes of social control but also represents the conditions which would guide the development of each of these types of data by an altruistic participant from m. Like the other two types of participant, altruists bear the full costs of producing any unit of information but they also recognize all potential benefit increases or decreases to those sharing their interests and all resource savings or expenditures which a unit of information might disclose. Accordingly, when objectives conflict the marginal benefits of information are the same for these participants as they are for society. Thus, for example, when the interests of a private trade association or public agency were the sole concern of collective action, their plans and proposals might provide sufficient control capability. If they behaved altruistically they would voluntarily develop the information society needed and should have to direct collective means to their ends.

Proposition 2. *When planning would reveal that the benefits of action could be increased and the resource costs decreased or when it would reveal that the scale of action should be changed, the plans and proposals of ambivalent participants will not provide an adequate basis for controlling collective action.*

Two types of ambivalent participants were distinguished earlier: (a) those who appraise a unit of information in terms of all cost changes but only a fraction of the benefit changes it reveals, and (b) those who take into consideration the totality of benefit changes and only a fraction of the cost changes a unit of data indicates. The former may be called cost conscious and the latter benefit conscious ambivalents. Consider the motivations of the latter first. A benefit conscious participant will use the following conditions to guide his data development:

$$B_x - pR_x = D_x$$

$$B_h - pR_h = D_h.$$ (4.2)

When expectations are positive, such a participant underestimates the value of pre-decision data, for he takes into account only a fraction of the resource savings $-R_x$ it permits. Accordingly he will produce less pre-decision data about the problem (including data about his objectives), problem environment, and alternatives than would be socially desirable. Because he produces less pre-decision data, such a participant may perceive greater marginal benefits and smaller marginal costs for any given quantity of feedback than society would and therefore may rely more heavily on it in his planning.

When expectations are mixed, a benefit conscious participant will either overestimate or underestimate the marginal benefits of information. With increasing expectations the benefit increases B_x from expanding the scale or changing the technical characteristics of action to the degree suggested by a unit of data exceed the resource expenditures R_x which that unit also indicates must be made to obtain these benefits. Because he considers only a fraction p of these resource expenditures, a benefit conscious participant expects greater net marginal benefits from pre-decision information than does society and therefore produces more of it. And the smaller p is—it may be zero in many cases—the more likely is such a participant to overestimate the value of a unit of information. For this reason the plans of such a participant will be misleading; they will propose a course of action which from a societal perspective is too extensive in scale. To illustrate, consider figure 4.1 in which the curves MB and MC represent the expected marginal benefits and expected marginal costs of any scale of action A. The curve pMC represents the portion of the marginal costs a benefit conscious participant takes into account. In the absence of planning, society might implement scale of action A_1. Through planning and the development of problem, problem environment, and alternatives data it would discover, however, that the scale of action could be expanded to A_3. If at this point the costs of the last unit of information collected were equal to the difference between MB and MC, planning should terminate and scale of action A_3 should be implemented. However, beginning at A_1 a benefit conscious participant might be led by planning to propose scale of action A_4, at which point for him the cost of the last unit of data was equal to the difference between MB and pMC. From a social perspective this is an excessive scale of action, for its marginal costs exceed its marginal benefits. Consequently participants who do not recognize the full resource costs of expanding the scale of action may misdirect society, possibly causing it to overinvest scarce resources in unwarranted scales or levels of action. For example, as a consequence of its planning a hunting club or conservation group seeking a decision which will benefit its members alone will propose action at a scale which is too

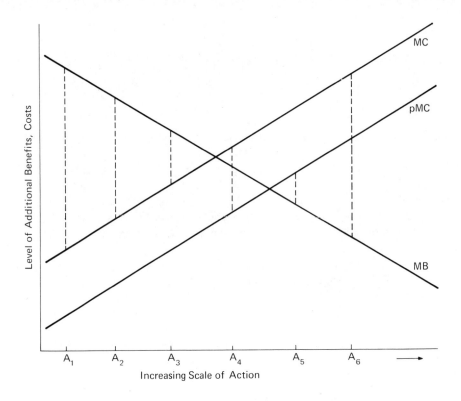

Figure 4-1. Information Produced by a Benefit Conscious Participant Given Increasing Expectations about the Value of Information.

great. Net benefits to society may be increased by implementing a smaller scale of action than that suggested by such a participant.

Two issues arise in interpreting figure 4-1. First, since society would not be led by a rational decision making procedure to the optimal scale of action (i.e., that scale at which *MB* equals *MC*), is it any worse off when it implements the scale proposed by a benefit conscious participant? The answer, of course, depends on the value of p. If p is zero or is very small, such a participant's proposals could be quite wasteful of resources, much more so, in fact, than the scale of action A_3 is wasteful of opportunities to expand the welfare of some citizens. Second, will not the plans and proposals of such a participant contain enough information to permit a decision center to determine the optimal scale of action? The answer depends in part on empirical observation: do participants communicate several alternative proposals or just one? The New York City school decentralization debate suggests the latter. However even if a participant communicated each unit of data he developed, this might not provide a basis for distinguishing the best response to a problem. In underestimating the resource costs of action, a participant may be led in practice to investigate technologically different courses of action from those a society should implement. Figure 4-1 is based on the assumption that this is not the case, that a benefit conscious participant, starting with a preplanning appraisal that suggests A_1 is the best response to the problem, will be led to investigate the same courses of action society should in its planning. But, because such a participant takes into consideration only a fraction of the resource costs of action that society would foresee, he may be induced in his planning to investigate different alternatives. Not only will this distort the alternatives data he develops but it may also adversely affect his problem and problem environment data. A participant's definition of the problem and his selection of environmental conditions for investigation are influenced by the alternatives he explores. Consequently, even if fully communicated, the information developed by benefit conscious participants when their objectives are the sole ends of collective action may not provide society with adequate control capability.

With decreasing expectations, the marginal benefits of pre-decision information in (4.1) are the difference between resource savings $-R_x$ and the benefit losses B_x expected to arise from contracting the scale of action to the extent indicated by a unit of information. Because benefit conscious participants consider only a fraction of the resource savings but anticipate all benefit decreases which a unit of data suggests, they underestimate the marginal benefits of information. Again they propose courses of action which are too extensive in scale but in this case because their plans are based on inadequate data. Starting from scale of action A_6, society might seek information until the point at which planning indicated A_4 as most desirable. At that point, however, the resource savings perceived by a benefit conscious participant, pMC, would be less than associated benefit losses. Such a participant might terminate his planning when A_5 was indicated, producing less data than is socially desirable and suggesting a scale of action which required an unwarranted level of resource expenditures.

Cost conscious participants are induced to produce data to the point at which

$$pB_x - R_x = D_x$$

$$pB_h - R_h = D_h.$$

(4.3)

When planning would indicate that the benefits of action can be increased and the resource costs reduced, such a participant underestimates the marginal benefits of any type of pre-decision data because he considers only a fraction of the benefit increases it reveals. Consequently he produces less of any type of information prior to action, and since he therefore perceives greater benefit increases and resource savings and smaller costs of production for any unit of feedback he may be inclined to rely more heavily on it in his planning than is socially desirable. The same is true when planning would reveal that the scale of action should be increased; cost conscious participants again underestimate the marginal benefits of pre-decision data. They consider all resource expenditure increases but only a fraction of the benefit increases and therefore base their plans on inadequate problem, problem environment, and alternatives data, proposing courses of action which are too limited in scale. On the other hand, when planning would indicate that the scale of action should be contracted, cost conscious participants overestimate the marginal benefits from information. They take into account all cost savings but only a fraction of the benefit losses from reducing the scale of action to the extent indicated by any unit of data. Consequently their plans propose courses of action which are too limited in scale.

In sum, cost conscious participants may develop plans which are based on insufficient data and which are misleading. Both of these shortcomings worsen as the fraction p declines, for these participants will expect fewer benefits from any unit of data and recognize a smaller proportion of the benefits lost from contracting the scale of action.

Proposition 3. *When planning would reveal that the benefits of action could be increased and resource expenditures could be reduced, the plans and proposals of myopic participants will not provide an adequate basis for controlling collective action. However, given sufficiently restrictive behavioral assumptions, the plans and proposals of these participants may be adequate when planning would disclose that the scale of action should be changed.*

A myopic participant will take into account only a fraction of the benefit and resource expenditure changes indicated by any unit of information. For planning purposes such a participant collects data in accordance with the conditions

$$qB_x - q'R_x = D_x$$

$$qB_h - q'R_h = D_h.$$

(4.4)

Because q and q' are positive fractions less than one, myopic participants will underestimate the marginal benefits from information when expectations are positive but may not do so when expectations are increasing, given a sufficiently small value of q'. To illustrate, let $\bar{x}$ be the unit of pre-decision data satisfying (4.1), that is, $\bar{x}$ is the last unit of pre-decision data which society should acquire. Then $B_{\bar{x}}$ and $R_{\bar{x}}$ are the benefit and resource expenditure increases indicated by this unit of data and $D_{\bar{x}}$ is its cost. If q' is less than or equal to

$$\frac{R_{\bar{x}} - (1 - q)B_{\bar{x}}}{R_{\bar{x}}}$$

(4.5)

a myopic participant will foresee net marginal benefits from information which are equal to or greater than those society expects. Substituting this value of q' into the first relation of (4.4) yields

$$qB_x - \frac{R_{\bar{x}} - (1 - q)B_{\bar{x}}}{R_{\bar{x}}} R_x = D_x$$

The unit of x which satisfies this relation is $\bar{x}$, demonstrating that for the specified value of q' a myopic participant may develop socially desirable quantities of data. Note, however, that such a value of q' may not exist and is in fact less likely to exist the smaller is q. The denominator of (4.5) is positive, and for the numerator to be positive $R_{\bar{x}}$ must exceed $(1 - q)B_{\bar{x}}$. But from (4.1), $B_{\bar{x}}$ exceeds $R_{\bar{x}}$ by an amount given by $D_{\bar{x}}$, and thus the smaller is q, the more likely the numerator of (4.5) is to be negative.

With decreasing expectations a myopic participant will generate information in quantities equal to or greater than that which society should collect if q has a value less than or equal to

$$\frac{B_{\bar{x}} - (1 - q')R_{\bar{x}}}{B_{\bar{x}}} \qquad (4.6)$$

where $\bar{x}$ is again the unit of pre-decision data satisfying (4.1). Substituting this value of q into the first relation of (4.4) indicates that the value of x satisfying that relation is also $\bar{x}$. However because the denominator of (4.6) is negative, the numerator must also be negative, and this implies that benefit decreases $B_{\bar{x}}$ exceed $(q' - 1)R_{\bar{x}}$. Yet with decreasing expectations, resource savings $-R_{\bar{x}}$ exceed benefit losses by an amount given by $D_{\bar{x}}$. Thus the smaller is q', the more likely the numerator of (4.6) is to be positive and the less likely a myopic participant is to base his plans and proposals on sufficient information.

By considering a sufficiently small quantity of resource expenditure increases or benefit decreases a myopic participant may foresee marginal benefits from planning of the same magnitude as those society would anticipate when expectations are mixed. The conditions under which they might do so are, however, quite restrictive, and in most problem situations they may not be met. Consequently it would appear that the plans and proposals developed by myopic participants will not provide the control capability society needs. This does not necessarily imply that these participants will rely more heavily on feedback. Given sufficiently small values of q and q', values for example which are consistent with (4.5) and (4.6), they may intend to develop less feedback than would be socially desirable. Lastly observe that as q and q' diverge, the behavior of myopic participants begins to resemble that of ambivalent participants. As q approaches one while q' remains constant, myopic participants behave like benefit conscious ambivalents while, when the reverse is true, they behave like cost conscious ambivalents.

Summary

When objectives are in conflict a decision center discriminates; it rules that the interests of only one segment of society are relevant in determining the response to a problem. Expressways that intrude into community parks, urban renewal projects that decimate low-income neighborhoods, and exclusionary zoning ordinances suggest that discrimination among competing interests and an objectives configuration of conflict are not rare in public decision making. Under these circumstances participants in plural decision-making processes frequently may not generate the control capability society needs. Only those whose behavior can be described as altruistic will prepare plans and proposals with sufficient pre-decision data and intend to rely on feedback to a socially desirable degree. The plans prepared by myopic and ambivalent participants will either be based on insufficient data or will propose courses of action which, from a societal perspective, are too restricted or too extensive in scale. Decisions based on these plans are thus likely to waste collective resources. Or they will not be as effective as they should be; they will fail to advance the interests of beneficiaries to the extent justified by a consideration of the resource costs of action and the costs of planning. One exception to this conclusion is the group or organization that succeeds in forestalling collective action. When inaction is, from a given participant's standpoint, the best response to a problem, all preplanning estimates of the value of information may be negative and any reassessments of these estimates are likely to remain negative. Such a participant may therefore develop little or no information; and when its interests dominate collective action, society needs little or no information. Another exception to this conclusion is the group or organization whose preplanning appraisal of a problem leads it to propose the socially most desirable response. Under such circumstances all possible findings from planning might dictate the same course of action, in which case neither society nor such a participant would have any inducement to acquire information. If this, however, were not the case only altruistic participants would acquire socially desirable quantities of information. Though suggesting perhaps the best response to a problem, the plans and proposals of ambivalent and myopic participants would be based on inadequate information; from a societal perspective too much uncertainty would surround them. In general society can depend only on those participants who behave as altruists to generate the data it needs to direct collective action solely to their ends.

Mutually Consistent Objectives

When the interests of different segments of society are mutually consistent, contributions to the objectives of some participants can occur simultaneously with contributions to the objectives of others. For this reason the analysis of mutuality contrasts sharply with that of conflict. To control collective action when objectives conflict, information is needed which will eliminate uncertainty about the objectives of only one segment of society, about alternatives which will make contributions to these objectives, and about environmental conditions affecting these alternatives. Quite clearly, society and participants who will be the beneficiaries of collective action confront the same uncertainty. As the preceding analysis suggests, whether participants will voluntarily generate the data society needs depends upon whether they behave as altruists. By contrast, when objectives are mutually consistent uncertainty for society implies ambiguity about a greater range of potential objectives, factual characteristics of the problem, environmental conditions, and consequences of action than it does for any participant. Society is concerned with the different ends of several of its members, but an individual participant is motivated to produce information only by his own goals and objectives. Society seeks to accomplish more with any response to a problem than any participant seeks to obtain from it and, therefore, confronts greater uncertainty and requires more information than any individual participant may voluntarily produce.[5] Consequently whether a plural decision-making process will generate the data needed to control collective action when objectives are mutually consistent depends not only upon the motivation and behavior of participants but also upon whether in the aggregate they perceive the uncertainty confronting society.

Three cases may be distinguished for analysis, each reflecting different assumptions about the manner and extent to which participants recognize the uncertainty surrounding the collective response to a problem. First, suppose that the response to a problem has separable parts, each of which can be designed independently of the others to make contributions to the objectives of a distinct participant. Suppose further that the uncertainty confronting the design of any of these component parts is different. Thus the response to a problem is in effect a set of separate decisions, each making contributions to the objectives of a different segment of society and each requiring that distinctly different types of problem, problem environment, and alternatives data be developed. Here the conclusions of the preceding analysis of conflict are relevant. Each participant, finding his ends served by only one of a set of projects constituting the response to a problem, is concerned about the uncertainty surrounding that project. In the aggregate participants perceive the uncertainties surrounding the response to the problem, and if each behaves like an altruist they will collectively generate the data society needs. This leads to the following proposition.

Proposition 4. *Participants who behave as altruists will, in the aggregate, generate the data needed to control collective action whenever the uncertainty about the problem, problem environment, and alternatives confronting society can be subdivided into mutually exclusive sets, each of which is in its entirety the concern of some participant.*

The two conditions specified in this proposition must hold simultaneously before society can depend upon participants to produce the data it needs. As the analysis of conflict reveals, if the behavior of participants can be described as ambivalent or myopic project decisions based on their data cannot be controlled to the degree that is socially desirable. Either participants will not make the investment in information that is justified by its value to society or the data they produce may be misleading. In addition, as the subsequent analysis will reveal, whenever the same range of uncertainties confronts several participants having different concerns they are not likely to produce the data society should have.

Suppose now that the response to a problem should not or cannot be designed as a set of separate projects but is an integrated whole lacking distinguishable parts. Here the uncertainties which participants perceive as affecting or limiting the advancement of their ends may differ markedly from that confronting society. Participants become involved and develop problem, problem environment, and alternatives data to eliminate uncertainty about the best way to preserve and enhance their own ends. Yet society may need information about environmental conditions and alternatives which affect the interests of all participants simultaneously. An excellent example is provided by Banfield, who found in the South Side Chicago branch hospital dispute that each participant "was too much committed to the solution implied by its own ends to look for one which would serve the interests of all."[6] Thus the information provided by participants may be of little value for the control of collective action where objectives are mutually consistent. This suggests the following proposition.

Proposition 5. *For individual participants to produce socially useful information, the uncertainty they perceive must correspond to that confronting society to some degree. Likewise, for society to obtain the control capability it needs through plural decision-making procedures, the uncertainty surrounding its response to a problem must be perceived in its entirety by some combination of participants.*

The conditions of this proposition introduce the third case to be analyzed. Here the uncertainty confronting society is assumed to be of two types: that of concern to participants individually and that of concern to two or more participants jointly. Thus, for example, when a community attempts to control the pattern and character of its future development, the same problem environment and alternatives data may be sought by environmentalists and a taxpayers association. Both may be interested in information about the consequences (traffic flows, water usage, potential flood hazards) of any alternative configuration of land uses, and both may be interested in information about environmental conditions (topography, soils, sources of water). But neither may be interested in information about the objectives of the other or the factual aspects of the problem as perceived by the other.[7] Similarly neither need be concerned about the full range of environmental and alternatives uncertainties considered to be important by the other. Environmentalists might be concerned about the ecological aspects of areas to be developed, whereas a taxpayers association might not. On the other hand, a taxpayers association might be concerned about the fiscal impacts of any developmental scheme, whereas environmentalists might not. For society, however, uncertainties about all of these factors might limit the control of collective action.

Notationally the third case may be presented as follows. In the society of M members let $\bar{B}_x$ and $\bar{B}_h$ represent the changes in benefits to the members of the set $\bar{m}$ indicated by a unit of pre- and post-decision data respectively.[8] Then for society three sets of interdependent conditions may be relevant to the production of data:

$$B_x + \bar{B}_x - R_x = D_x$$

$$B_h + \bar{B}_h - R_h = D_h$$

(4.7a)

$$B_x - R_x = D_x$$

$$\text{(4.7b)}$$

$$B_h - R_h = D_h$$

$$\bar{B}_x - R_x = D_x$$

$$\text{(4.7c)}$$

$$\bar{B}_h - R_h = D_h$$

The first of these establishes the amount of information that should be developed to eliminate uncertainties affecting the contributions a public program or policy will make to the objectives of individuals from both m and $\bar{m}$. Moreover, it refers to information which participants from both m and $\bar{m}$ would acquire in developing their plans and proposals. Participants from both m and $\bar{m}$ would, for example, be jointly interested in information about general environmental conditions, general characteristics of any alternative, and consequences of action affecting their mutual interests. The second and third conditions determine the amount of information that should be developed to eliminate uncertainties affecting the extent to which collective action advances the ends only of the members of m or only of the members of $\bar{m}$. They refer to information which a participant from m or $\bar{m}$ would acquire to reduce his separable or individual uncertainties about the best response to a problem. Thus in the third case participants collectively perceive the uncertainties surrounding the societal response to a problem; they investigate alternatives and environmental conditions which would be relevant in determining the course of action a collectivity should take. The information they need and develop to prepare plans and proposals can, however, be divided into two categories: joint data of interest to all participants and separable data of interest to a single participant.

The preceding analysis of conflict indicates that society can depend only on participants who behave as altruists to produce the separable data it needs for control purposes. In their planning only altruists will produce the information eliminating uncertainty about their ends and those environmental conditions and characteristics of any alternative affecting contributions only to these ends in accordance with relations (4.7b) and (4.7c). Thus the following conclusion emerges.

Proposition 6. *When objectives are consistent, only the plans and proposals of altruists will with certainty be based on the quantity of separable data that society would need for control purposes.*

While altruistic participants will reduce their separable uncertainties to the degree that is socially desirable, the question is will they also voluntarily produce the quality and quantity of joint or mutual information that society should possess before action is taken? The answer to this question is summarized by the following proposition.

Proposition 7. *When planning would reveal that the benefits of action could be increased and the resource costs reduced, altruists will develop plans with insufficient* *joint data. When planning would reveal that the scale of action should be changed, the plans of altruists will also be prepared with insufficient joint data or will propose courses of action which are too limited in scale. Thus the plans of altruists will not provide an adequate basis for controlling collective action.*

Altruistic participants from m, like ambivalent and myopic participants from this set, do not consider the benefit changes $\bar{B}_x$ which a unit of joint data reveals. Consequently when expectations are positive or increasing, they will not take into account the benefit increases which members of the set $\bar{m}$ will obtain from a decision based on an additional unit of joint problem environment or alternatives data. From a societal perspective they will underestimate the marginal benefits of this information and produce less of it in their planning than is needed for control purposes. With decreasing expectations altruists from m neglect the benefit losses $\bar{B}_x$ associated with decreasing the scale of action but take into consideration all resource savings. They may thus expect greater marginal benefits from information than would actually exist; for this reason their plans will propose courses of action which are too restricted in scale.

If they do not produce joint problem environment and alternatives data to the degree required by society altruists may also not generate separable or individual data to the degree required. Joint and separable data about the problem, problem environment, and alternatives together establish the expected benefits from and resource costs of action. The less data of either type available, the less is the discriminatory power provided by the other and accordingly the less valuable it is. The greater are those mutual uncertainties that an altruist shares with other participants about environmental conditions and alternatives, the less valuable is a unit of data reducing his individual uncertainties about normative and factual aspects of the problem, environmental conditions, and the consequences of any alternative. Alternatively, the more precise the information an altruist develops about such joint uncertainties as future demographic conditions, the more valuable will be information reducing his individual uncertainties about the problem, problem environment, and alternatives. Consequently, because an altruist does not generate sufficient joint data, he may also not develop adequate separable information.

The relative amount of feedback altruists will intend to produce is difficult to assess for positive and increasing expectations. Because in both cases they generate less pre-decision data, altruists expect greater benefit increases and greater resource expenditure changes from any unit of feedback. On the other hand, they neglect the benefit increases $\bar{B}_h$. Conflicting forces such as these do not complicate the analysis of an altruist's reliance on feedback when expectations are decreasing. Since they neglect the benefit decreases $\bar{B}_h$, altruists expect greater marginal benefits from feedback; however, information generated in accordance with these expectations would be misleading from a societal perspective for it would be focused on courses of action which were too limited in scale.

With respect to the behavior of ambivalent and myopic participants, propositions 2 and 3 suggest that they are likely to underestimate or overestimate the value of separable data. For this reason whatever the quality of their joint data their plans are not likely to provide adequate control capability. Yet it is instructive to analyze their development of joint information in some depth to determine how it interacts with separable data to affect the control capability developed in plural decision making.

Proposition 8. *When planning would reveal that the benefits of action could be increased and the resource costs reduced, both ambivalent and myopic participants will develop plans and proposals with insufficient joint data.*

Ambivalent and myopic participants do not recognize the benefit increases $\bar{B}_x$ and $\bar{B}_h$ which members of the set $\bar{m}$ will obtain from a decision based on an additional unit of joint problem environment and alternatives data. In addition, these participants may take into account only a fraction of the benefit increases B_x or resource savings $-R_x$ which a unit of such data enables. Thus they will underestimate the marginal benefits of this type of information when expectations are positive and in preparing their plans and proposals will not develop sufficient amounts of it. Because each participant also fails to generate adequate amounts of separable information when expectations are positive, collectively their plans fail to provide a satisfactory basis for controlling collective action. This and the preceding proposition suggest that even though many participants from m and $\bar{m}$ may be involved, the joint data of each will be insufficient when expectations about the value of information are positive and objectives are mutually consistent. Because the shortcomings of any participant's joint data are not rectified by the deficiencies of another's, society will not obtain adequate control capability through plural decision-making procedures under these circumstances.

Proposition 9. *Under restrictive behavioral assumptions benefit conscious participants may base their plans and proposals on sufficient joint data when planning would reveal that the scale of action should be changed. Neither their plans nor those of cost conscious participants may provide an adequate basis for controlling collective action, however.*

Given increasing expectations, benefit conscious participants will produce as much or more joint data than society needs prior to action if p is less than or equal to

$$\frac{R_{\bar{x}} - \bar{B}_{\bar{x}}}{R_{\bar{x}}} \tag{4.8}$$

where $\bar{x}$ is that unit of pre-decision data for which (4.7a) holds. Substituting this value of p in (4.2) reveals that the last unit of data which a benefit conscious participant would generate can also be $\bar{x}$. Thus for the specified value of p a benefit conscious participant may develop socially desirable quantities of joint data. Note that the denominator of (4.8) is positive and that for the numerator to be positive resource expenditure increases $R_{\bar{x}}$ must exceed benefit increases $\bar{B}_{\bar{x}}$. If the resource expenditures $R_{\bar{x}}$ needed to expand the scale of action to the degree indicated by the unit of data $\bar{x}$ do not exceed the benefit increases $\bar{B}_{\bar{x}}$ to the group $\bar{m}$, benefit conscious participants will not base their plans and proposals on adequate joint data even if they act as though p had a value of zero.

The amount of feedback a benefit conscious participant would intend to produce under increasing (and, as will become obvious, decreasing) expectations is difficult to analyze. There is, in particular, no reason to suppose that the value of p specified by (4.8) will lead a participant to rely on feedback to the extent that is socially desirable. However, the smaller p is the more a benefit conscious participant may tend to rely on feedback in his planning because he perceives a smaller proportion of the costs of using any unit of it.

With decreasing expectations about the value of information, a benefit conscious participant from m will produce as much or more joint data than society needs prior to action if the fraction p is equal to or greater than (4.8). With decreasing expectations B_x and $\bar{B}_x$ are both negative and $-R_x$ is positive. Since from (4.7a) resource savings $-R_{\bar{x}}$ exceed benefit decreases $B_{\bar{x}}$ and $B_{\bar{x}}$ by an amount $D_{\bar{x}}$, it will always be possible to find an appropriate value of p such that with decreasing expectations socially desirable amounts of joint data are produced by benefit conscious participants.

By taking into consideration a sufficiently small proportion of resource expenditure increases or a sufficiently great proportion of resource savings, benefit conscious participants may expect marginal benefits of the same magnitude as those society would foresee from joint problem environment and alternatives data. Consequently they could base their plans and proposals on adequate quantities of this information. Yet given a value of p specified by (4.8), a benefit conscious participant will (according to proposition 2) incorrectly appraise the marginal benefits of separable data about the problem, problem environment and alternatives and for this reason is likely to propose courses of action which require socially unwarranted resource expenditures. When planning would indicate that the scale of action should be expanded, overestimation of the value of information leads to plans proposing courses of action which from a societal perspective are too extensive in scale. Consequently even though a benefit conscious participant will base his plans on sufficient quantities of joint data, his proposals will be affected by his perception of the value of separable data when expectations are increasing. With decreasing expectations and a value of p specified by (4.8), a benefit conscious participant will underestimate the value of separable data. Thus although he may generate adequate joint data he will not perceive the full resource savings indicated by any unit of separable data. Accordingly he will again tend to propose courses of action requiring socially unwarranted resource expenditures.

Only under restrictive behavioral assumptions will a benefit conscious participant base his plans and proposals on sufficient joint data. Yet no value of p will induce such a participant to propose precisely that course of action which from a societal perspective constitutes the most desirable response to a problem. With increasing or decreasing expectations the separable data a benefit conscious participant produces will not be that which society would collect, and for this reason, though his plans might be based on adequate joint data, they will not constitute a sufficient basis for the control of collective action.

Consider now the behavior of cost conscious participants from the set m. When expectations are increasing, such participants will never produce joint data in the quantity and quality needed prior to action for they will always expect smaller marginal benefits from it than society would. Not only do these participants ignore the benefit increases $\bar{B}_x$, but they also take into account only a fraction p of the benefit increases B_x that a unit of data indicates. Moreover, they also underestimate the value of separable data when expectations are increasing (see proposition 2). In general, as p decreases they perceive fewer benefits from expanding the scale of action, and the quantity of both the joint and separable data they produce declines. They will thus propose courses of action which are too limited in scale. These participants may also not intend to produce adequate amounts of feedback. For the same reason that they underestimate the value of pre-decision data they underestimate the value of feedback. What feedback they do produce will also be directed to the analysis of courses of action which are too restricted in scale.

With decreasing expectations cost conscious participants associate smaller benefit losses than does society with the contraction of the scale of action to the degree indicated by each unit of data. They therefore expect higher marginal benefits from each unit of joint information and are likely to produce more of it than is socially desirable. This is also true with respect to the separable data they generate. Consequently they will use both the separable and joint data they develop to analyze and evaluate alternatives which are too restricted in scale and they will propose courses of action which make too few contributions not only to their objectives but also to those of other participants.

Proposition 10. *Under restrictive behavioral assumptions myopic participants may base their plans on sufficient joint data when planning would reveal that the scale of action should be changed. These plans, however, may not provide an adequate basis for controlling collective action.*

Given increasing expectations, myopic participants will produce as much or more joint data than society needs if q' is equal to or less than

$$\frac{R_{\bar{x}} - (1 - q)B_{\bar{x}} - \bar{B}_{\bar{x}}}{R_{\bar{x}}} \tag{4.9}$$

where $\bar{x}$ is that unit of pre-decision data for which (4.7a) holds. Substituting this value of q' into (4.4) reveals that the last unit of joint data which a myopic participant would generate is also $\bar{x}$. Given the specified value of q', myopic participants underestimate the resource expenditure increases associated with expanding the scale of action to the extent indicated by a unit of information. They thus anticipate marginal benefits from each unit of information of the same magnitude as those society would anticipate. The required value of q', however, may not exist and is in fact less likely to exist the smaller is q. The denominator of (4.9) is positive, and for the numerator to be positive resource expenditure increases must exceed the benefit increases $\bar{B}_{\bar{x}}$ plus $(1 - q)$ times the benefit increases $B_{\bar{x}}$. But (4.7a) suggests the reverse will be true the smaller q is. From (4.7a) the sum of these two benefit increases exceeds resource expenditure increases by an amount given by $D_{\bar{x}}$. Thus the smaller is q, the more likely the numerator of (4.9) is to be negative. Lastly, the value of q' given by (4.9) may not be equal to that specified by (4.5). The latter governs the development of separable data, and unless it is equal to the former a myopic participant will not generate socially desirable quantities of joint and separable data when expectations are increasing.

With decreasing expectations a myopic participant will develop as much or more joint data than is socially desirable if q has a value less than or equal to

$$\frac{B_{\bar{x}} + \bar{B}_{\bar{x}} - (1 - q')R_{\bar{x}}}{B_{\bar{x}}} \tag{4.10}$$

where $\bar{x}$ is again the unit of pre-decision data satisfying (4.7a). By substituting this value of q into (4.4), the last unit of x which a myopic participant would produce can also be shown to be $\bar{x}$. However, because the denominator of (4.1) is negative, the benefit decreases $B_{\bar{x}}$ and $\bar{B}_{\bar{x}}$ must exceed $(1 - q')R_{\bar{x}}$ if the specified value of q is to be positive. From (4.7a), with decreasing expectations resource savings exceed the sum of both benefit losses by an amount given by $D_{\bar{x}}$. Thus the smaller q' is, the more likely the required value of q is to be negative and the less likely a myopic participant is to generate the joint data society needs. Again if the value of q given by (4.10) is not equivalent to that given by (4.6) it will not be possible for myopic participants to generate socially desirable quantities of joint and separable data even though both values of q may be positive. Observe that a similar problem arises with the production of feedback. The values of q and q' which would induce myopic participants to generate sufficient joint and separable data prior to action may not engender the same results for feedback. While values of q and q' which would insure adequate development of feedback could be presented, they could not be compared with (4.5), (4.6), (4.9), and (4.10). Consequently it is impossible to ascertain to what extent myopic participants might intend to rely on feedback.

By considering sufficiently small proportions of the resource expenditure increases or benefit losses associated with expanding or contracting the scale of action to the degree indicated by a unit of data, myopic participants may base their plans on sufficient joint data. However, only if the values of q and q' specified in (4.9) and (4.10) equal those specified respectively in (4.5) and (4.6) will myopic participants also base their plans on appropriate quantities of separable data. Consequently only under extremely restrictive conditions will the plans and proposals of myopic participants provide a sufficient basis for controlling collective action.

Summary

When their interests are mutually consistent, taxpayer associations and chambers of commerce, private and public welfare organizations, automobile associations and private firms, historical preservationists and recreation associations, hunting clubs and educational organizations, and other combinations of participants may but generally do not appear to be likely to generate sufficient information to control collective action. Even if the uncertainties participants perceive correspond in the aggregate to the uncertainties surrounding the collective response to a problem, the control capability of plural decision making cannot be asserted. Participants either will not generate sufficient joint data in their planning or will do so only under restrictive behavioral assumptions. Yet even if they do so they may not produce adequate separable data, in which case they will propose courses of action which do not constitute a socially desirable response to a problem. Consequently their plans will not provide an appropriate basis for controlling collective action.

Inconsistent Objectives

Like conflict, inconsistency arises when contributions to the objectives of some participants are achieved at the expense of the interests of other participants. In contrast to conflict, it requires that the decision center consider the consequences for some but not necessarily all of those segments of society not positively served by collective action. These consequences may arise in two ways. First, the response to a problem, while benefiting some, may impose social costs on other segments of society. Thus widening a major thoroughfare by removing on-street parking may aid rush hour motorists but adversely affect contiguous commercial interests. Second, changing the scale or technological nature of the response to a problem may advance the interests of some segments of society but only with a loss in the positive contributions action will make to the objectives of others. In this sense inconsistency may imply compromise; for political or other reasons a decision center may conclude that the best response to a problem is a program or policy which advances the interests of all participants to some extent but the interests of no one participant fully. To do this the benefits some participants could obtain from collective action must be sacrificed or compromised so that the interests of others can be advanced.

Both types of inconsistency may result in the production of plans and proposals which are irrelevant, that is, useless for the control of collective action. In the case of compromise, a good example is provided by Meyerson and Banfield in their analysis of an early public housing controversy in Chicago.[9] They indicate that the proposals developed by both proponents and opponents of public housing were of little use in determining the compromise decision ultimately made by the Democratic party leadership and ratified by the city council.[10] Though based on information which was rudimentary in comparison with the ideals of comprehensive planning,[11] the plans prepared by proponents were still directed at a scale of action far more extensive than that finally approved. In contrast, the plans of opponents, based on even more rudimentary data, suggested a scale of action which was far more limited. Compromise in such circumstances does not imply control. Both proponents and opponents failed to perceive the ends of collective action as they would finally be established by the decision center and therefore did not produce data which eliminated the uncertainties surrounding the public program finally adopted. While the data they produced illustrated the range of possible objectives and may have outlined the range of alternatives, it did not provide the control capability needed to direct means to the eventual ends of collective action.

Consequently the usefulness of plural decision-making procedures when objectives are inconsistent depends, as it does when objectives are consistent, upon participants' recognizing the uncertainties surrounding the collective response to a problem. When objectives were consistent this meant that a participant would investigate alternatives advancing not only his own interests but also the interests of those other participants to whose objectives collective action would eventually make contributions. In addition, this meant that any alternative which increased the benefits such a participant obtained from collective action must also increase the benefits other participants obtained. These two conditions insure only that a participant perceives the uncertainties surrounding the societal response to any problem and that, starting from his preplanning appraisal of the problem, he will order the alternative courses of action in the same way society would. Whether he will propose that course of action which from a societal perspective constitutes the best response to a problem depends on the amount of joint and separable information he produces. When planning would reveal that the preplanning scale of action should be expanded, each additional unit of data will suggest a larger scale of action. Likewise, when planning would reveal that the preplanning scale of action should be contracted, each additional unit of data will suggest a smaller scale of action. Thus if a participant expects the same marginal benefits from joint and separable information that society would foresee, he will produce the same amounts of these two types of information as those society would acquire for control purposes. He will therefore be led to propose that course of action which from a societal perspective is the best response to the problem. The preceding analysis of mutuality suggested, however, that even if they perceive the uncertainties surrounding the societal response to a problem participants are not likely to generate appropriate amounts of joint and separable data. Accordingly their plans are likely to propose socially unwarranted courses of action.

The same conclusion holds for situations in which the objectives of participants are inconsistent. Before analyzing these situations, two characteristics of an inconsistent objectives configuration which distinguish it from mutuality must be discussed. First, to analyze the behavior of participants some of the notation developed earlier must be redefined. Suppose that in the society of M members the ends of the set of m individuals can be advanced only at the expense of the remaining $\bar{m}$ individuals. Then when it is negative $\bar{B}_x$ represents the social costs of action or the decreases in the benefits to the members of $\bar{m}$ revealed by a unit of information. If

$\bar{B}_x$ is positive, it may be defined, as before, as representing the benefit increases revealed by a unit of data or as representing the potential reductions in the social costs of action that it indicates are possible. As before $\bar{B}_x$ and B_x are assumed to be expressed in commensurable units. Second, from a societal perspective information cannot be classified as separable whenever planning would show that only if the social costs rose could the benefits of action be increased or whenever it would show that only by reducing these benefits could these social costs be decreased. Under these circumstances any unit of data a participant collects for his own planning purposes not only suggests changes in the benefits of collective action but also reveals or implies changes in the social costs. Thus all information a participant develops will in a sense be joint; it cannot alter the gains he and those who share his ends obtain without simultaneously altering the level of social costs imposed on or the benefits obtained by other segments of society. Separable information, or information which affects only one participant's gains from collective action, might be developed whenever planning would indicate that benefits can be increased at the same time that social costs can be decreased, or whenever it would indicate that benefits should be decreased and social costs increased in order to obtain resource savings. In either of these situations changes in benefits do not require changes in social costs or vice versa, but both benefit and social cost changes do require resource expenditure changes. Thus all information need not be joint; some information that a participant might develop for planning purposes could reveal only benefit and associated resource expenditure changes while still other information might indicate only social cost and associated resource expenditure changes.

The following analysis considers seven possible conclusions which might emerge from the application of a planning process to produce information in a situation where objectives are inconsistent. Each of these seven conclusions represents a different configuration of the conceivable benefit changes (B_x), resource expenditure changes (R_x), and social cost changes $(\bar{B}_x)$ that might be revealed by a unit of information.[12] The first three cases to be analyzed are those in which separable data might be developed, and thus the conditions (4.7a)–(4.7c) describe the point to which joint and separable data should be collected for control purposes.

To begin with, starting from a participant's preplanning appraisal of the best response to a problem planning might reveal that the benefits of action could be increased (B_x positive) at the same time that both resource expenditures and social costs could be reduced ($-R_x$ and $\bar{B}_x$ also positive). This is the formal equivalent of the previously analyzed case of consistent objectives and positive expectations. Thus propositions 7 and 8 are applicable, and they suggest that whether participants act altruistically, ambivalently, or myopically they will not base their plans and proposals on sufficient joint and separable data. Accordingly the following proposition holds.

Proposition 11. *When planning would disclose means of increasing the benefits and reducing both the resource and social costs of action, participants will develop* *insufficient joint data and their plans and proposals will therefore not provide an adequate basis for controlling collective action. Under these circumstances only altruists will develop sufficient separable data; both ambivalent and myopic participants will underestimate its value.*

Second, planning may disclose that by increasing resource expenditures (R_x positive) the social costs of action could be reduced ($\bar{B}_x$ positive) and the benefits of action could be increased (B_x also positive). This is the formal equialent of the previously analyzed situation of consistent objectives and increasing expectations. Thus propositions 7, 9, and 10 are applicable. They indicate that under sufficiently restrictive behavioral assumptions myopic and benefit conscious participants may generate sufficient joint data, but then may not prepare plans with appropriate quantities of separable data. Cost conscious participants will underestimate the marginal benefits of both types of information, while altruists will not develop sufficient joint data. Thus the following proposition:

Proposition 12. *When planning would indicate that the benefits of action could be increased and the social costs could be reduced by increasing resource expenditures, the plans and proposals of participants will not provide an adequate basis for controlling collective action.*

Third, planning might suggest that resource expenditures should be decreased ($-R_x$ positive) even though the benefits from action will decrease (B_x negative) and the social costs of action will increase ($\bar{B}_x$ negative). Because this is the formal equivalent of the previously analyzed case of consistent objectives and decreasing expectations, propositions 7, 9, and 10 are again relevant. They indicate that under sufficiently restrictive behavioral assumptions myopic and benefit conscious participants may generate adequate joint data but then may not prepare plans with sufficient separable data. Because they overestimate the marginal benefits of joint and separable data, the plans of cost conscious participants will propose courses of action which are either too restricted in scale or impose excessive social costs. Lastly, the plans of altruists may also impose excessive social costs, for these participants will overestimate the marginal benefits of information. Thus the following proposition:

Proposition 13. *When planning would indicate that resource expenditures should be reduced even though the social costs of action might increase and the benefits decrease, the plans and proposals of participants will not provide an adequate basis for controlling collective action.*

The last four conclusions which might emerge from planning can be analyzed together; they reflect situations in which every unit of information suggests either benefit and social cost increases or social cost and benefit decreases. The conditions (4.7a) describe the point to which information should be produced. The implications of each of these four conclusions can be presented as follows:

Implications of Data (for):

Case	Resource Expenditures	Social Costs	Benefits
1	decrease	increase	increase
	($-R_x$ positive)	($\bar{B}_x$ negative)	(B_x positive)
2	decrease	decrease	decrease
	($-R_x$ positive)	($\bar{B}_x$ positive)	(B_x negative)
3	increase	increase	increase
	($-R_x$ negative)	($\bar{B}_x$ negative)	(B_x positive)
4	increase	decrease	decrease
	($-R_x$ negative)	($\bar{B}_x$ positive)	(B_x negative)

The analysis of these four possible conclusions can be conducted, as were the preceding analyses, in terms of the behavior of participants from the set m. Results obtained for the behavior of these participants will apply to the behavior of participants from $\bar{m}$, assuming that they perceive the uncertainties surrounding the collective response to a problem. The reason for this is straightforward. The four possible conclusions from planning can be subdivided into two sets, depending upon whether information indicates that resource expenditures can be reduced (cases 1 and 2) or that resource expenditures must rise. In case 1, information indicates that resource expenditures can be decreased and the benefits of action can be increased by imposing additional social costs on the members of $\bar{m}$. In case 2, information would reveal that resource expenditures and social costs can be decreased if the benefits obtained by members of m are reduced. Thus cases 1 and 2 are mirror images; in 1, planning indicates that interests of members of m should be advanced at the expense of the interests of members of $\bar{m}$, while in 2 it indicates the reverse. Analyzing the behavior of participants from m with respect to both will yield results equivalent to those obtained from an analysis of the behavior of participants from $\bar{m}$ with respect to both.

The same is true for the second set of conclusions except that here planning indicates that resource expenditures should be increased. In case 3 information suggests that increased benefits to members of the set m can only be obtained at the expense of increased resource expenditures and increased social costs. In case 4 information reveals that the social costs should be reduced even though resource expenditures must be increased and the benefits of action obtained by members of m decreased. Consequently cases 3 and 4 are also mirror images; analysis of the behavior of participants from m with respect to both produces results similar to those obtained by analyzing the behavior of participants from $\bar{m}$ with respect to both.

Inspection of the chart and the relations (4.7a) suggests the following propositions about participant behavior.

Proposition 14. *When planning would reveal that the social costs of action could be reduced by increasing resource expenditures and decreasing the benefits obtained* *by members of* m, *no participant from* m *will generate any of the joint data society needs.*

The conditions assumed by the proposition are those of case 4, in which the beneficiaries of any data that might be developed by a participant perceiving the uncertainties surrounding the societal response to a problem are members of the set $\bar{m}$. Whether they would otherwise act altruistically, ambivalently, or myopically, participants from m are not motivated to develop information in this situation. Thus for society to obtain the joint data it needs it must look to those who suffer the social costs of action. The behavior of participants from $\bar{m}$ in this situation parallels and can be described by the behavior of participants from m under the circumstances of case 3.

Proposition 15. *When planning would reveal that by increasing both the expenditures for and social costs of action the benefits to members of* m *could be increased, cost conscious and myopic participants may under restrictive behavioral assumptions generate adequate joint data but the plans of altruistic and benefit conscious participants will not provide an adequate basis for controlling collective action.*

In this situation all participants from m ignore the social cost increases which would attend any increase in the benefits they obtained from increasing the scale or changing the technological nature of action. Thus altruists and benefit conscious participants, who take into account all benefit increases and all or a fraction of the resource expenditure increases, overestimate the marginal benefits of information, producing more of it than is socially desirable and proposing courses of action which impose excessive social and resource costs. Because they consider only a fraction of the resource expenditure increases indicated by a unit of data, benefit conscious participants are more likely to analyze alternatives imposing excessive social and resource costs than are altruists.

Though both cost conscious and myopic participants also ignore the increased social costs of action, they perceive fewer benefit increases. For sufficiently small values of p and q, their neglect of the social costs of expanding the scale of action to the degree indicated by any unit of data may be counterbalanced by their perception of fewer benefits. Consequently cost conscious and myopic participants may prepare plans which provide adequate control capability.

As noted above the conclusions of this proposition apply to the behavior of participants from $\bar{m}$ in case 4, where participants from the set m had no motivation to generate data. Consequently when planning would reveal that the social costs of action could be reduced by increasing resource expenditures and decreasing benefits, the plans and proposals of cost conscious and myopic participants may provide an adequate basis for controlling collective action. The plans of altruists and benefit conscious participants will propose courses of action which reduce social costs beyond the level that is socially desirable.

For this and the remaining two cases, the amount of feedback that any participant would intend to collect cannot be assessed with any precision. The implications of the quantities of pre-decision data collected for the value of feedback must be known exactly where objectives are inconsistent before the tendency of participants to depend on it can be analyzed. The analysis developed here does not permit this, and thus whether participants who developed inadequate pre-decision data would also produce inadequate quantities of feedback or might tend to compensate by relying more heavily on feedback cannot be assessed.

Proposition 16. *When planning would reveal that resource expenditures could be reduced and the benefits of action increased by imposing additional social costs on the members of* $\bar{m}$, *ambivalent and myopic participants from* m *may under restrictive behavioral assumptions generate adequate joint data but the plans of altruists will not provide an adequate basis for controlling collective action.*

These are the conditions of case 1. Here all participants from *m* neglect the social costs created by expanding the scale of action or changing its technological characteristics to the extent indicated by a unit of data. For this reason altruists will always overestimate the marginal benefits of information, developing plans which propose courses of action that impose excessive social costs.

Whether benefit conscious participants will overestimate or possibly even underestimate the marginal benefits of information depends on whether the social cost increases $\bar{B}_x$ revealed by a unit of data exceed or are less than the resource savings $-R_x$ it also suggests are possible. Benefit conscious participants consider only a fraction of the resource savings a unit of data reveals, and when these resource savings exceed social cost increases this may offset their tendency to overestimate the marginal benefits of information because they neglect the social costs of action. But if the social cost increases $\bar{B}_x$ exceed the magnitude of resource savings $-R_x$, even a value of p of zero will not lead benefit conscious participants to evaluate a unit of data correctly. Similar conclusions hold for cost conscious participants. Their tendency to overestimate the marginal benefits of information because they ignore the social cost increases it suggests may be counterbalanced by their perception of only a fraction of the benefit increases it indicates. However, if the social cost increases $\bar{B}_x$ exceed the benefit increases B_x, even a value of p of zero would not lead a cost conscious participant from *m* to appraise the value of information correctly. Finally, for some combination of q and q' myopic participants may offset any tendency to overestimate the marginal benefits of information because they ignore the social costs it indicates. Observe, however, that sufficiently low values of both q and q' may lead myopic participants to underestimate the value of information.

Proposition 17. *Whenever planning would reveal that by decreasing benefits to members of* m *the resource and social costs of action could simultaneously be reduced, cost conscious and myopic participants may under restrictive behavioral assumptions generate adequate joint data but the plans and proposals of altruists and benefit conscious participants will not provide an adequate basis for controlling collective action.*

This is the second case above, in which all participants from m ignore the social cost decreases which arise from changing the technical nature or decreasing the scale of action to the degree indicated by a unit of data. The analysis of the behavior of participants from m here describes the behavior of participants from $\bar{m}$ under the conditions of case 1.

Both altruists and benefit conscious participants from m underestimate the marginal benefits of information because they consider all benefit decreases but neglect the social cost savings it reveals. They produce less data than is socially desirable and their plans propose courses of action which impose excessive social costs and require unwarranted resource expenditures. Cost conscious participants may not for sufficiently low values of p underestimate the marginal benefits of information. In this case their tendency to underestimate the marginal benefits of information by neglecting social cost savings is offset by their recognition of only a fraction of the benefit decreases a unit of data suggests. Observe, however, that if the social cost decreases indicated by a unit of data exceed the benefit decreases, even a value of p of zero will not prevent cost conscious participants from underestimating the marginal benefits of information. For sufficiently low values of q and q', myopic participants may correctly appraise the value of information. However, in this case, as in the preceding case, myopic participants may for any set of values for q and q' either overestimate or underestimate the marginal benefits of information. When they underestimate its value, their data may be inadequate and their plans will suggest a scale of action which imposes excessive social costs and requires excessive resource expenditures. When they overestimate the value of information, they will propose courses of action which reduce the benefits of action to too great an extent.

Summary

When objectives are inconsistent, uncertainty for society may imply ambiguity about a greater range of environmental conditions, a larger number of the consequences of any alternative, and a greater number of normative and factual aspects of the problem than it does for any participant. Two cases must be distinguished for analysis. In the first, the benefits and social costs of action may to some degree vary independently. Given any preplanning concept of the solution to a problem, planning discloses that the benefits of action may be increased at the same time that the social costs may be reduced, or it reveals the reverse. This situation closely parallels the situation in which the objectives configuration is that of mutuality and the conclusions about the information that participants will produce resemble those obtained for this objective configuration. Even if they individually recognize the uncertainties surrounding the societal response to a problem, no combination of participants will unambiguously generate the data needed to control collective action. Only under restrictive behavioral assumptions, whicy may not be tenable in any given problem situation, will participants expect marginal benefits from joint information of the same magnitude that society would foresee; but, even when met, these assumptions imply that participants will not correctly appraise the value of separable data. Thus even though they may analyze alternatives which might constitute the socially desirable response to a problem, participants may still, after they complete their planning, propose courses of action which either impose excessive social costs and yet generate insufficient benefits or which require excessive resource expenditures.

To illustrate, let the alternative preplanning solutions to a problem be indicated, as shown in figure 4-2. In each of the three diagrams the points on the vertical and horizontal lines represent different preplanning alternatives and the point S_m represents the alternative which a participant from m would consider to be the best response to the problem in the absence of planning. The horizontal line indicates the direction in which planning would take such a participant if he perceived the uncertainties surrounding the societal response to the problem, and the point S_1 represents the alternative which from a rational decision-making perspective would constitute the socially most desirable course of action. The vertical lines indicate the direction in which planning might take participants who do not perceive the uncertainties of significance in determining the course of action which for all segments of society is best. The diagrams are, of course, illustrative. They are not meant to suggest that in any problem situation there are an infinity of possible solutions because the number of points on a line is infinite. Nor do the vertical lines represent the only possible way in which participants might not perceive the socially significant uncertainties. Additional rays might have been drawn from the point S_m to suggest different, though still socially undesirable, directions in which planning might take participants. Lastly, the point S_1 in each diagram might actually be off the right-hand end of the horizontal line. That is, planning might reveal that an alternative not recognized prior to the initiation of information development activities might constitute the best response to the problem.

The three diagrams depict the results which planning was assumed to yield in propositions 11, 12, and 13. Proposition 11 suggests that all participants will base their plans on insufficient joint and separable data and therefore will propose courses of action to the left of point S_1 in diagram (a). Participant proposals will thus require unwarranted resource expenditures, will not generate sufficient benefits, and will impose excessive social costs. Propositions 12 and 13 suggest that participants who perceive the uncertainties surrounding the societal response to the problem will propose courses of action to the right or left respectively of S_1 in (b) and (c). Thus with respect to diagrams (b) and (c) participants will propose courses of action which do not provide sufficient benefits and impose excessive social costs or which require unwarranted resource expenditures.

In the second case, which may be viewed as representing a situation of compromise, if $\bar{B}_x$ is interpreted as the benefit losses sustained by members of $\bar{m}$ so that the interests of members of m may be advanced, the objectives of different participants are truly inconsistent and the benefits of action vary inversely with the social costs. In this second case society and any participant may evaluate any unit

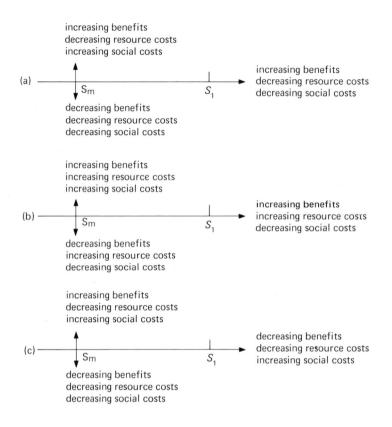

Figure 4-2. Alternative Benefit, Social Cost and Resource Expenditure Changes Revealed by Planning.

of data differently. When planning would show that their interests can be served further, participants who are the beneficiaries of collective action will tend to over-estimate the marginal benefits of information because they ignore the social cost increases it implies. But when planning would reveal that their interests should be served to a lesser extent, they will tend to underestimate the marginal benefits because they do not recognize the social cost savings it reveals. Only under restrictive behavioral assumptions, which may not be tenable in any problem situation, will the plans of beneficiaries be based on sufficient joint data. Similar conclusions hold for those adversely affected by collective action. Even if they perceive the uncertainties surrounding the societal response to a problem, they will not perceive marginal benefits from information of the same magnitude as those society would expect except under restrictive behavioral assumptions.

In general, whenever they incorrectly appraise the value of information, participants are likely not to perceive the uncertainties surrounding the societal response to a problem. In the first place, a tendency to underestimate or over-estimate the value of information will bias a participant's preplanning appraisal of the best response to a problem, and, as a consequence, some participants may perceive little value in planning when from a societal perspective substantial planning was justified. A participant who prior to planning takes an extreme position on the solution to a problem may find little value in information about other alternatives or the environmental factors which may affect them or his proposed solution. Because of his appraisal of the costs and benefits of action, no amount of information may alter his initial assessment. Second, starting from any preplanning appraisal of the best response to a problem, participants who overestimate the value of information will place a higher value than society on information about alternatives which advance their ends. They will ignore the social costs of these alternatives or the fact that to advance their ends contributions to the ends of other participants must be foregone. They thus may be led to investigate alternatives which from a societal perspective are undesirable, and accordingly their plans and proposals may be irrelevant for the control of collective action. Thus the plans and proposals of participants may be adversely affected by their incorrect appraisals of the value of information as well as by their failure to perceive the uncertainties surrounding the societal response to a problem.

In sum, when objectives are inconsistent society cannot depend upon participants in a plural decision-making process for information about courses of action which would reduce resource or social costs and/or increase benefits. Both those who gain and those who suffer from collective action are unlikely to propose those technological approaches or those scales of action which constitute the best response to a problem from a societal perspective. Pluralism, in other words, does not inherently generate the information and knowledge needed to find and implement that solution which is likely to be the best from the standpoint of benefits, resource expenditures, and social costs.

Information in a Public Decision System

To this point the control capability generated by plural decision making has been explored in terms of alternative assumptions about the expected value of information, participant motivations, and relative objectives configurations. The implications of public decision system structure remain to be explored. In general, the larger the planning field of a decision system, the less likely a decision center is to implement the plans and proposals of any given participant. Thus for most participants the central characteristic of involvement may be uncertainty. Unless a participant has sufficient power to insure that his plans and proposals will be adopted by a decision center, he is likely to view involvement as a gamble. For any given participant one outcome of this gamble may be a public policy or program which advances his ends, but another, perhaps just as likely, would be a program serving some other participant's interests, perhaps at the expense of his own. This uncertainty modifies a participant's expectations about the value of information, causing him to produce less of it than would otherwise be the case. A participant assured of decision center support for his proposal knows that whatever information he generates will affect the course of action implemented and accordingly that it will increase the benefits he obtains from collective action. But a participant who lacks the power or influence to determine the actions of a decision center cannot assume that his data will have any impact on the collective response to a problem and thus that it will in any way affect the benefits he obtains from collective action. Consequently the less assured a participant is of a favorable decision, the less valuable is a unit of information to him in developing his plans and proposals (for they may be valueless) and therefore the less data he is likely to collect.

Proposition 18. *The uncertainty inherent in plural decision making adversely affects the quantity and quality of data any participant will generate.*

The uncertainty which is inherent in open and advisory decision systems causes all participants to develop plans and proposals with less data than they would have used in the absence of this uncertainty. Participants who would otherwise generate inadequate data will produce even less. On the other hand, participants who would otherwise generate excessive amounts of data will be less likely to do so and correspondingly less likely to propose courses of action providing too few benefits or requiring unwarranted resource expenditures or imposing unjustified social costs.

Conflicting Objectives

Proposition 19. *In a closed decision system adequate control capacity will be provided only by altruists.*

This proposition follows immediately from propositions 1, 2, and 3. Even though there is no inherent uncertainty in a closed decision system, society may not rely on the plans and proposals prepared by the beneficiaries of collective action unless they behave altruistically.[13] Ambivalent participants either will not base their plans on sufficient information or will propose courses of action which are too limited or too extensive in scale. Myopic participants may generate sufficient data under restrictive behavioral assumptions; otherwise their plans and proposals are likely to be formulated with inadequate data. The politically powerful may in general not develop the data that should be available to direct collective means to their ends. They may tend to rely too heavily on feedback to correct the shortcomings in decisions. Consequently when power and influence are concentrated in the hands of a few, society may pay a double price. Not only may the interests of those who lack power be sacrificed, but also the collective action taken may waste resources unnecessarily. Ironically, the interests of the beneficiaries may also not be advanced to the extent that would be justified by a consideration of the resource costs of action and the costs of information.

In any problem situation decision centers in both open and advisory systems may also determine that the public response to a problem should make contributions to the objectives of only one segment of society. Because of the uncertainty inherent in such systems, the following proposition holds.

Proposition 20. *When the interests of only one segment of society are to be advanced by collective action, the plans and proposals of beneficiaries are more likely to be based on inadequate data in open and advisory than in closed decision systems.*

Participants who would base plans and proposals on inadequate data in a closed system will be more likely to do so in open or advisory systems where the outcome of involvement is uncertain. Consequently when the response to a problem would serve the interests of only one segment of society the information available in a closed system from beneficiaries may be superior to that available in an open or advisory system. On the other hand, participants likely to develop excessive quantities of data and therefore to propose unwarranted courses of action will be less likely to do so in these decision systems, but it is not possible to conclude that the decision made will therefore be better. Uncertainty in these systems may be so great that such a participant will base plans and proposals on inadequate data.

Consistent and Inconsistent Objectives

Before the implications of decision system structure can be analyzed for consistent or inconsistent objectives configurations, the uncertainty inherent in an open or advisory system must be distinguished from the failure of participants to recognize the uncertainty surrounding the societal response to a problem. To some degree the two phenomena are interdependent. Thus in the New York City school decentralization debate they had the same source, the different ends that different participants pursued. In that debate the objectives of the demonstration school districts in Harlem and Brooklyn were clearly in conflict with those of the politically powerful teachers union. Community control of neighborhood schools, sought by the demonstration districts, imperiled not only the rights and prerogatives teachers had wrested from the central Board of Education, but also the future bargaining power of the union. A set of thirty neighborhood school boards would be much more difficult to bargain with and threaten than the single city board. Because of this conflict with a politically powerful adversary the demonstration school districts were uncertain about the consequences of involvement and this quite possibly adversely affected their preparation of plans and proposals. Moreover, because they did not consider the objective of teacher job security important, the demonstration school districts also failed to perceive the uncertainties surrounding the societal response to the problem. The state legislature ultimately decided that the teachers' interests were important. When it did, the plans and proposals of the demonstration districts became virtually useless for the purpose of directing collective means to ends. This example of participant failure to perceive the uncertainty surrounding the societal response to a problem is perhaps gratuitous. No observer would have expected the demonstration school districts to analyze alternatives serving the teachers' interests, and it was inevitable that either their plans and proposals or those of the teachers would become irrelevant for control purposes. However this example does illustrate the common source of two distinct factors which restrict the utility of a participant's information for control purposes.

Proposition 21. *The quality and quantity of both the joint and separable data upon which the plans and proposals of participants are based will be adversely affected by the uncertainty inherent in advisory or open decision systems.*

The uncertainty inherent in an open or advisory system may induce every participant to believe that his involvement can be successful, and so all may participate under the assumption that their interests will be advanced by the collective action ultimately taken. If all participants anticipate a favorable decision, when a decision adverse to the interests of some participants is made, the decision center will not have available information about means of minimizing the negative impacts of its choice. Moreover, even where a participant discerns that his interests may be sacrificed so that the interests of others may be advanced, he may critically evaluate and oppose the plans of these participants rather than develop the separable data which would indicate how his losses could be reduced or limited.[14] More generally, as noted above, the uncertainty inherent in an open or advisory decision system will inhibit the incentive of any participant to produce information. Participants who are uncertain about the action a decision center will take will anticipate fewer benefits from planning and will base their plans and proposals on less joint and separable information than would otherwise be the case. They will thus appraise the value of information at less than its value to society for reasons which have nothing to do with their perspectives on a problem but which are associated directly with the nature of plural decision making procedures.

Proposition 22. *The uncertainties inherent in open and advisory decision systems make it less likely that the restrictive conditions under which ambivalent and myopic participants would generate socially desirable quantities of data will be met.*

Given sufficiently small or large values of p, ambivalent participants who would underestimate the marginal benefits of information will not do so. Similarly, given appropriate values of q and q', myopic participants may correctly assess the marginal benefits of information. However the pluralism of an open or advisory decision system makes every participant uncertain about the success of his involvement and thus his actual gains from planning and thereby makes it less likely that the restrictive conditions under which ambivalent and myopic participants might generate adequate data will prevail. To illustrate, if a myopic participant appraised his chances of successfully influencing the outcome of collective action at one in ten, he might appraise the marginal benefits of information at one-tenth of their actual value. Under these circumstances no set of positive values of q and q' might lead him to develop socially desirable quantities of data.

Proposition 23. *The partisans in a mutual adjustment process, even if they do not employ an incremental planning process, may base their plans and proposals and thus their decisions on inadequate information.*

The preceding propositions contain implications for what Lindblom has called partisan mutual adjustment when that term implies bargaining or negotiation. [15] These two decision-making procedures occur in open decision systems in which the distinction between the decision center and the planning field is blurred. Individual members of the decision center may be partisans who are committed to advancing a particular set of ends and who may look to one particular participant in the planning field for their information. Other members of the decision center may be independent; they may either develop their own information or form their proposals after exploring the viewpoints of several members of the planning field. In addition, while each member of the decision center may have the power or legal authority to oppose action, no single member possesses sufficient authority or power to determine it. In some cases any member of the decision center may be able to block action; then, the cooperation of all members is needed to implement a response to a problem. In such decision systems the members of the decision center must bargain or negotiate.

Two cases may be distinguished. In the first, a majority of the members of a decision center cooperate to advance their ends, which are mutually consistent. For expositional convenience assume that those involved in a bargaining or negotiating process are partisans. Thus bargaining and negotiation occur among partisans in order to form a coalition which can advance their mutually consistent ends. Under these circumstances the processes of bargaining and negotiation should serve to focus the attention of coalition members on uncertainties which from a societal perspective are important in determining the ultimate response to the problem. In other words, the information developed by all partisans should be relevant. In addition, the uncertainty inherent in an open decision system may not adversely influence their planning activities. Through successive rounds of bargaining or negotiation partisans will more clearly perceive the compatibility of their interests and thus may become ever more certain of a favorable decision. But, as propositions 6 to 10 suggest, only under restrictive behavioral assumptions will partisans base their plans and proposals on adequate joint data and only those who behave as altruists will produce adequate separable data. Although bargaining and negotiation may induce partisans to perceive the uncertainties which from a societal perspective surround the response to a problem and although these procedures may counteract the uncertainty inherent in an open system, they do not insure the availability of socially desirable amounts of information. As a consequence, irretrievable opportunities to advance the ends of the various members of a coalition may be lost and public resources may be wasted.

In the second case, the interests of all parties to a bargain or negotiation are not consistent. The ends of some partisans are incompatible with those of others. To increase the benefits one partisan obtains from collective action may require that the benefits others obtain be decreased; or to advance the ends of some partisans may require that social costs be imposed on others. Again the processes of bargaining and negotiation should induce partisans to perceive the socially important uncertainties surrounding the response to a problem, but they will not in this case reduce decision system uncertainties. Until a bargain is concluded or negotiations are completed uncertainty will prevail among partisans about their gain from involvement, and this may adversely affect their planning activities. Individual partisans will be uncertain about what their adversaries will demand, what concessions they might make, and what demands will cause them to terminate the bargaining or negotiating process.

In addition, even in the absence of any inherent decision system uncertainty partisans may not develop sufficient information to discern the response to a problem which from a societal perspective is most desirable. The various parties to a bargain, for example, begin with different plans and proposals for solving a problem. The information upon which these plans and proposals are based may be quite rudimentary, consisting of little more than a preplanning appraisal of the problem, or it may be somewhat more elaborate. In the latter case, propositions 1 through 3 suggest that only altruists will, from a societal perspective, initiate a bargain fully understanding the benefit and public resource expenditure implications of their proposals. Through bargaining partisans eliminate their differences of opinion; they discover how they must modify their original plans and proposals if a decision which will positively affect all bargainers is to be reached. Concessions are made—benefits are foregone and social costs are accepted—so that action which is expected to have net positive consequences by all partisans can be implemented. In other words bargaining establishes the distribution of the benefits and the social costs generated by the collective response to a problem. In some cases information beyond that used by partisans in determining their original proposals for action may be immaterial to the decision made. The resolution of distributional issues, of who gets what, and consequently the determination of the benefits created by and the level of resource expenditures associated with the collective response to a problem will depend primarily on the bargaining skills of the various partisans. In other cases partisans may engage in planning activity while they are bargaining in order to explore and expand upon the alternative proposals under discussion. In these situations the question arises what, from a societal perspective, will be the quality and quantity of the information developed and will the plans and proposals advanced by partisans constitute appropriate solutions to the problem? Again propositions 1 through 3 suggest that only altruists will fully comprehend the benefit and public resource expenditure implications of the alternative proposals they might advance during the course of a bargaining process. But propositions 11 through 17 also might be descriptive here. Propositions 11 and 12 suggest that when in a bargaining (or negotiating) situation a solution is possible which would improve the position of all partisans simultaneously or which would decrease the social costs imposed on one partisan and increase the benefits obtained by others, the information developed by all partisans might well be too imprecise or rudimentary to permit them to perceive this solution. Proposition 13 suggests the same conclusion for the situation in which, from a societal perspective, resource expenditures should be reduced even though as a consequence the benefits all partisans obtained would decline, or the social cost imposed on some would increase and the benefits obtained by others decrease. Partisans may, of course, not perceive or accept the societal implications of information in these situations and thus bargaining (and negotiation) would yield results which were socially undesirable. Propositions 14 and 15 suggest that when, from a societal perspective, resource expenditures should be increased to further the ends of one partisan, only this partisan is likely to produce any information or information which is useful for the purposes of controlling collective action. According to proposition 15 cost conscious and myopic partisans may be led to propose socially desirable courses of action while they are engaged in bargaining if, from a societal perspective, their ends should be advanced by the solution to a problem. Similar conclusions are obtained from propositions 16 and 17. Under sufficiently restrictive behavioral assumptions, both those partisans whose ends should, from a societal perspective, be advanced and those whose benefits from collective action should be reduced (in order to obtain resource savings) may prepare plans with sufficient information and thus in a bargaining (or negotiating) situation propose courses of action which constitute the most desirable response to a problem from the standpoint of the collectivity.

To the extent that they uniformly employ incremental planning processes the various parties to a bargain or a negotiation may not perceive or advance the course of action which is most desirable from a societal perspective. Even if they adopt a rational decision making approach to planning they may not generate sufficient information to comprehend the benefit and public resource expenditure implications of proposals serving their ends. Only under restrictive circumstances can they be expected to present proposals which constitute the socially most desirable response to a problem. On informational grounds, then, it is difficult to conclude that, as partisan mutual adjustment processes, bargaining and negotiation represent a desirable way for a society or collectivity to reach a decision.

Power and Influence

Proposition 24. *Because of the uncertainties inherent in an open or advisory system, a participant may find that the best use of resources lies in trying to increase power and influence rather than in trying to determine through planning the course of action most consistent with his ends.*

When a decision center concludes that the interests of only one segment of society should be served, the plans and proposals of most participants and the supporting data, even if of high quality, may be ignored. For this reason the political influence a participant can exert may be a more important determinant of his gains from involvement than the quality of his information. A very precise analysis of alternatives may be meaningless to a participant who lacks power, and thus instead of investing in the preparation of plans and proposals participants may be induced to spend resources promoting them. Rather than plan, they may hire lobbyists, undertake public relations campaigns, form coalitions (through bargaining and negotiation) to increase their political influence, pursue informal relations with decision center members, and otherwise attempt to improve the likelihood that their plans and proposals are those adopted. As a consequence, the likelihood that any collective action taken will eventually prove unsuitable and need revision is increased because resources are diverted by participants from the production of information to the establishment of political power or influence. Even though a decision advances a participant's ends it will be based on lower quality information and thus is more likely to yield lower net benefits.

In the extreme, lack of or an inability to develop political power and influence may dissuade many potential participants from involvement. If the gains foreseen from involvement and information development are not expected to justify the costs, non-participation will be a rational strategy.[16] Consequently the interests of some potential participants and their observations about the impact of any decision will not be available to a decision center. From a societal perspective the unequal distribution of political power and influence may exact a high price in terms of welfare foregone. In addition, it will impede the efforts of those who attempt to induce the uninvolved, the disaffected, to participate. Unless he can raise their expectations of success, perhaps by political activity on their behalf, a community organizer, for example, may never engender the involvement of non-participants in the public decision making process.

The school decentralization debate affords a view of the actual importance to participants of efforts to exercise power and influence. The teachers union, the mayor and the Board of Education had paid lobbyists in Albany promoting their plans. The union in particular waged an effective lobbying campaign and undertook an extensive public relations program during the course of the debate to explain its position. As a consequence, other participants such as the demonstration school districts were at a distinct disadvantage. Whatever the merit of their proposals, it was surely submerged by the extensive promotional activities of other participants.

Proposition 25. *The uncertainties inherent in an advisory decision system (a) engender pressures to convert such a system to an open system, (b) may limit the involvement of many participants to an ineffectual level for control purposes, and (c) increase the likelihood that an issue will cycle.*

By definition an advisory decision system is one in which no participant exercises political influence or power and at the outset the decision center displays no preferences for any solution to a problem. As noted above participants may in such a context find planning less rewarding than attempts to exert pressure or influence on members of the decision center. Thus as an ideal an advisory system may be unstable, that is, it may always tend to evolve into an open system at best or a closed system at worst.

In addition, the uncertainties inherent in an advisory system may restrict the involvement of some participants to such a degree that their plans and proposals are of little or no value in controlling collective action. With low expectations of success from involvement participants will not commit substantial resources to planning but will be satisfied with limited amounts of data which establish only the general nature of objectives, environmental conditions, and the consequences of any course of action. For many participants the initial unit of data obtained from a planning process may be the first and only unit to justify its costs. Thus even though the marginal benefits of information to society may be very large, participants in advisory decision systems may base their plans and proposals on very little information. For example, limited political power as well as limited real resources may account for the rather vaguely defined proposals minority groups and organizations present as non-negotiable demands. Even though the gains from a favorable decision might be substantial, these participants will employ simple planning processes producing only small quantities of data because their expectations of successful involvement are low. As a consequence when a decision center does act in accordance with the information provided by these participants the decision it makes is quite likely to be imperfect and in need of revision. The inadequacy of the information upon which its decision is based undermines the efforts of the decision center and reduces the gains which those who are politically and economically weak obtain from collective action.

The same can be true in open decision systems. The analysis of the New York City school decentralization debate suggests that the plans and proposals of the demonstration school districts do not critically examine the problem of increasing community involvement in educational decision making. Many factors which would either improve or limit the contributions made to that objective were left unexplored in the plans of these participants. Being new elements in the New York City political environment, they were at a relative disadvantage compared to other, more politically powerful and better financed participants in the debate. Perhaps because they did not expect their plans and proposals to be adopted, they were unprepared to invest substantial resources in the information upon which they were based.

Because of the uncertainties inherent in an advisory (and an open) system, issues may tend to reappear. This is even more likely to the extent that the beneficiaries of action divert resources from planning to the pursuit of power and influence. Because an initial response to a problem in such a system is thus likely to be based on inadequate data, opportunities to make contributions to objectives will be lost and collective resources may unnecessarily be spent trying to correct imperfections. Moreover, there is no assurance that through successive iterations a solution to a problem will emerge. Programs which have failed to fulfill initial expectations are legion, but public programs whose initial shortcomings have been corrected through reliance on feedback are few in number. Also, nothing in the formal nature of a public decision system insures that feedback will be generated or if generated that it will be used.[17] Participants may be satisfied with an imperfect response to a problem, or a decision center may refuse to respond to feedback. Thus because of the uncertainty inherent in an advisory system society is more likely to implement plans and programs which will never successfully respond to a problem and which will waste both opportunities and resources.

Proposition 26. *Expanding the number of participants in an open or advisory system may reduce the quality and quantity of data produced by all.*

The involvement of additional participants in an open or advisory decision system increases the uncertainty of all about their gains from participation. Thus the openness or permeability of a planning field does not seem to serve a significant control purpose. While they may improve a decision center's conception of the range of objectives that might be appropriate ends of action or the range of alternatives that might be implemented, participants who previously were not involved may increase the uncertainty inherent in an open or advisory decision system and thus adversely affect the informational bases of the plans developed by others. In addition, the tendency to form competitive groups which reflect the same general interests but differ in their interpretation and specification of details may adversely affect the development of information in a public decision system. Needless duplication may result when essentially similar interests become fragmented into distinct organizational and group structures. For example, different conservation clubs in a region may all become concerned about the same proposal for an industrial park or waste treatment facility. Each of these groups may find participation in a public decision system fruitful. But unless those with similar interests combine their resources, the decision center will receive redundant data of a lower quality than that justified by the aggregate interest in the problem situation.

Proposition 27. *Control capability in an open system should, other things being equal, excede that in an advisory system.*

The possession of power or influence by some participants positively affects the data they develop and therefore improves the likelihood that means will achieve ends, or that collective action will be controlled. An open system may have many of the control negating characteristics of an advisory system. Its openness may not be a virtue; issues may tend to cycle; potential participants may be dissuaded from involvement; and participants may find resources better used in the promotion rather than in the preparation of plans. Yet all these shortcomings may have a smaller impact in an open system. Participants who possess some power and influence are assured that their plans will receive some recognition. They may thus appraise the value of information more highly than they would in an advisory system and therefore will be less likely to base proposals on inadequate data.

Conclusions

The invisible hand of self-interest which in classical economics insures efficient resource utilization is not apparently as effective in plural decision making. The plans and proposals voluntarily developed by participants will not provide adequate control capability for four reasons. First, some participants may not recognize the totality of benefit and resource expenditure changes indicated by a unit of data. Another way of stating this is to say that the benefits obtained by participants from involvement—the contributions to objectives, the decreases in social costs, the resource savings—are a public good. Whatever course of action makes these benefits available to a participant makes them available to all sharing his ends. But participants in plural decision-making processes may not take into account the totality of benefits which might be associated with their planning activities. Participants who behave ambivalently acknowledge only a fraction p of either the total benefit or the total resource changes indicated by a unit of data, while participants who behave myopically take into account only a fraction of both. As a consequence, in the development of separable data or where the objectives configuration is that of conflict, both of these participant types will base plans and proposals on inadequate data and/or suggest courses of action which are too limited or too extensive in scale.

Secondly, the plans and proposals of participants will not provide adequate control capability because the representatives of different segments of society do not recognize their joint interest in the same type of information. Separately they do not acknowledge the full implications of any unit of data for benefit, social cost, and resource expenditure changes. Separately, therefore, they may not develop adequate amounts of joint data and/or will propose courses of action which in scale or technology do not constitute an appropriate response to the problem confronting society. In a plural society deficiencies such as these in the information developed by participants appear inevitable and are likely to increase in extent as the number of different interest groups and organizations in the society increases.

Third, participants fail to provide adequate control capability because of the uncertainties inherent in open and advisory decision systems. Because of these uncertainties even altruistic participants may not evaluate a unit of information at its full value to society. In addition, participant activity to reduce the uncertainty inherent in a decision system and to increase the probability of a favorable decision may occur at the expense of information development. Participants may find the possession of power and influence more instrumental in obtaining their ends than a well-analyzed plan. To the extent that they do, society's control capability is weakened, resources are likely to be wasted and the effectiveness of collective action is reduced.

Fourth, participants may not perceive the uncertainties surrounding the societal response to a problem. Whenever collective action would serve the ends of several distinct segments of society simultaneously, individual participants may analyze alternatives which would advance only their ends. They thus would not produce relevant alternatives data and, because their alternatives data was not useful for control purposes, their problem environment and problem data might also not be useful. Similarly, where objectives are inconsistent participants may ignore the social costs of action and in so doing analyze and evaluate alternatives which impose excessive social costs. These courses of action will be evaluated more highly by participants than society because information about them will be more valuable to a participant than to society. For society the best course of action may be that providing fewer benefits but also imposing fewer social costs or requiring smaller resource expenditures. While participants may investigate these alternatives to some degree, they will expect greater marginal benefits from information about socially undesirable alternatives and will focus their investigations on them.

Thus the preceding analysis casts doubt on the often asserted effectiveness of plural decision-making procedures in generating the information needed to control collective action. In particular, it neither supports the contention that a plural decision-making process will "bring all relevant considerations to the fore and . . . give them the attention they deserve,"[18] nor does it support the contention that such processes necessarily cope "with the inevitability of omission and other errors in complex problem solving."[19] Participants, because they incorrectly appraise the value of information, will not develop their plans and proposals to the extent that is socially desirable and may direct their plans to the analysis of socially unwarranted courses of action. They will fail, from a societal perspective, to give relevant factors the attention they are due and will overlook socially important aspects of a problem situation. Even though a large number of participants may be involved as members of the planning field of a decision system, the aggregate joint and separable data available for control purposes will be inadequate; the shortcomings of any participant's joint or separable data are not rectified by the deficiencies of another's. However, the preceding analysis suggests but does not prove that society cannot depend upon the solutions to a problem advanced by participants; in particular instances participants may succeed in generating the control capability a society should have. For example, in the absence of decision system uncertainties participants who behave as altruists may base their plans and proposals on adequate information; and when restrictive behavioral assumptions hold, participants who act ambivalently or myopically may also generate the plans and proposals needed for control purposes. But in general a society cannot rely on the data voluntarily provided by participants.

Finally, when some of the other problems of plural decision making, those assumed away here for analytical convenience, are recognized, it is not obviously superior, as is often contended, to centralized planning. Not all segments of society affected by the response to a problem may be represented in a participatory process. Equally not all participants may have the resources needed to participate and develop data; Lipsky notes, for example, that the effectiveness of relatively powerless protest groups is limited by their lack of financial resources and technical expertise.[20] Still other participants may perceive a participatory process as a convenient forum for the airing of ideological issues, in which case their plans and proposals may not be designed with the intent of directing means to ends.[21] In addition, the problems of irrelevant data, withheld data, incorrect data, and of integrating plans and proposals developed by different participants plague plural processes.

Consequently the superiority of pluralism to centralized planning may be questioned. Under the best circumstances society cannot depend upon plural processes. And it would seem that the only claim which could be substantiated for these procedures is that they insure that a wide range of uncertainties about the problem, problem environment, and alternatives will be made apparent and, perhaps, be openly discussed. However, in any problem situation not all of these uncertainties will be relevant, and information about those that are cannot necessarily be assumed to provide an adequate basis for controlling the collective response ultimately made to a problem. The preceding analysis suggests that both in quantity and quality the information voluntarily generated by participants in plural decision making processes will be deficient for control purposes.

Chapter Five
An Empirical Investigation of Plural
Decision Making

The following examination of the New York City school decentralization debate is undertaken to provide some empirical insight into the effectiveness of plural decision-making procedures. It is also presented to illustrate some aspects of the preceding conceptual analysis and to assess to what extent the abstraction which is inevitable in such an analysis may have resulted in misleading conclusions.

As noted earlier, by 1967 the idea of decentralizing the New York City school system had many antecedents.[1] City school system organization had been reviewed and evaluated for approximately thirty years before the state legislature asked the mayor to prepare plans for a system of community school districts. Most of these studies suggested that decentralization would improve the delivery of educational services, that is, that it would have a positive effect on student academic achievement. Instead of supporting this conclusion with the results of empirical analyses, however, most of these studies cited the shortcomings of the centralized system—its cumbersome web of regulations which tended to stultify initiative and innovation, its insensitivities to the varying needs of schools in different neighborhoods, the difficulties encountered by parents in finding an administrator who would take responsibility for and interest in the functioning of programs in which their children were involved, the needless delays in implementing even the most limited changes.[2] Logically there is nothing wrong with this. If it is maintained that centralization implies low educational attainment, the conclusion that high achievement implies decentralization follows by an elementary logical principle.[3] Centralization in and of itself, however, does not necessarily imply low quality education. It is not a sufficient condition for poor scholastic achievement. Many other variables are involved, and it is misleading to emphasize one and ignore the others. [4]

Community involvement was also seen as an end in itself.[5] In New York City it would put the poor, for the first time, in some control of their environment and in the position of being responsible for their own futures. It was a means of breaking the immensity of the city down, of making government more accessible and responsible to the individual citizen. It was a mechanism by which citizens could initiate and propose rather than react to governmental programs. In a city of almost eight million, it could represent a long overdue reform of a school system of over one million students; it would bring the decision making for an essential urban service directly in contact with consumers. While appealing, this argument is also somewhat narrowly constructed. It underestimates the need to supplement the redistribution of authority and power with the creation of community institutions for the exercise of that power. Community participation requires thought and planning beyond the redistribution of raw power from bureaucrats and administrators to citizens. Attempts to improve citizen participation could easily be subverted by political, social, and organizational factors at the community level. A poorly designed organizational form, an indifference to participation which arises more from the exigencies of poverty than disinterest, or a strong, politically motivated local community faction could undermine the best intentions of any plan for citizen involvement.

As the following discussion will reveal, the school decentralization debate did not remedy the deficiencies of previous studies. Instead of analyzing the potential effectiveness of decentralization in terms of the objectives of quality education and citizen involvement, it focused on a distributional issue: how much authority should local school boards have to allocate resources and set policy for neighborhood schools? Community involvement could have been achieved by a variety of alternatives, which ranged from an administrative reorganization to make an essentially centralized structure more accessible to parents to local control of community schools. These alternative forms may be regarded as a continuum:

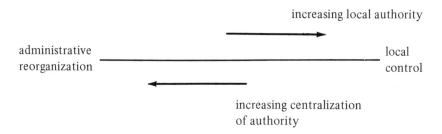

increasing local authority

administrative   local
reorganization   control

increasing centralization
of authority

Each point on the continuum represents a different distribution of authority between a central citywide school board and a set of community school boards. Under local control, a community school board would have unquestioned authority to allocate educational resources and set educational policy but it would not have the authority to determine the size of its budget. This would depend upon the total funds allocated by the mayor, the City Council, and the Board of Estimate to the entire school system and the community board's share of those funds (probably determined in accordance with a formula.) Under a reorganized administrative structure, access of parents to administrators would be improved and clear lines of authority would be established, but parents would be limited to an advisory role in the formulation of educational policy. At best they would have only the opportunity to comment on or ratify decisions which would be made by administrators. While all decisions might not be made in a central bureaucracy, those that were made in community school districts would be determined by the administrative personnel there, not by elected representatives of the parents.

The 1967 Legislative Action

From the very beginning school decentralization was a controversial issue. Legislators from other areas of the state opposed Mayor Lindsay's initial proposal to have the city system considered as five separate borough systems because, while state aid for their school districts would not increase, aid for New York City schools might increase by more than $100 million annually.[6] This proposal was also opposed by State Commissioner of Education Dr. James E. Allen and New York City Superintendent of Schools Dr. Bernard Donovan.[7] Five separate independent bureaucracies would compound administrative problems, unnecessarily complicate the coordination of citywide and special programs, restrict effective neighborhood involvement and integration across borough lines, and introduce undesirable political influences into educational decision making.[8] The Allen-Donovan opposition to the mayor's proposal made the already divided legislature hesitate. To obtain better information and reduce uncertainty, the legislature directed the mayor to prepare and submit a plan for the "development of educational policy and administrative units within the city school district" by December 1, 1967.[9] Even this was not entirely satisfactory; both Commissioner Allen and the Board of Education objected that city educators and not the mayor should prepare the December 1 plan.[10] The board further responded to the situation by unveiling its own decentralization proposal. Prepared in early February and revised after public hearings in March,[11] it was publicly approved by the board on April 19, 1967. As part of the proposal the board announced its intention to experiment with various forms of community involvement on a limited basis. Accordingly, in July 1967, it created three experimental school decentralization districts, one in Ocean Hill-Brownsville (Brooklyn), one in Harlem, and one in the lower East Side (Manhattan).[12] The first of these was to have a major role in the teachers strikes of 1968.

The Proposal Developed by the Mayor's Panel

In late April 1967, the mayor established a panel of experts, formally called The Mayor's Advisory Panel on Decentralization of the New York City Schools, to prepare the plan requested by the legislature, and by early November it had completed its task. Its plan, entitled *Reconnection for Learning*,[13] asserted that before educational quality could be improved all participants in the educational process—teachers, parents, students, administrators—had to be reconnected. And this, in the panel's opinion, could only be accomplished by a fundamental realignment of power and authority within the school system.[14] Consequently the redistribution of power rather than any concepts of political representation or educational theory became the basic tenet of the panel's plan to improve scholastic achievement and increase citizen involvement.

Problem Information

Proceeding under the premise that "an effective redistribution of responsibility in the public school system is essential,"[15] the panel analyzed several objectives in addition to those specified by the legislature as the ends of any decentralization proposal (quality education and community involvement). The rights and welfare of school administrators and teachers,[16] integration,[17] and efficiency [18] were also considered by it as potentially appropriate to the problem situation. With respect to teachers and administrators the panel concluded that New York City could not "afford to approach the government of its schools as a problem in the protection of vested interests."[19] In particular it felt that the teachers union "could collaborate with all decentralized local school boards"[20] and indeed would have to if authority was to be redistributed according to its plan. Integration should be "advanced as far as practicable"[21] in a decentralized system, but it was not to determine the characteristics of such a system. The panel argued that efforts to integrate the school system had been less than successful and that, in any case, integration was itself only one of several alternative means to the end of quality education. Not only did it feel that decentralization would be a more effective means to this end but also that in the long run community involvement would improve educational quality and thereby bring white middle class parents back to the city and their children into its school system.[22] Lastly the panel rejected efficiency as an objective. Acknowledging that a decentralized system would cost more to operate than a centralized one, it argued that, even at an incremental cost of $100 million, community involvement would be a good investment.[23] To put such a level of costs in perspective, it amounted in 1967 to 10 percent of the school system budget and would have consumed all but $8 million of the additional state aid that would have been obtained from decentralization. In sum, the panel would not allow the costs of community involvement to influence its proposal.

Thus of the five objectives it had initially considered as appropriate, the panel rejected one, efficiency, outright and relegated two others, integration and the welfare of teachers and administrators, to a position of secondary importance in evaluating any realignment of decision-making authority. Yet the redistribution of power from the central school board to a set of community school districts was not an end in itself. While the panel believed in citizen participation, it also sought "to keep the advantages without the disadvantages of the size and variety of the city's school system."[24] The plan it prepared was designed with two objectives primarily in mind, quality education and citizen involvement;[25] as the following discussion will suggest, however, the contributions this plan would make to either were quite doubtful.

In its plan the panel also provided information about an important factual dimension of the problem: the scholastic achievement of system students. The panel found that the average city student was not as well educated as the average student in the state or nation. In 1965 more than half of the students found to be below the state's minimum educational competence standards were from the city, although city school enrollment was only 35 percent of the state total. In 1967 approximately one-third of city students were a year or more behind the average student in the nation in reading and arithmetic skills. Only two-thirds of the students in the class originally scheduled to be graduated in 1967 were graduated.[26]

Problem Environment Information

Complementing this description and juxtaposed with it was an elaboration of four main aspects of the problem environment: (a) physical and related school system conditions, (b) changing ethnic composition of the student population, (c) organization of the school system, and (d) personnel policies. The panel observed that

1. the fastest growing boroughs, Richmond and Queens, lacked specialized high schools and that the last of these constructed by the city was the Bronx High School of Science in 1938;
2. approximately one-thirteenth of the 1.1 million students attended overcrowded schools;
3. approximately 16,000 teachers were "permanent substitutes" lacking standard licenses;
4. more experienced teachers were to be found in predominantly white schools than in black or Puerto Rican schools;
5. daily teacher absences averaged about 3 percent of the total teaching staff. In addition, approximately 500 classes lacked a permanent teacher throughout the year.[27]

Two longitudinal analyses were undertaken by the panel. One related the failure of integration policies to the changing ethnic proportions in student enrollment and total population. From 1954 to 1964 black and Puerto Rican students increased from 30 to over 50 percent of the total enrollment. This reflected a similar change in the city's population, which in turn was representative of demographic change in other large cities. Whites had migrated to the suburbs while blacks and Puerto Ricans had in-migrated. These population shifts, in part, defeated policies to improve school integration.[28]

The other longitudinal study assessed problems of teacher recruitment and advancement. The panel noted that the procedures for examining prospective teachers worked quite well when originally designed. They provided the system with outstanding personnel and were appropriately restrictive when the system itself was able to attract and retain the very best. Since the early 1930s, however, teacher recruitment had become very competitive. And for some time the system had not been able to attract or retain superior personnel. Qualifying city examinations had become an impediment. They were given at odd times of the year, and failure to pass them would deprive even an applicant certified by the state of financial rewards received by regular teachers. Moreover, aggressive, competent teachers were discouraged by their relatively limited chances for rapid advancement in the city system.[29]

The tradition that hobbled teacher recruitment also stultified system performance. Administrators were often bound to rigid conformance with inflexible standards and prevented from working together in the best interests of students. The panel stated that

the school system is heavily encumbered with constraints and limitations which are the result of efforts by one group to assert a negative and self-serving power against someone else. Historically these efforts have had ample justification, each in its time. To fend off the spoils system, to protect teachers from autocratic superiors, to ensure professional standards

... interest groups have naturally fought for protective rules. But as they operate today these constraints bid fair to strangle the system in its own checks and balances.[30]

This traditional concern with power and its preservation had in fact fragmented the school system into many quasi-autonomous decision-making units. Each was a "center of responsibility" with the authority to respond to some set of system needs; yet in their uncoordinated, undirected state they were collectively impotent and inert.[31] In addition, the size of the system worked against effective parental involvement, and the distant layers of bureaucracy above teachers and principals thwarted originality and innovation. Bureaucrats at central headquarters were too far removed and too busy to appreciate and understand the range of community school problems that existed. The needs of ghetto communities were, for example, different from those of middle-class communities and could not be met by the same programs, but, according to the panel, the central administrative staff did not recognize this: "Even when new programs and practices are promulgated, they tend to be designed uniformly for schools throughout the city."[32]

Information About Alternatives

When the panel began to design a system of community school districts, several alternatives had already been suggested. The Temporary Commission on City Finances had proposed four: educational parks, a borough school system, strengthened local school boards, and fifteen city school districts.[33] In addition, at least two participants in the decentralization decision system, the Public Education Association and the Board of Education,[34, 35] had promulgated their own plans. After its review of these alternatives and of a Louisville, Kentucky, design, [36] the panel decided to construct its own.

In the plan that it presented the panel called for a fairly extensive but not complete redistribution of decision-making authority from the central Board of Education to not less than thirty nor more than sixty community school boards. [37] Though community school boards were required to honor existing tenure and contract rights, they were given the authority to appoint the teachers, administrators, and supervisory personnel they needed with the restriction that all personnel had to meet qualifications established by the State Board of Regents and the State Commissioner of Education. The plan established, however, the rights of new teachers to tenure and the rights of existing teachers to promotion, to transfer between schools in any district, to transfer between districts, and to a hearing before being removed from a permanent appointment. Community school boards were also given the authority to allocate financial resources to different educational needs, to lease and furnish property for educational uses, and to approve general courses of study for their school districts. With respect to these powers the panel was at points almost euphoric in its visions of the initiative and innovative energies, pent up in New York City residents for years because of the rigidities and insensitivities of the centralized system, that would be released in a system of community school districts. "A district," it observed, "could authorize exchange programs with foreign countries" or "designate a cluster of schools for a sustained experiment . . . with a particular style of education . . . it might not wish to employ throughout the district." [38]

Although it recommended that the existing centralized administrative organization be dispersed throughout the community school district system, it nevertheless saw a role for a central education agency which would conduct research into educational programs and encourage cooperation among school districts. Such a central agency would establish citywide salary schedules and aid school districts in their recruitment and potential teachers in the job placement process. It would also be involved in allocating by an equitable formula the city educational budget to community school districts and would be responsible for the analysis of the educational attainments of students in the decentralized system.

With respect to the objective of community involvement the panel proposed that delegate representatives from local schools, not the parents themselves, elect six of eleven community school board members.[39] To prevent the domination of community boards by political clubs the mayor would have the power to appoint the other five members from lists maintained by the central education agency. The panel also recommended that parent-teacher groups be strengthened in schools and that community boards be required to make annual reports and furnish information to parents on demand.

In its plan the panel also attempted to maintain flexibility. It permitted districts and communities to remain under the authority of the board of the central education agency—to reject, in effect, the opportunity to assume local control. It empowered the central education agency to alter district boundaries of its own accord, and it suggested that the State Commissioner of Education should have the power to authorize referendums within communities to change the method of electing community board members. Moreover, a transition commission was to be made responsible for determining many important aspects of a decentralized school system which the panel had neglected: new educational standards, precise district boundaries, plans for reassigning the administrative staff employed at the Board of Education, fiscal guidelines for community boards, procedures for reporting district budgets and transferring students, and the decentralization of adult education and summer programs.[40]

The Mayor's Plan

The mayor received the panel's plan in early November 1967. After public hearings, which were lightly attended, and informal discussions with teachers and parents, the plan was given to his advisors on educational policy for review and evaluation.[41] The result was a revised version which the mayor submitted to the legislature in early 1968.[42] In this plan the mayor stated that citizen participation was only a means to an end.

> The reason for establishing community school districts is not simply to give citizens more control over their schools; they are proposed only in

order to provide the framework in which citizens and educators can work together on a radical improvement of educational quality in all parts of the city.[43]

While the plan reflected a concern for integration and the rights of those affected by decentralization, it essentially reiterated the panel's philosophy that to improve quality education the distribution of power within the school system had to be altered. In it an unresponsive, centralized administrative organization was associated with scholastic deficiencies and community involvement was viewed as positively affecting scholastic achievement.

The mayor's plan altered the panel's design for a system of community school districts in several minor ways. Community boards were not to assume control of city high schools immediately. Their ability to do so would be reviewed three years after the system had been decentralized. Local boards were required to prepare long-range plans, and the budgetary process was modified. A nine-man central board, rather than the New York State Commissioner of Education, was made directly responsible for the enforcement of educational standards. The temporary transition commission was required to determine the number of school districts, and the central board together with the State Commissioner of Education was given authority to revise school district boundaries. Finally, greater emphasis was placed on the need for a training program which would "give participants in the community school system the strength, perspective and knowledge to grapple with the highly complex, often sensitive issues that inevitably will confront them."[44]

Given the time available to prepare a plan, both the panel and the mayor's educational staff would appear to have performed admirably. The panel completed its planning within a period of six months, and the revisions undertaken by the mayor required another month to accomplish. Thus in a period of seven months two proposals had been developed in accordance with planning processes which were essentially participatory in nature for redesigning a school system of over one million students.[45] These time constraints were not eased, moreover, by an abundance of financial resources. The mayor's panel received $50,000 from the city and approximately $50,000 worth of services from the Ford Foundation. Together members of the mayor's educational staff spent about seventy man-days debating and revising the panel's proposals.[46]

In comparison to the resources available for other planning activities in the city, those available to the mayor's panel were small. Including the services provided by the Ford Foundation staff they amount to less than ten cents for each of the students enrolled in city schools and less than one tenth of one percent of the $100 million the mayor expected annually in additional state aid. In comparison to other city expenditures for information the resources made available to the panel for school system reform were surprisingly small. During the late 1960s the city spent $1 million for *several* studies of its housing needs and problems (centered primarily on the impact of rent control and the abandonment problem) and allocated almost $400,000 to a study of pollution-free cars.[47] In July 1970, Frederick O'R. Hayes, Budget Director for the City of New York, apparently informed the mayor that the $5.3 million spent in 1969 for management consultant contracts had saved the city over $100 million.[48] Yet for a plan which promised to improve educational quality and community involvement and to increase state aid by over $100 million, the city could afford only $50,000.

The Teachers Union Proposals

Two major position papers, two bills in the 1969 state legislature, a myriad of statements by Albert Shanker, United Federation of Teachers president, and pamphlets by his staff attest to teachers union interest in the decentralization decision. The first comprehensive union proposal appeared in late 1967 and was in many respects a reaction to the panel's plan. The union accepted the redistribution of authority as a valid end in itself but maintained it would conflict with the goal of quality education. The myopic nonprofessionals who would control public schools would prevent innovative teachers from employing advanced instructional techniques and improving the relevance of subject matter. Integration and efficiency were emphasized, and the welfare of teachers and supervisors was rigorously defended. Thus with the exception of quality education, the union appears to have reversed the panel's general assessment of objectives. The union did not elaborate upon the factual dimensions of the problem; in particular, while it noted the declining educational achievements of city students, it did not discuss their academic deficiencies in any detail.

Problem environment data was also contained in the union's proposal. Physical and organizational aspects of the school system were criticized, and aspects of the problem environment which would restrict the effectiveness of the panel's plan were discussed. Given a choice of assignment within a decentralized system, teachers and supervisors would seek employment in the "most favored" communities, leaving those most in need to fight over the rejects, "if indeed, they were fortunate enough to receive any applicants at all."[49] Teachers might be hired or fired on the basis of such noneducational factors as race, favoritism, political philosophy, or conformity with community prejudices. Referring to tenure as "a precious teacher right" which might not survive a predicted formal attack by elected community school boards, the union also foresaw harrassment of teachers by local vigilantes to such an extent that tenure would for practical purposes become a meaningless aspect of employment in a local school district. In addition, it observed that educational innovation had not normally been the hallmark of local community participation; in most instances it was a product of state and federal imposition of programs and requirements on local boards and had emerged most frequently in large consolidated school districts.

The union's design for community school districts differed in many important respects from the panel's proposal. Direct election of all eleven local school board members and fifteen school districts or less were proposed, while the budgetary policy-making and other powers of local boards were substantially altered. Community school boards would not have the power to disburse funds for teachers' salaries, to select textbooks, or to participate in the design of curriculums, but they would be allowed to advise professionals on the courses of instruction they thought desirable. Having fought over the years to establish its bargaining power vis-à-vis the city Board of Education and to promote the image of teachers as professionals, the union was opposed to any form of decentralization which would fragment the school system into independent decision-making units and give community leaders authority over matters of interest to teachers. On the other hand, to improve any school system that might emerge as a consequence of the decentralization debate, the union recommended several procedural innovations: trained administrators in the system's bureaucracy, increased use of paraprofessionals, more complete utilization of community resources, and education of some students at home. Accompanying these was a set of programs to improve teacher quality and decrease student deprivation, which included a teacher internship program, special funds for exceptional children, universal preschool programs, and more funds for special facilities to teach children with physical, emotional, or mental problems.[50]

After publication of its 1967 plan the union continued to generate information about citizen participation in educational decision making. In December 1967 union president Shanker asserted that large numbers of teachers would leave the system if the panel's plan was adopted, and in September 1968 he suggested that parents were more interested in information about their children, their academic strengths and deficiencies, than in the authority to determine curriculum and select system personnel.[51] A large number of pamphlets and documents modified or reiterated ideas developed in the union's 1967 plan or presented ideas which were to appear later in its 1969 proposals.[52]

Three documents, two legislative bills, and one general proposal, were released by the union in 1969. Of the two bills, one outlined a procedure for electing the city Board of Education through proportional representation, and the other specified a rather precise procedure for removing personnel in a system of fifteen school districts.[53] The general statement for school system reform supported these two bills. In this document the union asserted "that decentralization is only a system of organization which . . . is *educationally* irrelevant,"[54] but later it averred that "in a system as large as ours, some decisions cannot and should not be made at central headquarters."[55] This plan differed very little from the 1967 plan, with one exception. Nonprofessionals would be allowed, through some unspecified device, to bring formal complaints against teachers on nonprofessional matters.

The planning process employed by the union was essentially participatory, involving union delegates from each of the city's schools. Actual resource costs of the plans were minimal. The union maintained a staff of special research assistants and lawyers to develop information, and union delegates contributed their time freely at meetings. In both 1968 and 1969 the union spent from $30,000 to $50,000 in addition to the real resource costs of its plans to promote its position on decentralization. These expenditures could and would have been expanded had the situation justified so doing.[56]

In sum, the union as a participant in the decentralization decision system developed data primarily to preserve its self-interest. But this does not gainsay its value to the legislature. Without this information the decision center would not have known to what extent teacher interests would be affected or could be protected by the collective decision to decentralize schools. Interestingly, analysis of union plans and proposals indicates that in 1967 the value of more precise information was underestimated. The 1969 bill, produced after the strikes of 1968, carefully outlines grievance procedures and the rights of teachers when charged with malfeasance. Whereas the 1967 plan indicates the general interests of teachers in these matters, it does not detail a procedure for protecting them. The strikes of 1968, which occurred in part over the issue of teacher rights, appear to have impressed upon the union the value of better information about its own interests.

Plans Prepared by the Demonstration School Districts

When the city Board of Education indicated in the summer of 1967 a willingness to experiment with increased citizen involvement in educational decision making, members of the teachers union joined with local leaders in Harlem and Ocean Hill-Brownsville to plan and organize the demonstration school districts in these communities. But by that fall deep conflicts between the objectives of these two groups became apparent, and the union members withdrew. The local groups sought the ability to determine who would teach in local schools and were interested in educational experimentation. Union members were interested in the teachers' right to tenure, the preservation of grievance procedures, which had been difficult to establish, and the expansion of a compensatory education program entitled More Effective Schools. These fundamental differences were intensified by racial differences; Jews comprised the largest proportion of teachers in New York City, and the residents of the demonstration school districts were predominantly black.

In the spring of 1968 the governing board of the Ocean Hill-Brownsville Demonstration School District informed nineteen teachers and administrators in its schools that they were being transferred out of the school district. A majority of the district's teachers then went out on strike in support of their colleagues and were still on strike when the school year ended in June. During the summer unsuccessful attempts were made to reach an accord between the Ocean Hill-Brownsville district and the teachers union; a citywide teachers strike was called over the matter in September, and the teachers did not return to the schools until mid-November.

The strikes of 1968 were a grievous source of friction between the demonstration school districts and the union. Racial slurs and invective were commonplace, and even after the fall strike was settled violence and civil disobedience erupted in the demonstration school districts. The strikes and the acerbic dispute that accompanied them have been the focus of many commentaries on community involvement,[57] but understanding these disputes and the personalities, proclivities, and penchants of the principal combatants contributes little to present purposes. Moreover, the strikes tend to obscure the contributions the demonstration school districts made to the decentralization debate.

In the spring of 1967, a group called the Harlem Parents Committee released a plan outlining institutions for increased citizen involvement in educational policy making.[58] Nominally the plan was concerned with quality education. It did specify a District Education Commission, which was to be responsible for curriculums, educational innovation, research, and evaluation, but its most important contribution was a detailed design for citizen involvement. Salaried positions such as school aide, classroom aide, teacher helper, and family-school intermediary were integrated with a design for parent organizations which specified the structure of certain working committees for dealing with community school system problems.

The essence of the Ocean Hill-Brownsville community plans may be found in three documents, two prepared in 1967 and one presented in the spring of 1968. In early 1967 a steering committee of community people, parents, and teachers formed to develop plans for and to negotiate with the Board of Education about an appropriate community voice in the administration of a new community school facility. This group became the progenitor of a larger group which later developed a proposal for increased citizen participation in the administration of Ocean Hill-Brownsville schools. The preamble of this plan states,

> The parents of Ocean Hill-Brownsville are determined that they shall no longer tolerate the abridgment of their right to have a voice in improving the educational lot of their children. They are imbued with a determination to bring to an immediate and permanent halt their voicelessness in matters pertaining to their schools.[59]

The plan elaborates the procedures for selecting a governing board, the functions and duties of such a board, and the qualifications and functions of a unit administrator. Specific educational objectives and proposals for achieving them are not presented, although a need to evaluate the total educational program is acknowledged. A structure for the governing board is suggested, but no other proposals for community involvement are made.

In July 1967, the Board of Education designated the Ocean Hill-Brownsville community an experimental school decentralization district. The community elected a governing board in August, and by early October it had promulgated a statement of objectives. The governing board asserted community interest in teaching staff stability, smaller class size, increased professional and paraprofessional services, new and improved educational programs, enriched programs, new schools, and more freedom for "professional staff to plan and institute curriculum change." [60] With this statement of purpose the new local governing board moved to solve the two major problems it faced: a need to design for community involvement and a need to design for quality education. In the spring of 1968 it decided that to solve both problems it needed more power and authority than had originally been granted to it by the Board of Education. It requested the authority to select assistant principals, to plan and renovate schools, and to purchase textbooks and other supplies.[61] Throughout the teachers strikes of 1968 the governing board and its administrators defended and enlarged this request.

The governing board's proposals contain little information on its experiences with programs to improve educational quality and procedures to increase community involvement. By early 1970 approximately sixteen educational programs for students and sixteen general community education programs had been implemented or proposed. Though potentially useful, the information describing and analyzing these programs does not seem to have been presented to the legislature. Similarly, information which the legislature could have used to understand the design of participation seems to have remained in Ocean Hill-Brownsville. Many programs to involve parents in the educational process were instituted in the district. Over 300 parents were directly employed in community schools, and many others were instructed by professionals in how to aid their children at home.[62] Groups of parents were organized to act on or analyze educational and related community problems; given the designation of "task force," they participated in the design of educational curriculum and the development of programs for involving other community residents. Finally, an open door policy in administration, a substantial community relations program, and activities sponsored by a community education center were used to encourage participation. Neither the effectiveness of these programs nor their structure was ever reported to the legislature.[63] Thus the main contribution of the Ocean Hill-Brownsville Demonstration School District to the decentralization debate was a statement of purpose and a proposal for redistributing decision making authority.

Plans Developed by the Board of Education

The Board of Education possessed the power to decentralize the city school system to a limited degree, and on April 19, 1967 it adopted a policy to strengthen the thirty existing local school boards, which at that time possessed only advisory powers.[64] District school superintendents were required to consult more with their local school boards over a greater range of issues before taking any action themselves; in addition, they were allocated certain discretionary funds and given greater freedom in curriculum innovation and the use of staff. According to Alfred A. Giardino, vice president of the Board,

> The vesting of authority, money and personnel in the local district with power to make final decisions in many areas of administration should expedite administration and more fully reflect local needs.[65]

In this same policy statement the board also announced its intent to establish demonstration projects in more advanced forms of decentralization. These projects would develop new approaches and techniques for "teacher training and instruction, and for increasing parental and community involvement."[66] In other words, these experiments were to provide the board with information about alternative designs for community involvement and innovative programs for increasing quality education.

In the spring of 1968 the board completed a major proposal for decentralization which could be implemented only with legislative action.[67] The plan recognized five objectives: quality education, integration, efficiency, community involvement, and the welfare of teachers and administrators. In the plan the board contended that contributions to the objective of quality education would require dependent, not independent, local school boards and district superintendents. A city Board of Education and superintendent of schools were necessary to coordinate, instruct, maintain standards in, and control city schools. Under the proposal some powers, such as the appointment of district superintendents and the granting of tenure, were to be given to local school boards immediately. The board requested authorization from the legislature to delegate other powers such as budgetary control to local school boards at those points in time when they appeared to be ready to assume them and doing so appeared to be consistent with the maintenance of minimum educational standards. The board was willing to allow the local school boards to have a more effective voice in the determination of curriculum, educational programs, and textbooks. In addition, increased funds were requested to combat the effects of deprivation through more extensive compensatory educational programs, and the coordination of health, housing, employment, and recreation services was suggested as necessary to relax nonschool constraints on scholastic achievement. However the plan suggested no mechanisms for increasing community involvement nor did it contain any concrete proposals for improving quality education. To correct these deficiencies the board was prepared to rely on feedback.

> It is our intention to monitor this plan as it proceeds in order to make whatever modifications are necessary to accomplish our purposes—the improvement of instruction and closer and more meaningful involvement of parents and community.[68]

To some extent the board's willingness to rely on feedback is attributable to the nature and organization of the resources available to it. The members of the board were overburdened by ordinary system problems. Almost without staff of their own, they had little ability to develop a thoughtful, comprehensive plan. With a tight budgetary constraint they could not easily hire consultants to develop such a plan, and they were unlikely to obtain one from the bureaucracy. At central headquarters the immense volume of day-to-day work was compounded severely by rules and regulations which required tedious cross-checking.[69] Moreover, administrative positions were more likely to be filled by ex-teachers than by trained personnel. According to Rogers,

> the practice of assigning former classroom teachers to positions at headquarters is partly responsible for the bureaucratic ineptitude. There are teachers in auditing, zoning, human relations, demographic research, programming and data processing, and guidance counselling, who have little or no technical training.[70]

These factors alone may account for the board's reliance on feedback, or its uncertainties about the success of any proposal that it might make, and hence, its uncertainty about the value of information, might account for this reliance. Uncertainties about the best way to increase community involvement and academic achievement could be eliminated once the legislature had acted to give the board and its administrative personnel the authority to decentralize the system. What was the point of clarifying uncertainties about community involvement and quality education if in the end some other set of administrators, perhaps those in a system of independent community school districts, would reap the rewards of such information? There is still another possible explanation. As a participant in the decentralization debate the board and its administrators may have been more concerned with saving the centralized school system structure than with advancing either community involvement or quality education. If this was the case, the board's primary objective was one other than those it suggested in its initial proposal and it therefore did not need, nor did it develop, detailed information about how those objectives might be achieved even under a centralized system.

In the spring of 1968 the legislature passed a compromise bill which required that a new plan for school system decentralization be prepared, this time by the Board of Education, which at the request of the mayor was expanded from nine to thirteen members. Known as the Marchi bill after John J. Marchi, a conservative state senator from Staten Island, this legislation also allowed the Board of Education to delegate any or all of its powers to existing local school boards and to the three demonstration school districts. In mid-July 1968 the mayor appointed five new members to the board, each of whom was thought to be favorably disposed toward decentralization of the school system. The expanded board acted quickly to decentralize the school system to the extent it thought to be desirable. At the end of the month the superintendent of schools sent a memorandum to board members outlining possible forms of decentralization, and, after tumultuous public hearings in late August, the board approved a plan to delegate increased power to local school boards including its demonstration school districts.[71] This proposal was approved in mid-October by the Board of Regents, and by December the board had a detailed statement of guidelines promulgated for local school boards.[72]

By the end of January 1969 the Board of Education had completed a plan for school decentralization which viewed the redistribution of power from the central Board of Education to a set of thirty local boards of education as an end in itself.[73] Little is said about the goal of quality education. While community involvement is ambiguously associated with improved scholastic achievement, as a minority report observed, no evidence is presented to support this relationship.[74] Structures and programs for bringing parents into the schools, such as those employed by the Ocean Hill-Brownsville governing board, are not included. The design for participation was limited to two requirements. First, local school board members were not to be elected at large but as the representatives of different schools in a community school district. Second, in all schools parent-teacher associations were required which would have an advisory role in the formulation of budgetary, personnel, and other policy and with which principals, community superintendents, and community school boards would have to establish working relationships.[75] The plan ignores the efficiency objective but emphasizes integration as a socially important goal. Priority was placed on protecting the rights of tenured teachers. Grievance procedures required by state law were outlined "to make it absolutely clear that tenured employees would continue [in a decentralized system] to be protected by ... statutory procedures."[76] Procedures for appointments and promotions which were used throughout the state in school districts of less than 400,000 total population were adopted in the plan as relevant to each of the thirty community districts in a decentralized system.

The plan gave community school districts the authority to establish curriculum and educational programs subject to state requirements and minimum Board of Education requirements and the authority to employ personnel who met state standards. The districts also had the authority to disburse funds for educational services and equipment but were to have primarily an advisory role in the construction of new educational facilities, that is, in the allocation of the capital budget. But community school districts would have the responsibility for providing school lunches and undertaking repairs and maintenance on existing facilities. Powers not given to the community school districts remained in the hands of the city Board of Education. Because city high schools were often not comprehensive but specialized in the provision of vocational or of academic training, they individually attracted students from areas of the city which were larger than any community school district. Accordingly they were to remain the responsibility of the city board until they were converted into comprehensive schools, at which time the local school districts would be given the authority for operating them. Responsibility for the capital budget and for negotiations with the teachers was also left with the city board, and it was given the task of preparing an objective formula by which the city educational budget would be allocated to the community school districts.

In sum, the plan prepared by the enlarged thirteen member Board of Education focused on the redistribution of decision-making authority from the city Board of Education to a set of thirty local school boards. But the purposes of this redistribution were all but neglected. No evidence was presented to indicate that it would have any impact whatsoever on educational quality or that it would in fact lead to citizen involvement in educational decision making.

Information Developed by Other Participants

Numerous other groups and organizations participated in the decentralization debate either by preparing plans and proposals or by expressing opinions about the relative merits of various proposals. Though it is not a comprehensive assessment, the following discussion illustrates the range and diversity of this involvement in sufficient depth to permit analysis of the quality and quantity of data voluntarily developed by the participants in the debate.

The Educational Associations

In New York City two groups, the Public Education Association and the United Parents Associations, have traditionally attempted to influence the formulation of city school board policy. Both became involved in the decentralization debate by expressing opinions at public hearings and presenting plans and proposals to the state legislature.

The Public Education Association viewed the problem of decentralization primarily as one of giving greater decision-making authority to thirty local school boards, which prior to 1967 had by state legislation only an advisory role in the development of educational policy at the community level. In a plan presented in early 1967 it proposed that local school boards be permitted to appoint district superintendents of schools who would be responsible to them "for all educational and administrative matters which have been delegated to the district[s] . . . and to the [city] Superintendent of Schools for all other matters."[77] The association felt that the primary cause of failure in the centralized school system was the accountability of the district superintendents, who were responsible for implementing all educational programs in a local school district, to the Board of Education. By making these supervisory personnel accountable to local school boards, they would be positively induced to design and modify programs to meet local needs. The district superintendent would, with the local board's advice and consent, appoint school principals and would, subject to the limitations of city Board of Education personnel policy, assign, transfer, and remove teachers. In addition, the local school board and district superintendent were to be given authority, again subject to city board guidelines and regulations, for the purchase of supplies, maintenance of buildings, and the development of curriculum. Thus in many respects this proposal resembles that developed by the mayor's panel, and in January 1968 the Public Education Association gave qualified endorsement to the mayor's proposal for school decentralization. Its reservations about this proposal centered on the power it gave the mayor to appoint members of local school boards (five of eleven) and the power it gave him to allocate funds to these local boards. The association observed that "no Governor in the country may modify his state aid formula without legislative action but under [the] proposed plan the Mayor is not even required to hold a public hearing" to modify the formula in accordance with which community school district budgets would be determined.[78]

The United Parents Associations viewed decentralization as a means of improving the quality of educational programs, but it also maintained that in making parents more significant partners in the educational process a "degree of centralization [was needed] . . . to assure curriculum standards, . . . to protect against discrimination, favoritism or influence peddling, to achieve maximum integration, . . . to establish . . . standards for tenure, and to protect against . . . self-interest groups gaining control of . . . schools."[79] Parents, the association felt, did not want politics intruding into the educational process and did want a central education authority to whom they could appeal when disputes arose in community school districts. Moreover, while it was important to have community school district personnel, and in particular a community school district superintendent, accountable for their actions and decisions to a local school board, it was not necessary to decentralize administrative services which could be more efficiently provided on a citywide basis. Thus under the United Parents Associations' plan a central board would be responsible for construction and maintenance of educational facilities, for the provision of major services and operating needs (lunches, fuel, equipment), for negotiating contracts with the teachers union, and for the development of a formula for determining the funds to be allocated to community school districts in any fiscal year. Subject to citywide standards and regulations, local school boards would be responsible for curriculum, for the selection and acquisition of texts, for appointing a school district superintendent, and for the recruitment, assignment, and promotion of teachers. Thus the association's plan leaves substantial powers with a central Board of Education but attempts to introduce some flexibility at the local level into the educational decision-making process.

The United Parents Associations saw parental involvement in educational decision making in two perspectives. First, it felt that parents alone should be involved in the elections of local school board members. Second, it foresaw, as might be expected, parents associations in the schools as having a basic and important advisory role to the district superintendent, principals, and local community school board. In the formulation of educational and administrative policy all three were "required to consult regularly with elected representatives" of the parents associations from each community school.[80]

Interestingly, from 1968 to 1969 the associations' position on the composition of local school boards and the election of representatives to them changed. In 1968 it advocated that parent assemblies in each community school elect one representative to a District Selection Panel. This panel would then elect six members to the local school board, and three other members would be appointed by the central board. The purpose of this was to insure that no community group dominated local elections. In 1969, however, it advocated direct election of all nine local school board members by parents.[81]

Other Citywide Participants

A number of other groups with citywide membership became involved in the decentralization debate. Some of these, such as the Liberal party, had at best a broad concern with the functioning of the school system, while others, such as the African-American Teachers Association, had a more focused interest. What the Liberal party advocated was not so much a plan as it was an outline for decentralization. Very little is said about increasing community involvement other than a suggestion that a majority of local school board members be elected by parents and the remainder by the general electorate of a community.[82] While the party reaffirmed its traditional interest in "quality integrated education," its proposal suggested only that greater expenditures (at the time they were nearly $1,000 per student—a sum exceeded by few suburban school districts) needed to be made for education. On the other hand, four of the thirteen points in its proposal deal with the appointment, advancement, and grievance procedures for teachers and administrative personnel. Curriculum would be established and a district superintendent would be appointed by local school boards subject to city Board of Education and state standards. "Clear guidelines" were advocated for distinguishing the responsibilities of local school boards and a central board of education. In sum, the plan is in most respects general but is specific with respect to the interests of teachers, who constituted a politically powerful segment of the city populace.

The proposal advanced by the African-American Teachers Association demanded *"self control, self-determination and self-defense for schools in black and Puerto Rican communities."*[83] The association demanded an end to segregated education, a term it defined as education in schools "controlled by outsiders whose only interest is exploitation."[84] Its plan was in essence quite simple. The Board of Education was to relinquish all power and authority to local governing boards. Thus these boards would become completely responsible for the appointment, advancement, and recruitment of personnel, the expenditure of funds, the establishment of curriculum, and other matters. Relationships between local school boards and parents were to be developed by salaried parent coordinators. The association's ideas were more a manifesto than a proposal, more a rhetorical statement than a design for action. The mechanics of decentralization on a citywide scale, the procedures for electing local school boards, the achievement of quality education were neglected in favor of a strong position on the redistribution of authority.

Similar demands for complete community control were voiced by the Teachers for Community Control and the City-Wide Coalition for Community Control of Public Schools.[85] Both of these groups were organized in response to the decentralization debate. The coalition, which was comprised of several organizations seeking local control of schools,[86] specified that community school boards must have complete control over the disbursement of all funds and that all community school district personnel were to be accountable to these boards for their performance. Election procedures were to be established by local community school boards. The teachers' group maintained that "under community control, there is absolutely no reason why teachers will not have the same rights and tenure protection they now have."[87] They also expected salutary effects on quality education from local control, and, though they admitted that integration would not be advanced in a set of locally controlled school systems, they observed that it had been frustrated in the centralized system.

The Anti-Defamation League of New York, long a proponent of school desegregation, also favored school decentralization, although not to the degree advocated by proponents of community control. The league maintained that each local community was part of a greater citywide community and that for this reason "all delegations of power and authority . . . must be subject to standards, controls, audits and evaluations which are centrally administered on the City and State levels."[88] Like all other participants the league specified a redistribution of powers between local school boards and a city board. Its proposals deal primarily with the development of curriculum and the personnel policies of local school boards (the merit system and teacher rights were to be protected), but relatively little is said about their budgetary powers.[89]

Supervisory Associations and the Board of Examiners

For many participants in the school decentralization debate the supervisors at central headquarters, school district superintendents, principals, and the Board of Examiners were the villains in the school system. Because they were accountable to supervisors in the Board of Education central offices, district superintendents were often insensitive to the different needs of community schools. The panel, for example, observed that for supervisors in the central headquarters

> Rules, regulations, and multiple channels require so much cross-checking . . . that little or no time is left for exposure to schools in their community setting . . . . Failure to adapt changes to local needs and capabilities often prevents changes from taking root widely . . . . The lack of adequate contact with the local scene also impedes the spread of innovative practices that are first developed on a pilot basis in a few schools.[90]

Thus district superintendents were unlikely to find a sympathetic or comprehending ear for change or innovation at the board's main offices and, since their advancement depended upon evaluations made by supervisors there, they were unlikely to press for programs adapted to local needs. Given this organizational environment, school principals had only limited ability and little motivation to introduce creative educational programs. The Board of Examiners was a branch of the Board of Education charged by law with protecting the merit system. No potential teacher, whatever his educational qualifications, could be certified to teach in the New York City school system without passing an examination given by the board. Promotion was based on these tests and new appointments to the position of principal or superintendent had to be made from the top three individuals passing an appropriate board exam. Thus effective control of personnel, the recruitment, appointment, and advancement of teachers, would not belong to local school boards in a decentralized system if the Board of Examiners retained its statutory authority.

Having profited from the merit system established by the Board of Examiners, the supervisors, district superintendents, and principals supported it. The Council of Supervisory Associations recommended "a form of decentralization, increasing autonomy and flexibility in specified activities for individual schools and their districts but retaining central coordination and support."[91] Primarily this meant that the central board would retain most of the authority for curriculum change, certification of teachers, the establishment of qualifications for advancement, and the disbursement of funds. With respect to the goal of community involvement, the council suggested *"a close working partnership between parents and the professional staff based on a clear understanding of their respective roles."*[92] This meant that while "in general" professionals might be accountable to parents for their decisions, they could "be held specifically accountable for their effectiveness and their performance only to the fellow professionals and experts who supervise and rate them."[93] The supervisors also favored greater expenditures for education on the grounds that this would improve educational quality, and they saw their proposal as being more conducive to integration than the panel's.

The High School Principals Association took the position that "decentralization should mean greater community involvement in education, not immediate community control over details of policy and planning."[94] It further added that "true decentralization should result finally in delegating a wider degree of authority and responsibility to the school principal."[95] The association stressed the need to clearly differentiate the responsibilities of parents and local school boards from those of professional educators, and it recommended decentralizing the city system into five borough systems. The registered voters in each of the boroughs were to elect nine individuals to a borough board who would then elect a chairman. The five chairmen would constitute a city board of education responsible for appointing a city superintendent of schools and passing on matters of broad educational policy. The borough boards would in turn appoint borough superintendents and would have total supervisory authority over the activities of the local school boards. Local school board members would be elected by parents; they would appoint a community school district superintendent but would be concerned primarily with implementing policies of the borough board. On budgetary matters local school boards were to consult school principals, and on general policy matters they were to consult the parents' associations and the professional staff. The role of the principal was stressed in the association's plan. Principals were, for example, to select new staff for their schools from lists of certified teachers prepared by the Board of Examiners and were to have funds to carry out minor maintenance operations, and it was the principal who had the authority for adjusting curriculum to the needs of his school.

In contrast to these two proposals was the approach to decentralization taken by the Association of Black School Supervisors and Administrators.[96] This association advocated complete community control of local schools as the best means for increasing the scholastic achievement of children. A set of four reports from principals to local school boards and superintendents on curriculum, staff training and evaluation, and educational programs was recommended in order to insure accountability of educators to the citizens of the community school districts in which they were employed. Teacher job security and grievance procedures were supported, but in turn more critical evaluation of teacher performance in the classroom was advocated. A greater exposure of students to black history and culture was also suggested. Finally, the association condemned the Board of Examiners as "outmoded, prejudicial and ineffective,"[97] and it proposed reliance on state certification of personnel for appointment and promotion.

For its own part the Board of Examiners attempted in the debate to establish the role it could play in a decentralized school system. During the course of the debate it apparently implemented changes in its testing procedures which made them more efficient and less objectionable. It noted that central selection and assignment of teachers in a decentralized system might prevent the best teachers from leaving the areas where they were most needed for positions with wealthier school districts. "There is nothing," it noted, "inconsistent between decentralization and a centrally functioning Board of Examiners."[98] The merit system could and should be preserved in a decentralized system and with it, of course, the Board of Examiners.

The Board of Regents

In the spring of 1968 the state Board of Regents presented its guidelines for the decentralization of the school system.[99] This plan emphasized the objective of quality education, observing that decentralization should

> raise and maintain the level of educational achievement for all boys and girls, with special attention to those who, for whatever reason, are failing to acquire the most fundamental tools of elementary education.[100]

Full participation of parents and the delineation of the proper role and responsibilities of professional educators were subsidiary objectives. The plan specified that the registered voters in a community school district were to elect local school board members, whose terms would be staggered to preserve continuity. The local school board was given the authority to appoint a district school superintendent and to grant tenure to new teachers; state certification of teachers was to be the minimum qualification for teacher appointment. Each local school board was also to develop local councils of parents and professionals, which in turn were to have advisory powers. The regents proposed larger districts than those advocated by the panel. They foresaw approximately fifteen local school districts because of the high administrative costs, and the problems of responding to change, of desegregating the schools and of finding suitable lay leadership in a more fragmented system. In areas of extremely low educational achievement, a central board was to have the power to establish temporary smaller school districts which had responsibility only for elementary and intermediate schools. Authority for curriculum was not discussed, and, though local school boards were to have maximum control in budgetary matters, no specific proposals were advanced. Instead the regents suggested that a central Board of Education should prepare proposals for this and other matters not covered in its plan.

The regents' plan initially appeared likely to be accepted by the legislature, but in the end the Marchi law was adopted. This law required the regents to evaluate the plan developed by the Board of Education, and therefore in February 1969 the regents issued their evaluation, noting that they had not had sufficient time to examine this plan in detail.[101] Most of the comments made by the regents were of minor significance. They felt that the board's method of electing local school board members who would in effect represent the different schools in a district would result in the election of the politically motivated and not those spurred by an interest in the schools; yet they suggested no alternatives. They noted certain inconsistencies between the board's proposals and existing state legislation and suggested in each case that the board's plan be brought into conformance. They further suggested that it was unnecessary for the central board to establish curriculum standards in addition to those imposed by the state. But in the areas of quality education and imporved community involvement they made very few recommendations, and these were the areas in which the board's plan was weakest.

The Legislature

In the spring of 1968 the legislature received plans from the mayor, the union, the demonstration school districts, the Public Education Association, the

United Parents Associations, the Council of Supervisory Associations, and the state Board of Regents. Almost uniformly these plans contained little of substance about how the objectives of quality education and community involvement would be advanced by any form of decentralization. While the majority of the plans postulated procedures for preserving the rights and welfare of teachers and administrators, few were explicit about the future of integration in a decentralized school system. With respect to the efficiency objective there was substantial difference of opinion; some participants thought it important and others did not. Given the ambiguity and disagreement about ends, the disagreement about means was to be expected. The plans which gave greatest support to the status quo were prepared by the board and the union; less conservative were the proposals of the Board of Regents, Public Education Association, and the United Parents Association. More extensive change was proposed by the mayor, and radical change was advocated by the demonstration school districts.

As a result the legislature was confused and uncertain about the best response to the problem. In hearings held by the Senate Standing Committee on the City of New York, Senator Albert Lewis (from New York City) branded the proposals for decentralization as "experimental in every conceivable fashion,"[102] and wondered what their educational impact would be. In those same hearings Senator Seymour Thaler (also of New York City) asked a proponent of decentralization whether the legislature would not be "better advised to mandate . . . a few experiments giving them full leeway and power . . . rather than risk the entire system."[103] At a different set of hearings Senator Thaler asked a different witness, "Is it your opinion that we dare tamper with the whole system on such a dramatic level" without any evidence of the consequences of decentralization?[104]

To some extent this legislative conservatism may have been prompted by the fact that many legislators would be seeking reelection that November. A decision in the spring on an issue as controversial as decentralization could complicate the efforts of incumbents in the fall. But to some extent the legislature as a body appears to have been in doubt about the best response to the problem. In a letter, Assemblywoman Cook, chairman of the Education Committee, said,

> I believe it is a fair statement to say that in early 1968 most legislators were uncertain about the correct course to take and they regarded the Marchi law as a temporary measure.[105]

The Marchi law itself reveals a certain amount of legislative uncertainty. It begins by stating that

> The need for adjusting the school structure in the city of New York to a more effective response to the present urban educational challenge requires the development of a system to insure a community oriented approach to this challenge. The state's dedication to and success with the principle of maximum local involvement in education suggests that it may be effective in a city having over one-third of the pupils in the state.[106]

However, although it believed in general that increased citizen involvement was desirable and would positively affect the educational process, the legislature was not sure which of the plans it had received was best. Dourly it observed, "Numerous plans for decentralization have been advanced" and then requested "that a detailed program for decentralization be formulated by the board of education of the city of New York against the background of urban educational problems in the city."[107]

The plan to be prepared was to "take into account the educational needs of the communities and children involved, special needs of areas of low educational achievement, [and] the ability of the community to assume the required responsibilities and initiative."[108] It was, in other words, to be concerned about both quality education and citizen involvement in educational decision making. In addition, the Marchi law specified some of the information that should be developed. Among the uncertainties the legislature wanted clarified were

1. the number of districts, restricted however to between five and thirty;
2. the size of community boards and the manner of selection and terms of members, with the requirement that a majority must be elected;
3. powers, functions, duties and staff of community boards.

Additionally, the legislature specified the procedures for selecting the city board in any decentralized system, its powers and those of its superintendent. To facilitate community involvement during the planning period, 1968–1969, the legislature allowed the existing lay board to delegate any or all of its powers to local school boards including the experimental districts. And in accordance with the mayor's wishes it enabled the expansion of the existing board from nine to thirteen members. While the procedures for protecting rights and welfare of teachers were to be investigated, integration and efficiency were not added as objectives.

After constructing several "compromise" bills, the legislature passed on April 30, 1969 a law decentralizing the New York City school system into a system of between thirty and thirty-three community school districts.[109] This law defines the powers of community boards, community superintendents, a new city board of education, and a chancellor of city schools. It specifies procedures for

1. electing community board members;
2. determining members of the new city board;
3. effectuating the transition from a centralized to a decentralized system;
4. hiring, assigning, promoting, and disciplining personnel;
5. constructing and disbursing the budget.

Approximately one-eighth of the sixty-four page bill is devoted to the specification of regulations governing teacher appointment and removal. The registered voters in a district were to elect by proportional representation the members of a community school board, and they in turn were given the authority to appoint a community superintendent, subject to state certification requirements, and, subject to city board standards, select textbooks and instructional materials, and establish curriculum. In general, community school boards would be permitted to employ only those individuals certified by the Board of Examiners to possess appropriate qualifications. An exception was made for school districts seeking personnel for schools which ranked in the fifty-fifth percentile or below on the annual citywide reading tests. For these schools community boards would be able to appoint teachers who met minimum state standards and had passed the National Teachers Examination. The disbursement of funds credited to local school boards was to be the task of the city treasury; only upon the signed order of the city director of finance could a community school district superintendent expend any funds, and the community school boards were given only advisory powers with respect to capital expenditures. To improve citizen involvement community boards were required to establish a parents' or parent-teacher association in each school under their jurisdiction. Community superintendents were required to maintain close relationships with these associations and provide them with information and advice. Lastly, for those details of a decentralized system not covered by the law, and to implement the actual process of decentralization, the legislature mandated a five-member interim Board of Education to be replaced by July 1970, at which time the process of decentralization was to have been completed, by a seven-member city board.

In sum, the legislation passed in 1969 does not constitute a substantial redistribution of authority. At most, control over curriculum, personnel, and budgetary matters was shared by local school boards with the city board or the city director of finance. But local boards were no longer restricted to an advisory capacity, and district school superintendents were responsible to them, not an administrator in the central office of the board, for their actions, decisions, and the implementation of educational programs. Initiative and innovation could surface in such a system, but the contributions that this system or any other type of decentralized system would make to the objectives of quality education or citizen involvement were unknown. The plans and proposals of participants in the school decentralization debate were not based on sufficient information to determine the consequences of legislative action with respect to these objectives.

Useful Information

It is one thing to have objectives such as the legislature did in 1967 and 1968 and quite another to understand how aspects of the material environment can be molded to obtain them. In the spring of 1967 the legislature made a value commitment to two objectives, quality education and citizen involvement; it then sought information, plans and proposals, which would direct its efforts to obtain them. In 1968 it reaffirmed its commitment to these objectives and made an even more specific request for information. But the participants in the decentralization debate appear to have ignored both requests; their plans offer little evidence that decentralization in any form would improve educational quality or increase citizen involvement. In a sense the school decentralization debate is a good example of a discussion of appropriate values which lacks facts. Though incrementalists may respond that facts and values are not ordinarily distinguished by decision makers, the fact is that participants in the debate were not decision makers; they were advocates for a cause and therefore in the position of reaffirming values. From a social perspective and for the purpose of controlling collective action through plural decision-making procedures, the issue is whether they supplemented these values with sufficient facts to direct means to ends. This is not to require, however, the complete elimination of uncertainty. In most problem situations there is probably no way to know with certainty what will happen when collective resources are directed toward the attainment of collective goals. Yet information can be developed, facts can be generated which will significantly reduce uncertainty. It is this type of information and facts in this sense which appear to be conspicuously absent in the decentralization debate.

Problem Information

Participants in the debate did discuss the general merits of several objectives at length and did thereby insure that the values they considered most important were acknowledged in the public forum. Yet their discussion may be faulted in two respects. First, the objectives suggested by participants did not from a societal perspective constitute the most thorough definition of the normative aspects of the problem. Education does more than provide a student with the ability to read and write; it contributes to the "social goals of a democracy," as Francis Keppel, former United States Commissioner of Education, observed.[110] Of these goals only integration was specified by participants. Any contributions decentralization might have made to reducing the drug addiction problem or the problem of juvenile delinquency would never have been recognized because these goals themselves were not recognized. Suppose, for example, that a decentralization proposal which called for active involvement of parents in the schools could have been structured in such a manner (e.g., through the establishment of after-school and weekend recreational opportunities) to reduce the problem of juvenile delinquency. Important contributions to this goal, which was the general concern of all but the central concern of none of the participants, could have been lost simply because it was not advocated as relevant.

Second, little progress was made in the debate beyond a general discussion of appropriate objectives. Objectives such as quality education, integration, and community involvement were never defined in operational, measurable terms. With respect to the first of these objectives this is somewhat ironic. Several quantitative indices such as reading test scores were available and were used with great effect to demonstrate the failures of the school system. Nor were the complex interactions and conflicts among the possible objectives which any decentralization plan might satisfy ever elaborated. When the union claimed,[111] for example, that decentralization would divert "hundred of millions . . . from the frontlines of the educational battles . . . to offices in the rear,"[112] it provided at most only a very limited basis for viewing the relative importance of the objectives of efficiency, quality education, and community involvement. Similarly, when the Board of Education asserted that "more community involvement must not harm the basic forces and conditions that permit integration," [113] it raised the specter of adverse consequences of some forms of decentralization for this goal without noting the positive contributions that might be made to quality education or community involvement. The question might be asked should not some contributions to these two objectives be obtained at the expense of integration? Those who would answer this question affirmatively, however, did not provide the information to determine to what extent these two objectives should be advanced at the expense of desegregation. They were as dogmatic and therefore as uninformative as the board. Although their problem information clearly reveals the incompatibility of various objectives in a decentralized system, it provides only the most limited basis for determining to what extent contributions to one objective should be sacrificed for contributions to another.

Problem Environment Information

From the outset substantial uncertainty existed about the precise effect environmental conditions had on the scholastic attainment of New York City students. Perhaps because it began by assuming "that an effective program of decentralization would help the school system,"[114] the panel concluded that the centralized, institutional form of the Board of Education, which had once been appropriate, was an important explanatory factor. In its opinion the educational bureaucracy had become rigid with age and was incapable of responding to contemporary educational problems. Several qualifications can and must be appended to this inference.

First, the system was flexible and innovative. In recognition of the more difficult educational problems they confronted, over three hundred ghetto schools had been designated special service schools, making them eligible for supplemental funds. Prior to the panel's report a number of special educational programs had been implemented: compensatory reading programs, the Higher Horizons project, [115] the More Effective Schools program,[116] after-school study centers, all day neighborhood schools, and computerized and team teaching. A centralized organizational form had not, therefore, completely incapacitated the system's response capability. Second, the panel's own analysis suggests that the system's main organizational problem was an inadequate and inefficient mechanism for control. The checks and balances instituted to preserve it from graft and political interference created a set of independent fiefdoms within the school system.[117] This analysis is amplified by Rogers, who cites the following deficiencies of system organization:

1. multi-leveled chain of command;
2. fragmentation within levels impeding communication and coordination;
3. empire building and strong informal organization within units which compelled conformity;
4. strict interpretations of powers and authority;
5. subversion at lower levels of intent of policies formulated by the board.[118]

Under these conditions the system was actually run by the administrative bureaucracy. Moreover, with little or no staff of their own board members were dependent on it for guidance and recommendations. John Lotz, a member of the board, made the following comments about his ability to control:

> I have administered $70 million as chairman of the board, $70 million worth of federal money in new projects. I have yet to see an evaluation I could hand to a layman and say that this program is good or bad. [119]

As a member of the board Lotz voted for over 7,000 promotions and 300 transfers without ever seeing a resumé or an evaluation.[120] He observed, "There are no evaluations of any consequence in our system."[121]

Thus the institutional context within which educational services were delivered in New York City was neither rigid nor in fact centralized. Substantial attempts to improve educational quality had been made; and a chaotic organizational structure had combined with the dependence of an unsalaried Board of Education on administrators to prevent centralized control. The panel recognized the impotence and inertia of the administrative bureaucracy, but its proposal for decentralization does not logically follow from this observation. *Any* reorganization which defined channels of authority and provided board members with more information and staff would have improved the board's control capabilities and thus system adaptability and flexibility. In short, a *properly* designed and functioning centralized system could have had many of the educational advantages of a decentralized community school districts plan. Such a system also could have economized on the need for scarce administrative expertise, an aspect of the problem environment which no participant investigated. While the union's assertion that the best teachers and administrators would not seek employment in the most impoverished community school districts was factually unsupported, it does raise the question of whether the number of skilled administrators needed in a decentralized system could be found and, if not, what would be the implications for the functioning of such a school system? Would not most competent, innovative administrators seek and be able to find employment in the physically safer and probably less frustrating environment of a suburban school district? How much of an improvement would decentralization make if this were the case?

Other environmental factors which might affect scholastic achievement were also left unanalyzed by many participants. With respect to some of these factors the panel simply made the following observation:

> Reorganization will not give New York the additional funds it needs to improve schools in all parts of the city. It will not wipe out the generations of deprivation with which hundreds of thousands of children enter the schools. It will not meet the great deficits in health and welfare services that beset many families. It will certainly not wipe out the poverty and physical squalor to which too many children return when they leave school every afternoon. It will not wipe out the shortage of qualified, imaginative, and sensitive teachers and supervisors. It will not automatically provide insights into the uncharted terrain of the basic mechanisms of learning and teaching.[122]

Yet a very large body of literature indicates that racism, poverty, disease, unemployment, and poorly educated parents interact to affect scholastic achievement. Havighurst, for example, has suggested that student performance is positively associated with socioeconomic class.[123] A number of other researchers have concluded in independent studies that the scholastic performance of a middle-class child is associated with the characteristics of his home life: the educational attainments of parents, their interest in and involvement with his education, and the physical educational resources found in such a home environment.[124] The Coleman Report, one of the largest social science investigations ever undertaken, also indicates that family background is positively associated with educational achievement and that disadvantaged students often begin school with less advanced verbal and nonverbal skills than other students.[125] No attempt was made to develop or discern the extent to which these findings might explain or account for the New York City school system experience. In other words, no attempt was made to estimate the extent to which scholastic failure in the public school system was associated with the socioeconomic characteristics of the student population. Perhaps even more significant, since proponents of decentralization argued that the system's size accounted for academic failure, was the fact that no attempt was made by any participant to ascertain whether these findings might hold for the private and parochial schools in New York City. Rogers states that in 1967 parochial schools enrolled approximately 450,000 students from the city's five boroughs.[126] Surely, from somewhere in this smaller school system enough data could have been collected to ascertain the extent to which socioeconomic and home environment characteristics might be associated with scholastic achievement. Comparing this information with similar information for the larger public school system might have been useful in understanding the contributions decentralization could make to quality education.

When participants did refer to research findings on the factors affecting scholastic achievement they did so selectively and uncritically. For example, to support its proposal for decentralization the panel cited the Coleman Report finding that academic achievement is associated with a student's interest in schooling, his feeling of control over his environment, and his self-concept.[127] Community involvement in educational decision making, the panel argued, could induce students to regard the schools as agencies which, being controlled by their parents, had an interest in and a clearly defined responsibility for their academic achievement and which therefore could be expected to positively influence their scholastic development. Consequently student interest in education might be strengthened through decentralization. Moreover, community involvement could induce a feeling of self-confidence and of control over a portion, at least, of the environment. However, while these attitudinal variables were important, they were not the sole determinants of scholastic achievement. Coleman concluded that

> Taken alone, the attitudinal variables account for more of the variation in achievement than any other set of variables (all family background variables together, or all school variables together). [128]

Thus Coleman isolated two other sets of variables, one reflecting a student's family background and the other reflecting characteristics of the school, including student body characteristics, that the student attended. In addition to being important determinants of scholastic achievement, these two sets of variables might also be expected to influence attitudes. A student's self-confidence, sense of control over his environment, and interest in schooling is probably affected by his classmates, their aspirations, their achievements, and his family background, the tangible successes of his parents, their interests, and their aspirations. Without knowing the extent to which the academic achievement of city students could be associated with family socioeconomic conditions and school related factors and without knowing how these variables affected attitudes, the possible contributions of decentralization to the goal of quality education could not be estimated. Moreover, the general implications of the Coleman report findings on attitudes for the New York City school system are not clear. To illustrate, in reaction to the statement "Agree or disagree: Good luck is more important than hard work for success," 70 percent of the black students and 88 percent of the white students surveyed in the metropolitan Northeast gave the response indicating a high sense of control over their environment. [129] But what does this mean in the context of New York City? Does it suggest, for example, that at the maximum the sense of control of only 30 percent of the non-white and 12 percent of the white students could be affected by community involvement? A 1 or 2 percent variation in either of these statistics in New York City would involve thousands of students and thus significantly affect the potentials of community involvement.

With respect to the environmental factors which might affect contributions to the objective of community involvement, the investigation undertaken by the mayor's panel again was the most comprehensive. The panel notes that "the few studies that have analyzed school elections indicate that participation in voting for school boards is limited, particularly for ghetto communities."[130] It also warns that socioeconomic status and the level of education influence political participation; the higher either is, the more likely a person is to become politically involved. But the panel places its hope in another finding that where communities are homogeneous and organized the level of involvement of all potential participants rises. [131] Here again the analysis does not encompass the complete range of findings and for this reason the implications of the research cited for citizen involvement in educational decision making are not necessarily apparent. Almost five years prior to the debate Martin found that the bland issues raised in school board elections may account for voter indifference.[132] Lyke has observed that school board elections are rarely fought over issues,[133] and both Martin and Carter note that in general citizen concern with educational policy is low.[134] To the extent that these last findings are based on observations of middle-class suburban communities they may suggest even lower degrees of involvement and interest on the part of ghetto residents.

Several other findings from research into the general area of political participation would also appear to have been relevant to the issue of school decentralization. First, professional persons are most likely to become politically active, while laboring persons are "disinclined, on the whole, to become involved actively in politics."[135] This raises the question of who would represent whom in a community school district. In a system of thirty community school districts the average district would be responsible for the education of more than 30,000 public school children and be the place of residence of approximately 200,000 adults. Under these circumstances, would working-class parents be any more closely involved in educational decision making in a decentralized system where local school board members were primarily middle-class professionals than they would in a centralized system? Secondly, renters are less likely to vote than are homeowners.[136] In ghetto areas where most housing is not owner occupied this does not appear to augur well for citizen involvement.

Consequently those research findings which suggest that in homogeneous, well-organized communities lower-income residents might become involved need not necessarily apply to community school districts in New York City. School districts the size of those proposed by the panel (for example, from about 15,000–30,000 students and about 100,000–200,000 adults) would only with careful planning be homogeneous. Moreover, even if such districts could be obtained, it is doubtful that effective community involvement would naturally evolve around the schools and educational decision making. Educational policy is apparently not the type of issue which is of interest to or leads to the involvement of large numbers of people. In the absence of some policy or program for bringing citizens into the schools, involvement in a decentralized school system was not likely to be as extensive as many participants hoped. The very size of the school districts proposed might also impede success. A community of 100,000 or more adults is sufficiently large to submerge educational issues behind an abundance of competitive concerns, especially when that community is but a small part of a much larger entity. Such a community is also much more likely than a smaller community to have a cadre of middle-class professionals who could be expected to become actively involved in educational decision making, perhaps to the exclusion of "average" citizens. Thus after decentralization many citizens might still find themselves having very little relation to or involvement with the schools.

Alternatives Information

The plans and proposals of most participants were input-oriented; they specified what could be or should be done to reorganize the school system but did not indicate what might result. After two years of debate, any plan for decentralization promised, at most, only to redistribute power and authority in educational decision making. Other than the obvious fact that such a redistribution would be to the advantage of some participants and occur at the expense of others, the legislature was no more certain about the consequences of action in 1969 than it was when it first requested a plan for a system of community school districts from the mayor. Given the problem and problem environment data most participants produced, this is not surprising. General definitions of objectives and vague, imprecise conceptions of environmental factors do not facilitate or for that matter indicate an interest in the assessment of alternatives. What is surprising, however, is that no participant, neither those who expected decentralization to advance the objectives of quality education and citizen involvement nor those who viewed it primarily as a means of acquiring some power, foresaw sufficient benefits to justify the development of information which would even generally indicate the consequences of decentralization.

At the minimum, data for the achievement of students in school systems in cities of approximately 150,000–250,000 might have provided some insight into what could have been expected from community school districts of that size. Even more might have been learned from a detailed study of school districts across the country. In the early stages of the debate such a study was being conducted by William S. Vincent on the fiscal aspects of suburban school systems.[137] If extended and expanded, it might have provided insight into how poverty, disease, unemployment, poorly educated parents, school system size, and the degree of community control in educational decision making interact to affect academic achievement. Such a study might also have been quite useful in determining two characteristics of a decentralized system: school district size and the minimum distribution of power needed to produce educational benefits. However the legislature never received any information about either of these matters. In 1969 the most appropriate size of a community school district was a complete unknown; there was no information which suggested that for the purpose of improving educational quality one district size was even likely to be preferable to others. Accordingly how many school districts should be mandated in a city of approximately eight million residents and over one million public school students was a matter of guesswork. Equally as uncertain were the decision-making powers and authority to be granted to community school boards. Proponents never established any relationship between quality education and the powers they sought, and thus they failed to provide the legislature with a basis for viewing as of secondary importance the union's assertion that teachers' interests would be adversely affected by community involvement. Moreover, the union's charges, particularly those predictions of teacher harrassment which were according to the union based on local school board experience throughout the country, were never challenged. Thus the proponents of decentralization never provided evidence to support their claims or to refute the claims of those opposing them.

In 1968 Dr. Kenneth B. Clark urged that the discussion of decentralization return

> to the fundamental and critical problems of improving the quality of education for all children in our public schools and [increasing] measurably the reading and arithmetic abilities of educationally deprived children. Without the attainment of these goals, any and all decentralization plans will be the perpetuation of cruel hoaxes on the presently helpless children and parents of the ghettos and all other deeply concerned citizens of our city and state.[138]

Decentralization is neither a necessary nor a sufficient condition for the evolution and implementation of imaginative educational programs. Motivating students whose daily environment was poverty, discrimination, and a broken home to excel in mathematics, history, biology, or English was a complex problem for which innovative solutions could not be expected to appear *deus ex machina* in a decentralized system. Yet this apparently is what many participants seemed to think. Their proposals contained no evidence of the innovative capability of smaller school districts or of the success of such districts in educating the environmentally disadvantaged child. Nor did their proposals detail institutional mechanisms for coordinating the research, development, and evaluation of the various educational programs implemented in a decentralized system. Thus orderly, systematic citywide progress toward the goal of quality education was not assured. Equally likely to occur was duplication, lack of comparability of results, inadequate analysis and the reoccurrence in a decentralized system of the central board's lack of success with compensatory educational programs. After two years of debate the inherent potentials of a decentralized school system to advance the goal of quality education were unknown and the institutional mechanisms which would have fostered orderly progress toward this end in such a system were unexplored. No reorganization of the existing system could be justified on the grounds that by producing innovation and flexibility it would also induce greater scholastic achievement. The evidence to support (or refute) such a claim, indeed the evidence to support (or refute) the more limited claim that the local school districts in a decentralized system would in the aggregate be more innovative and flexible than the centralized system, was not made available by participants in the debate.

Just as uncertain in 1969 was the extent to which community involvement might advance the goal of quality education by positively affecting the attitudes of students. Participants did not know whether a majority of the city's students had a high or low self-concept, a positive or negative attitude toward education, a feeling of control or no control over their environment. Thus the potential of decentralization to affect scholastic achievement by changing attitudes could not be established. Moreover, no evidence was presented to demonstrate that, given the socioeconomic characteristics and the spatial distribution of the city's students, parental involvement in any system of community school districts could have the desired effects on attitudes. Predictions of favorable educational results were thus based on hope, not fact, faith, not control.

The data developed by participants was also not sufficient to determine where public policy might intervene, and in which areas of the city an interventionist strategy was most needed, to abet whatever benign effects decentralization might have on quality education. Most participants had only a general notion of the incidence of various adverse environmental factors on the public school population in New York City. While they may have been able to designate those areas of the city in which socioeconomic family factors and community conditions were most likely to exercise an adverse effect on scholastic achievement and student attitudes, they were not capable of differentiating between those factors and conditions which could and those which could not be positively affected by public policy. Thus they were not capable of advocating with any degree of confidence programs which might be necessary if decentralization were to affect scholastic achievement directly through a more innovative, dynamic educational approach or indirectly through its effects on student attitudes. Nor were they capable of discerning in which areas of the city an interventionist strategy was likely to be most successful.

With respect to the objective of quality education several other deficiencies in the plans and proposals prepared by participants may be noted. First, and perhaps most conspicuous, is the approach to accountability or the reconnection of parents and teachers. Participants defined accountability primarily in terms of the authority to appoint, promote, or discipline. Though this is important, it does not establish what accountability does mean, particularly with respect to the objective of quality education. It does not establish performance standards by which the effectiveness of a teacher may be judged and the validity of any attempts to hold a teacher accountable may be assessed. For this reason it raises the specter of lay interference in the educational process for parochial reasons which have little to do with the scholastic achievement of students. In addition, it does not necessarily insure creativity or innovation. It provides only a stick or negative incentive to teachers and administrators in a situation where a positive incentive or carrot was probably needed. It does not encourage teachers to take the risks associated with experimentation and innovation but may induce them to take an educationally conservative approach toward teaching. Evidence which might have suggested the merits or deficiencies of this approach or which might have revealed alternative approaches to accountability was not developed by participants. For example, an investigation of small school districts throughout the northeast or in the state of New York might have provided a basis for judging the consequences of this approach to accountability and might have disclosed alternative, perhaps preferable, approaches.

Second, the plans and proposals of participants do not contain projections of future demographic conditions and make no attempt to predict future need for or availability of resources. How well would any form of decentralization function when confronted with a massive imbalance in the school-age population in one or more districts? Would local boards spend their funds to educate students from other districts? Would middle-class students leave the city school system? How would teachers react to decentralization? What mechanisms might insure that the more impoverished school districts would be able to attract experienced teachers? Where would the numbers of devoted, imaginative, inspired teachers who were expected to appear by many proponents of decentralization be found? Once they had encountered the exigencies of teaching environmentally deprived students on a continuous basis would they retain their enthusiasm? Further, since sympathy with the plight of students does not necessarily imply success as a teacher, would those seeking and finding jobs in impoverished school districts be successful? Would the physical and personnel problems of the centralized school system, to which the mayor's panel called attention, be mitigated in a decentralized system? Could, for example, the 3 percent teacher absentee rate be reduced, or did it reflect illness rather than apathy? No evidence was provided by participants to answer these questions and thus to clarify the implications of a decentralized system.

Equally as important as information about the educational impact of decentralization was information about its potential contributions to the objective of community involvement. Yet the problem of effectively integrating parents or other community school district residents into the educational decision-making process was never clearly analyzed. Not one participant undertook a survey of community school districts outside New York City to ascertain how involved residents became with educational policy. No participant sought information about citizen involvement in school districts of a size roughly comparable to those he was proposing for New York City. For example, a number of participants proposed a system of approximately thirty school districts, yet none developed information about the representativeness of local school board members in districts of similar size even elsewhere in the state. Were such school boards representative, or did they appear to be removed from their constituents? Were the school boards dominated by one single, well-organized group, and, if not, what prevented domination? How involved actually were parents in the schools; did community involvement mean only an ability to elect local school board members or could something more be achieved? Did parents contribute effectively to the formation of educational policy, or did they acquiesce to the plans of teachers and administrators? This latter question is of course critical in the context of decentralization, for it raises the issue of whether in fact community residents would be any more likely to hold teachers and administrators accountable in a decentralized than in a centralized system. While this was presumed to be the case by many participants, there is no reason to suppose that administrators and teachers could not usurp the powers of a community school board.

Still other questions might be raised about any proposal for increasing community involvement. How representative would school board members elected in accordance with the procedures advanced by any participant be? For example, the plan advanced by the Ocean Hill-Brownsville Demonstration School District required that "parents from each school [in the district] . . . nominate and elect"[139] parent representatives who would in turn select five community school board members from nominees designated by various community organizations. Whether or not this constitutes an effective response to the problems of representation and involvement is not clear. Would this procedure overcome the apathy and indifference to educational matters which was widespread prior to the decentralization debate?[140] Could it be successfully employed in a system of community school districts, each of which was likely to be four times as large as the Ocean Hill-Brownsville Demonstration District (approximately thirty schools as opposed to seven)? How would residents and parents vote on educational policy in such circumstances, particularly in view of the fact that even in direct elections the main issue is often the personal qualities of the candidates?[141]

A number of participants foresaw substantial parental involvement in the educational process and from this a form of community organization. The panel suggests, for example, that through decentralization the school would become "the center of an organizational nucleus which would encourage participation."[142]

But it presents no evidence for this, though some might have been obtained by looking at suburban school districts. Even if the constituents of a school district were homogeneous by social class, divisive disagreements over the administration of schools could arise, destroying any nascent sense of community and alienating various groups from the schools. While some participants, such as the Ocean Hill-Brownsville Demonstration School District, did develop fairly extensive procedures for bringing parents into schools, their effectiveness in a citywide school system is uncertain. Even assuming that the programs developed in Ocean Hill-Brownsville for involving residents in educational decision-making were successful there, questions arise about their consequences in a decentralized system. To what extent did the novelty of involvement and the aura of a demonstration district account for the degree of success achieved? How extensive would citizen participation be once the entire school system had been decentralized or once the Board of Education and the teachers union could no longer be depicted as the villains in the educational process? Again, how effective would the Ocean Hill-Brownsville procedures be in school districts four times its size?

Finally, few participants confronted the difficulties involved in making educational policy a concern of citizens and a school board election issue. According to Lyke, effective community involvement in decision-making requires organizations and institutional mechanisms which will crystallize educational issues, communicate grievances, and generate a variety of perspectives.[143] Parent-teacher associations and other school related organizations perform this function to some degree, but they often are not sufficiently independent of the educaional bureaucracy and thus constrain citizen participation. Yet to involve parents in the formation of educational policy most participants specified either parent-teacher associations or a series of reports from administrators to community residents on the functioning of local schools. Both of these proposals could have had unanticipated consequences—they could have kept community residents dependent, at least to some degree, upon those whom they were trying to hold accountable for school system performance. An independent staff for local school boards which offered advice on educational policy, issues, and problems might have been a more expedient mechanism for providing residents with information in the formulation of school district policy. To exercise control, community board members and residents would need the resources to develop information and make analyses of their own.

Assessment

According to some proponents school decentralization had the potential to improve the scholastic achievement of many of the city's students. In addition, substantial benefits were to be obtained from improving citizen involvement in educational decision making. From this optimistic view of decentralization the consequences of inadequate data and an inferior decision would appear to be quite great. Since more than a million students and a large portion of the city's adult population would be the beneficiaries of any decision, large contributions to the objectives of quality education and citizen involvement might have been lost by even a small error in judgment. Yet to realize the benefits decentralization promised, the legislature had to base a decision on data which were imprecise and incomplete. In general the pre-decision data participants produced was not sufficient to allow the legislature to determine even a range of possible consequences from decentralization. While the discussion of appropriate objectives is in fact fairly extensive, participants did not provide a sufficient basis for determining even a satisfactory course of action (à la Simon[144]) or for discerning what values were actually inherent in any of the policy choices that might have been made (à la Lindblom[145]).

To construct the 1969 law the legislature had to use political judgment, intuitive notions, and subjective responses; there was no other basis for a decision. If implemented any plan for decentralization would have only one obvious accomplishment, the redistribution of power from the Board of Education to local school boards and their bureaucracies. But even this consequence of decentralization was uncertain in many cases. Speaking with respect to the panel's plan, perhaps the most thoroughly analyzed of all the proposals received by the legislature, Senator Lewis in 1968 made the following comment,

> One of the things that . . . behooves me to be absolutely against [this plan] is the fact that under [it] a temporary commission on transition will be established with three members and that . . . commission . . . has almost carte blanche to set up a system of decentralization without legislative controls.[146]

Consequently after two years of discussion and debate feedback would probably have been needed if collective means were ultimately to be directed to ends. However, as Pois notes, relying on feedback in educational decision making can be very costly; "irreparable damage" can be caused by superficial pre-decision analysis and evaluation.[147] The educational process is cumulative—skills not acquired in one grade retard learning and skill acquisition in another.[148] Not only because so many students were involved but also because the effects of an inferior decision were likely to be cumulative, substantially more pre-decision information than that produced by participants in the decentralization debate would have been desirable for control purposes. Even if an imperfect legislative decision could be corrected within a year, the academic achievement of possibly thousands of students might progressively fall short of what it could have been had a better decision based on better data been made. But the success or failure of decentralization was not likely to be established quickly. Time is needed to reorganize a large school system, to establish community boards, for them to appoint personnel and implement programs, and for these programs to have an impact. If at the end of this time the action taken appeared to be ineffective or not as effective as it might have been, then even more substantial contributions to the objective of quality education would have been lost.

The question of how much information is sufficient or adequate is, of course, difficult to answer. The preceding conceptual analysis suggests that information should be acquired to the point at which the cost of an additional unit equals the benefit obtained from that unit. Only indirectly, however, is this approach meaningful in analyzing the information produced by participants. It raises the question of what quantity of resources should be committed to developing the information for a decision which would affect over one million children and residential communities throughout the city of New York. Was $500,000, or less than $.50 a child, justifiable? Apparently not to individual members of the decentralization decision system. While all participants combined may have spent more than $500,000, there is no evidence that any one participant spent this amount. The most thoroughly investigated, most detailed proposal, that developed by the panel, was generated apparently at a total cost of $100,000. The more intensive investigations of the problem environment and alternatives that even $500,000 would purchase were not available. From a broad, decision-making perspective, however, it is conceivable that even more substantial expenditures were justifiable. The extensive shortcomings of the school system, the number of students who might benefit, and the potential of strong citizen involvement might have justified much greater expenditures on information for the analysis of alternatives, the investigation of environmental parameters, and the clarification of objectives. From a societal rather than a New York City perspective, even larger expenditures for data might have been desirable. Participants in the decentralization debate were confronting a problem which, as defined by the legislature, was probably present elsewhere in the state and the nation. If they had discovered a form of decentralization which advanced the objectives of quality education and community involvement, it might have served as a model for other cities. As Harold Howe, II, U.S. Commissioner of Education, suggested, the state of New York was calling for a reform which might be an appropriate approach to increased citizen involvement and scholastic achievement in a number of cities.[149]

This is not to say that more information would have completely eliminated uncertainty about the best response to the problem or insured any set of consequences. Even for decisions which require a smaller scale of action than decentralization entailed, mechanisms for precisely predicting the consequences of change do not exist. Whenever decisions depend upon predictions into the future or data which cannot be generated under controlled experimental conditions, certainty about their consequences is not possible. Yet better data than that actually available would have been useful to the legislature. As noted earlier, given the uncertainty about the implications of any form of decentralization for quality education and community involvement, individual legislators had little substantive basis for even rebutting the arguments vociferously advanced by the union, politically perhaps the most powerful opponent of decentralization. Even if one of the proposals advanced by a proponent of decentralization had actually constituted the best response to the problem, the legislature would not have been able to recognize it as such or defend it.

The data available to the legislature in 1969 may be viewed primarily as elaborating but not reducing the preplanning uncertainties surrounding the response to the problem. In the face of these uncertainties the legislature did make a decision, authorizing a system of thirty to thirty-three community school districts with some, though not extensive, power and authority in educational decision making. Assuming that this was the best response to the problem in the face of the uncertainty surrounding a decision, what might planning have demonstrated? Two possible answers are suggested by the preceding discussion of data developed by participants. First, planning might have demonstrated that a system of smaller school districts with greater decision-making authority could be expected to advance the objectives of quality education and community involvement to a significantly greater degree. Thus planning would have shown that the scale of action should be increased and, though at the same time costs might be imposed on teachers and administrators, that these costs were either slight or justified by the contributions to the two objectives. Equally, planning might have shown that the objective of quality education was more likely to be advanced in a reorganized though still centralized system without any particular loss in contributions to the objective of community involvement or any substantial costs being imposed on teachers and administrators. By giving members of the Board of Education the resources with which to exercise control over the administrative bureaucracy and by rationalizing the organizational structure of that bureaucracy, the effectiveness of the school system might have been increased. Further, by attempting to involve parents in the educational process in the way programs such as Higher Horizons or More Effective Schools had done in the past, some community participation, perhaps more than that likely to arise as a consequence of local elections for community school board members, might have been expected. Both of these programs stressed receptivity to parental concerns by teachers, counselors, and other school personnel, and under both attempts were made to aid and advise parents in their efforts to facilitate the education of their children. Programs similar to these in a properly functioning centralized system might have been expected to contribute substantially to community involvement and educational quality objectives. In addition, such a system might have possessed a greater capability than a decentralized system to advance the end of integration and might have been able to serve the end of efficiency. Though this end was considered unimportant by many, it was not dismissed by them in light of any assessment of the future availability of resources in the school system. In both 1971 and 1972 the requested budget for the school system was not appropriated, resulting in a curtailment of programs and services,[150] and in late 1972 the children in a community school district in Harlem boycotted local schools at the instigation of parents over the issue of inadequate budgetary funds.[151]

Alternative Interpretations

Resources

Several different interpretations of the school decentralization debate may be advanced. Perhaps the most obvious is that, in contrast to the assumption made in the preceding conceptual analysis, many participants did not possess the financial resources or expertise needed to improve their analyses or the degree of detail in their plans and proposals. Time was a critical factor for the panel but equally important were the limited financial resources which it had available. With increased resources the panel would have been able to develop a more thoroughly documented proposal even though it had only six months to prepare its plan.

Lack of resources may also have been a contributing factor in the case of the Board of Education. Overburdened by ordinary system problems and employing almost no staff of their own,[152] members of the Board of Education had little ability to develop a thoughtful, comprehensive plan. With a tight budgetary constraint they could not easily hire consultants to develop such a plan, and they were unlikely to obtain one from the bureaucracy under them. At central headquarters administrative positions were more likely to be occupied by ex-teachers than by trained administrators, and the immense volume of day-to-day work combined with restrictive rules and regulations to produce an organization which was perhaps incapable of responding to such a challenge. Not only could bureaucrats there not be expected to have a positive interest in developing a plan for decentralization, but it is also questionable whether they possessed the expertise to develop such a plan. For example, the demonstration school districts, which were promoted by School Superintendent Donovan as experiments in decentralization [153] and administered by central headquarters bureaucracy, would probably not, even in the absence of the teachers strikes of 1968, have generated useful information about educational reform. Plans for experimentation and the exploration of alternative approaches to community involvement were never fully developed for the demonstration school districts. The community residents elected to local governing boards were never given specific and different programs to encourage participation or improve quality education. Instead they were allowed to develop their own designs for both. In no sense were the experiments controlled; the results from the three districts probably would not have been comparable and would not have provided a basis for judging the merits of alternative approaches to school system reform.

Other participants may also have lacked sufficient planning resources. At best all that groups such as the Teachers for Community Control could offer would be opinion, while participants such as the Public Education Association, which did maintain a professional staff for the purpose of investigating educational issues, probably did not possess sufficient resources to adequately analyze an issue as significant as decentralization.

Motivations

Inadequate resources are not the sole explanatory factor in accounting for the information participants produced. Equally as important are their motivations. For some participants, such as the demonstration school districts, the redistribution of power and authority in educational decision making was an end in itself, and for many others, for example, the African-American Teachers Association, this aspect of decentralization was as important, if not more important, than its potential for advancing the goals of quality education or community involvement. Participants such as these would have had relatively little or no interest in developing data about the problem; problem environment, or alternatives. Quite rationally they would have employed incremental planning processes which do not emphasize the analysis of objectives, environmental conditions, or alternatives. With an end such as the redistribution of power, the implications of an alternative are relatively straightforward and priorities can be established by directly choosing among alternatives. Moreover, environmental conditions such as those which would affect contributions to the objective of quality education or community involvement would be of secondary or no concern.

The tendency of many participants to view decentralization in a political dimension, that is, as involving either the preservation or alteration of a structure of power, may be attributable to the fact that in New York City power to determine public policy and allocate public resources is fragmented among a large number of individuals, groups, and organizations. In a city in which "every decision of importance is . . . the product of mutual accommodation,"[154] it is perhaps natural to emphasize the political side of a problem situation. Issues which entail alterations in the distribution of power and authority affect the way in which problems are resolved on a continuing basis in the future and thus, in a city like New York, affect the ability of a large number of different interests to satisfy their maintenance and enhancement needs in the future. However, while this line of reasoning may account for the behavior of the Board of Education, the teachers union, the experimental school districts, and groups such as the supervisory associations, it does not explain why participants such as the education associations and the mayor's panel failed to develop the educational implications of decentralization. Nor does it explain why many other groups and organizations, whose maintenance and enhancement needs also would not be significantly affected by a redistribution of power and authority in educational decision making, did not more fully analyze the problem of bringing about effective community involvement. For example, the Teachers for Community Control, formed during the debate, probably would have disbanded after it no matter what the decision of the legislature, and, while the United Bronx Parents advocated community control, their maintenance and enhancement needs were not necessarily in conflict with those of the teachers union. In advocating community control the United Bronx Parents were seeking an effective form of parental involvement in the educational process. This objective conflicted with the maintenance and enhancement needs of the union but as long as there was a public educational system, groups like the United Bronx Parents and the educational associations would have continued to exist, to attract new members, and to attempt to influence policy.

The tenor of the debate may also have been established by the legislature when it ordered the mayor to "prepare a plan for the creation and development of educational policy and administrative units."[155] Redistribution of power would be an important element in any plan, and, particularly since it threatened a large, established bureaucracy, it is perhaps understandable that this aspect of any plan and not its implications for the two objectives specified by the legislature became the focus of the debate. The conclusion reached by the mayor's panel early in the debate that a redistribution of power and authority was necessary if all participants in the educational process were to be reconnected may also have affected the way in which participants viewed the issue of decentralization. In effect, the panel's plan may have become the model proposal; it may have been used by many subsequent participants as a standard to suggest what factors should be considered in their plans and what the substantive focus of a proposal should be. The union's adverse reaction to the panel's proposals may have further helped to focus participants' attention on the redistributive aspects of decentralization to the neglect of its potential implications for quality education and community involvement. Finally, the fight for power waged by the community school districts against the Board of Education and the teachers strikes of spring and fall 1968 may have contributed to the emphasis many participants placed on the redistributive aspects of decentralization. When it created the experimental districts the Board of Education established a set of vested interests whose maintenance and enhancement needs were inconsistent with its own and those of the teachers union. The strikes reflected this; the key issue in them was the relative power and authority of community school boards, the teachers, and the Board of Education.

With the exception of the panel, there is very little evidence that any participant investigated more than one alternative. It is as though each participant surveyed the range of preplanning uncertainties and determined that course of action which might be expected, in the face of those uncertainties, to best serve his ends. This to some extent may be evidence that many participants behaved myopically. However, because of the uncertainty inherent in the decision system further inferences cannot be made about the extent to which participant motivations can be described by the three conceptual categories of participant behavior advanced above. The decentralization debate occurred in an open decision system and was concerned with an issue for which the objectives of various participants were inconsistent. Participants disagreed about the importance to be accorded the objectives of efficiency, integration, community involvement, and the rights and welfare of teachers and administrators in a decentralized system. No participant was assured that through his involvement he would obtain his ends. Some participants, therefore, could have been acting altruistically or ambivalently but because they were uncertain about their success in advancing some of their ends may have been induced to develop only limited amounts of data about the means by which others such as quality education or community involvement could best be served. Thus participants such as the Teachers for Community Control or the United Bronx Parents, both of whom accorded little weight to the rights and welfare of teachers and administrators and placed correspondingly greater emphasis on community involvement in educational decision making, may have viewed their payoff from involvement as uncertain because of the conflicts which existed between their ends and those of the teachers union. Perceiving the importance of their plans and proposals to the maintenance and enhancement needs of the union, they may have anticipated its forceful opposition and reacted by limiting their commitment of resources to the development of information. Why attempt to reduce the uncertainties surrounding the impacts of decentralization on student attitudes, or attempt to predict the impacts of various forms of decentralization on quality education, or attempt to discover how effective community involvement might be engendered in a system of community school districts when decentralization might not occur and when in the end the maintenance needs of the educational bureaucrats at the board's central offices or the enhancement needs of the union might be, because of their political power and influence, a more important determinant of the action ultimately taken? Thus the distributional issue involved in decentralization and the unequal distribution of power and influence among proponents and opponents of decentralization prior to the debate may have combined to limit the information available to the legislature about the alternative ways to advance the ends of quality education and citizen participation in educational decision making. Politically powerful participants were threatened by decentralization and expected little or no benefits from such information while the proponents of decentralization, generally weaker politically, foresaw little or no value in such information because they did not consider a favorable decision very likely.

Two participants, the mayor and the Board of Education, may simply have perceived decentralization as a means of obtaining increased state aid for city schools, a perspective which would not require detailed planning. They may thus have silently agreed with the union when it claimed that decentralization was merely an organizational change,[156] and thus for both the aspect of decentralization which may have been most significant was the political—how much decision-making authority should be given to local school boards. Yet, as the panel demonstrated, the scholastic achievement of public school students was undeniably low and the school system, despite substantial budgetary expenditures, did not seem capable of reversing this. Therefore the question of educational quality as it relates to school system form was important. Equally important was community involvement and the degree to which it might be obtained under any form of decentralization. Thus a cynical or myopic view of the potentials of decentralization by the board and the mayor would seem to have been unwarranted and not an appropriate explanation of their behavior.

The plans and proposals of many participants might also reflect their feeling that the legislature could or would not use better information. The tendency of legislative bodies to make general laws, the tendency of legislators to evaluate issues on ideological grounds, the distribution of power among participants, and a lack of time on the part of individual legislators for evaluating plans and proposals may restrict the needs of a legislative body for information and its ability to use it.[157] A legislature may view its role as that of establishing the broad parameters, or as Etzioni would say the context, [158] of the response to any problem but leaving the details to an administrative body which may or may not be representative. Consistent with this legislative philosophy may be a concern by individual legislators for the ideological implications rather than the details or item aspects of any problem situation. The distribution of power among participants may also restrict the usefulness of data to a legislature. For individual elected officials the benefits, resource costs and social costs of action may not be as important a determinant of a decision as the power and influence of various participants. In addition, the limited time a state legislature may spend in session and the vast number of decisions it may be asked to make may restrict its ability to evaluate detailed plans and proposals. If they viewed the legislature in this light participants in the decentralization debate would not have been induced to expend substantial resources on planning. Instead they would have been led to undertake lobbying and other activities which would have allowed them to explain their ideas and proposals directly to individual legislators.

This perspective of the New York state legislature might not have been correct with respect to the issue of school decentralization, however. This issue was specifically focused on New York City. Concerned about the rising cost and declining quality of education in New York City, the legislature requested not once but twice that plans be prepared, and each time it mentioned the objectives of community involvement and quality education. Decentralization was also not an issue likely to be decided on narrow political grounds. Both the conservative and liberal factions of the state legislature may have found the idea of decentralization consistent with its general value perspective so that a decision by any individual legislator would not necessarily have been made on ideological grounds. Moreover, apart from New York City legislators who might have been expected to reflect the views of a particular set of New York City participants, many legislators may have been open minded, at the outset of the debate at least, about decentralization. As long as they were not excessively costly, the educational and community involvement aspects of any plan probably would have been reviewed fairly by individual legislators. Lastly the very involvement of so many other participants suggests that the legislature was receptive to information presented to it.

The Strikes

As a consequence of the strikes of 1968 the atmosphere surrounding the debate was at times poisonous. Value differences which ordinarily make it "difficult for participants to understand each other and therefore . . . harder to trust and tolerate each other"[159] became associated with the issue of race during the strikes. Thus instead of the orderly, rational process of informed debate, the discussion of decentralization was frequently characterized by invective. The merit of the plans and proposals developed by any participant was tarnished and cast in doubt because of suspicions about the underlying purposes of those proposals. Were they best viewed primarily as an attack on the black communities if prepared by the teachers union, and, if prepared by advocates of community control, were they best interpreted as a means of reducing the dominance of Jewish professionals in teaching and supervisory positions? Under these circumstances detailed plans and proposals may have been of no greater value than unsupported opinion. Any data a participant developed might have been dismissed as biased and distorted. Moreover, given the turmoil of the strikes and the recriminations which followed in their wake, some participants no doubt found the generation of information an emotionally dissatisfying, unrewarding task. But the strikes also appear to have demonstrated to many citizens the importance of school system reorganization. The Bar Association, the Urban Coalition, the United Bronx Parents, the American Jewish Congress, the Afro-American Teachers Association, the Liberal party, the High School Principals Association, the Confederation of Local School Boards, and the City-Wide Coalition for Community Control of Public Schools either participated in the decision system for the first time in 1968 or significantly increased their involvement in it. Attendance at public hearings improved. Hearings held by the Human Rights Commission in December 1968 and by the Board of Education in early 1969 were well attended, whereas those held by the Human Rights Commission in 1967 (concerning the panel's plan) were not. To a limited degree new groups also formed to participate in the decision system. The Citizens Committee for Decentralization of Public Schools, a group of prominent citizens, and the Teachers for Community Control, who opposed union views, became actively involved in the planning field in order to promote decentralization.

Postscript

In a smaller city than New York or for a smaller urban service system more information than was voluntarily produced by participants might not have been needed. The opportunity costs (contributions to objectives foregone) from an inferior decision would have been smaller and the value of precise specifications of goals and detailed evaluations of alternatives would have been less. Three years after the legislature's decision in 1969 it is still probably too early to reach a final conclusion about the form of decentralization it enabled. Nevertheless what can be said does not augur well. In the spring of 1972 the reading ability of city students, as measured by a standardized test, was on the average lower than in 1971.[160] Moreover, the community school district with the lowest average reading score was district 23, which encompassed the former Ocean Hill-Brownsville School District. [161] In the fall of 1972, Dr. Kenneth B. Clark, a former supporter of decentralization, criticized the decentralized school system asserting that in too many community school districts politics took precedence over education.[162] Parents in community school districts in Harlem and in a predominantly white section of Brooklyn have charged that their local school boards are unrepresentative and discriminate against them and their children.[163] Furthermore, an analysis of the school board elections in 1970 suggests that the Catholic Church was able with the teachers union to exercise a disproportionate influence on the results.[164] Lastly charges of corruption, malfeasance, and misuse of funds are beginning to surface.[165] This is not a very auspicious beginning for school reform, given its original objectives.

Chapter Six
The Provision of Adequate Control
Capability

Public decision systems, like the market mechanisms of economic theory, allocate resources to the production of goods and services; but while the self-interest of the buyers and sellers who participate in a market can be shown to lead unambiguously to an efficient allocation of resources,[1] the same conclusion does not hold in a public decision system. In general the self-interest of participants in a public decision system will not lead them to produce the information a society needs to control collective action. Whether broadly or narrowly defined, the self-interest of participants may lead them to appraise the value of information incorrectly and thus to prepare plans which are based on insufficient problem, problem environment, and alternatives information, or to propose courses of action which do not constitute the socially desirable response to a problem. In addition, uncertainties associated with the act of involvement, which arise in open decision systems because of an uneven distribution of power and influence and which arise in an advisory system because no planning field member possesses any power or influence, will adversely affect a participant's expectations about the value of information and thus the quality and quantity of data he develops. Participants may also not perceive, when objectives are either consistent or inconsistent, the uncertainties which from a societal perspective are important in any problem situation. Because of their narrower perspective they may investigate alternatives which do not constitute appropriate responses to problems confronting a collectivity. Finally, as the case study suggested, several other factors may have an adverse effect on the information generated by participants. The limited financial resources and technical skills participants possess will restrict the potentials of plural decision-making. The dynamics of debate and involvement and participant concern with political ends can destroy whatever information-producing capability might have otherwise existed. For all of these reasons participatory decision-making procedures may result in the implementation of public programs and policies which provide too few benefits, require too extensive resource expenditures, or impose excessive social costs.

Two Possible Approaches

Reliance on a Professional Planning Agency

If the participants in plural decision-making processes will not in general provide an adequate basis for controlling collective action, where will a society obtain the data it needs? It is tempting to suggest that every public decision system needs a professional planning agency which would be responsible for insuring that the decision center obtained the information a problem situation justified. In some decision systems this planning agency might do very little. The preceding analyses challenge but do not refute the frequently advanced hypothesis that participatory decision-making processes do generate adequate information. When objectives are in conflict in a closed decision system, altruists who would be the beneficiaries of collective action will provide adequate data for directing collective means to ends. Both ambivalent and myopic participants may, under restrictive behavioral assumptions, base their plans and proposals on sufficient information in open and advisory decision systems when objectives are consistent or inconsistent. In some problem situations participants may also generate adequate data because very little is needed or very little can be produced. In the former situation the decision to be made may be primarily of the "go–no go" variety and the concern of different participants may be primarily to prevent or to promote a single course of action. Here there are only two alternatives and the decision to be made may be more strongly influenced by distributional factors—who benefits, who gains—than by the question of relative effectiveness—who gains how much. Uncertainties about environmental conditions, the factual and normative aspects of the problem, and the consequences of implementing the single alternative may be unimportant. On the other hand, participants might produce adequate data in problem situations where it is very costly or difficult to develop or where time is an important factor limiting planning activity. If the first few units of information are relatively inexpensive or are quickly developed but thereafter successive units are prohibitively expensive or require time consuming analyses and investigations, participatory processes might be as effective as claimed.

In all other problem situations, however, a professional planning agency could be conceived as having a substantial role. It would have the function of protecting and/or advocating the interests of those segments of society who were unrepresented in the planning field. It would be responsible for suggesting objectives and ends which were overlooked by all participants though they might be the common concern of several. Using the plans and proposals prepared by other participants as a preplanning base, it might also be responsible for developing precise definitions of objectives and for providing the relevant facts about the problem environment and alternatives. The case study suggests that even if plural processes do not generate adequate data they are likely to raise some of the issues and make apparent some of the uncertainties surrounding the normative aspects of a problem. The primary failing of these processes is that they generate information of low quality and quantity about the problem environment and alternatives—imprecise and incomplete estimates of environmental factors and ambiguous, insufficient assessments of the consequences of action. They are less likely to fail to suggest the quantity of data or the types of information that should be collected to determine the normative aspects of a problem. Accordingly the primary functions of a professional planning agency would be to clarify the values advanced by different participants as being appropriate ends of collective action and to provide the facts which would be useful in directing means to these ends. While the planning agency would use the plans of participants as the basis for its activities, it would be responsible to the decision center for integrating and improving the normative problem data upon which these plans were based and for providing the relevant joint and separable problem environment and alternatives data needed to evaluate the courses of action they advanced.

Superficially such a proposal appears to possess several advantages. First, it establishes the role and function of professional planning as a publicly supported activity in a plural society. In particular it does not require that priority be given to the solutions to a problem evolved in isolation by a professional planning agency on the grounds that they are comprehensive or long range, for such an agency would in general present no proposals which were uniquely its own. It suggests that an open society needs a public agency which will facilitate the participatory procedures the society employs, not attempt to determine the outcome of these procedures by being involved in them primarily as another participant, albeit one advocating comprehensive solutions. Second, this proposal re-emphasizes an often ignored aspect of the ideal planning model, that the ends of collective action should be determined by elected officials, not civil servants. Thus in concept it does not put the planning agency at odds with the decision center or the power structure that may attempt to influence the decision center in any problem situation. Third, this proposal capitalizes upon the motivation of participants to produce data and thus their initiative and creativity. Participants provide the broad general preplanning basis from which professional planners begin the tasks of operationally defining objectives, analyzing alternatives, and exploring environmental conditions. Lastly it recognizes the potentially greater efficiency and effectiveness of a professional planning agency in developing information. Participation results in numerous small expenditures for information by many participants. In concept a public planning agency with both the resources and the responsibility for producing information could always undertake more extensive resource expenditures for the development of information than any participant and would as a consequence improve the control capability available to a decision center. Such an agency would correctly appraise the value of information and, since it would be preparing plans at the direction of the decision center, would be less affected by the uncertainties inherent in a decision system. In the decentralization debate, for example, a professional planning agency with adequate staff and other resources might after reviewing the plans and proposals of various participants have noted their shortcomings and in consultation with members of the legislature have attempted to remedy them. By supplementing the data produced by participants with that generated by professionals, the legislature would have had a better capability to deal with the realities of school system failure in New York City. Although professional planners would not have completely eliminated uncertainty about the best response to the problem, their information would have increased the likelihood of a successful response.

The preceding proposal commits a logical error which might be called the fallacy of the ill-defined alternative. Just as the failure of a centralized educational system does not imply a decentralized system, so the potential shortcomings of the plans prepared by participants do not imply that a public planning agency should belong to the planning field of every decision system. Establishing the nature of a problem does not simultaneously establish its apparent obverse as a solution. The members of the planning profession who staff city, regional, metropolitan, and other public planning agencies may not provide data which is superior to that produced by participants for two reasons. First, in order to improve the functioning of a public decision system a public planning agency would have to possess a reputation for impartiality and would need the cooperation of decision center members in determining the types and amounts of information to be produced. For example, although the issue of school system decentralization was not one likely to divide the New York state legislature on ideological grounds—it appealed to both liberals and conservatives alike—it is doubtful whether after the strikes both proponents and opponents in the legislature would have accepted the findings from any planning agency which was not widely regarded as impartial. Moreover, to develop specifications of objectives and determine the relative importance of various uncertainties, a planning agency would need to interact with members of the decision center. Otherwise it might find itself in the position of not perceiving the uncertainties surrounding the societal response to a problem.

In many problem situations and in many decision systems the planning agency might not be able to obtain the requisite cooperation of elected officials. Decision center members may not possess the time or be inclined to become involved with planning professionals to the extent required to aid them in the determination of relevant objectives, the appraisal of the various issues raised by participants, and the assessment of the various uncertainties surrounding the societal response to a problem. Whether a public planning agency could impartially provide information to a decision center is also open to question. Professional planners employed by public agencies have in a sense always been partisans; they have always been in the position of advocating a particular response to a problem. As Brooks and Stegman note, "it is clear that the benefits of the planner's activities have not been distributed equally . . . and that the black community has generally benefited least of all."[2] It is perhaps unreasonable to assume that a professional agency could be capable of completely impartial analysis and evaluation. Its members would be rare indeed if their interests were not aligned in some manner with those of some participants in a decision system.

Second, whether public planning agencies and professionals can actually respond to the informational deficiencies of plural decision-making procedures is doubtful. In the decentralization debate the public planning agencies of New York City were conspicuously absent; despite the need for better information they did not become involved. While political considerations (for example, a desire not to offend any potential source of future support) might account for their noninvolvement, even if these political factors were not present the public planning agencies of New York City might not have participated or made effective contributions to the debate. The planning profession lacks, as Altshuler has observed, a normative theory or code of conduct which would "define its purposes and explain why society should deem them valuable enough to occupy some of its most serious men."[3] Such a normative theory necessarily establishes the utility of the skills, knowledge, and procedures which the profession considers characteristic. To contribute effectively to the functioning of plural decision-making processes professional planners would need a normative theory which established their role as that of developing information to improve or supplement the data base for decisions which participants voluntarily provide. In addition, professionals would have to perceive the choice of a planning process not as an either/or decision between the polar extremes of incremental and rational planning but as a choice to be made from among a large set of alternatives, each yielding different qualities and quantities of data. The profession does not now have such a normative theory nor would its members appear to be generally concerned about the methodological issues surrounding their choice of planning process and the application in a given problem situation of the tools and techniques of analysis which comprise any process.

A review of the planning profession's theoretical literature for the period 1950–1970 suggests that the substantive focus of planning, not its tools, techniques, or process, has been the major concern to the profession. In the early 1950s the physical environment was viewed as the primary focus of professional activity and the physical urban environment in particular was viewed as the patient to which the profession ministered. As part of this conception the professional planning agency was to prepare a master plan for orderly growth, development, and change in the physical environment of man.[4] In the late 1950s and early 1960s traditional physical planning was replaced by comprehensive planning,[5] a conception of the plan as a flexible document in need of periodic revision, and a claim that the planning agency was the only branch of local government with a holistic or systemwide perspective. The comprehensive plan was an integrative device, coordinating the activities and plans of all branches of government. Its main orientation was physical and its main concern was the spatial allocation of private and public services and facilities. Aside from a growing commentary on the nature and potential function of planning agencies whose domain was the region [6] or metropolitan area,[7] the issues in the professional literature in the mid 1960s were advocacy and social planning. Advocacy planning [8] was an attack on the idea that in a plural society a unitary concept of the public interest could be developed to guide public policy. Social planning [9] required the professional to devise and evaluate public programs and policy for the direct amelioration of social ills. This was a different approach from that embodied in the concept of comprehensive planning, which viewed only those social and economic factors related to the physical aspects of the urban environment as being within the domain of the planner. Thus for the last two decades the planning profession has been more concerned with what it does, what issues it attacks, what interests it defends, than with how it does these things. While the question of process has received some general commentary, it has not apparently been as important a concern as the substantive focus of the profession. The question of the discriminating use of tools and techniques to accommodate the distinct informational needs of a given problem situation has not apparently been an issue.

In sum, integrating public planning agencies into plural decision-making processes would not appear to be an effective way of overcoming their informational shortcomings. Philosophically and methodologically the professionals who staff these agencies would not seem to be prepared at the present time for the task of improving the informational bases of collective action. And, even if they were prepared, the problems of assuring their impartiality and securing the cooperation and respect of decision center members remain to be solved.

Subsidized Information Development

An alternative means of improving the informational bases of collective action might be subsidization of the planning activities undertaken by participants. Trained personnel proficient in the production of information might be used to guide inexpert participants in the allocation of resources to information generation and to increase the planning resources of those who would otherwise be unable to produce information in the amounts needed for control purposes. Subsidized with publicly supported professionals and/or lump sum grants for planning, participants who would otherwise have based their plans and proposals on insufficient information would produce better data. A number of participants in the decentralization debate might have developed more precise specifications of objectives and more penetrating analyses of alternatives and environmental conditions if they had had available a few trained experts. Such a subsidy scheme has, however, several deficiencies. First, although subsidization would give all participants more or less equivalent capability to produce information, it would not necessarily induce participants to foresee the same benefits from a unit of information that society would anticipate. Subsidization reduces the costs of developing information but does not change a participant's appraisal of the marginal benefits of information. It does not correct, for example, the tendency of cost conscious participants to take into account only a fraction of the benefit changes indicated by a unit of information and, for this reason, does not correct their tendency to base plans and proposals on insufficient or inadequate data. Second, it does not reduce the uncertainties inherent in open and advisory decision systems, and these might affect the informational bases of participants' plans even though subsidies were granted. If a participant does not consider a favorable decision very likely he may not completely use his subsidy or may reduce personal expenditures he would have made for information even with the subsidy. In either case his plans and proposals will still be developed with information which from a societal perspective is insufficient. Third, it does not induce a participant to perceive the uncertainties surrounding the societal response to a problem. Lastly, if extended equally to all participants subsidies would be expensive and likely to yield redundant data whenever different participants sought information about the same environmental conditions and alternatives. For these reasons, subsidization of the planning activities undertaken by participants would not appear to be a desirable means of improving the control capability developed in plural decision-making processes.

Assessment

Information is a necessary condition for good decisions. The availability of it is enabling; the absence of it is incapacitating. With it problems and their solutions can be more precisely defined and understood; without it resources may be wasted implementing an ill-conceived response to an ill-defined difficulty. A democratic form of government can fail the majority of its citizens no matter how noble the intentions of its officials are simply because they lack adequate information. Democracy may mean very little if it does not possess the capability to effectively obtain ends. In the absence of information a democratic society is like a rudderless ship, drifting with the current, blown by the prevailing winds but making little or no continuous progress on any course. Through chance and luck such a ship may eventually arrive at some port, but the journey would have been more felicitous for its crew with an adequate control mechanism.

What is needed is an analysis and evaluation of the alternative means for developing information within the context of plural decision-making processes. The questions of how much information and who produces it are difficult to answer. It may well be that the price of democratic involvement is some loss in control capability and in the effectiveness of collective action. On the other hand it may be that the motivations of participants can be structured, possibly by some sort of subsidy scheme, to improve the data they voluntarily provide or that institutional arrangements can be devised whereby the plans and proposals prepared by participants can be improved so that they ultimately constitute an adequate basis for public decisions. Much might be gained by a conscious effort at designing the mechanisms by which a plural society could obtain the control capability to direct means to ends effectively. This study only demonstrates that a society cannot depend on participants to voluntarily provide this capability. The discussion above of possible responses to this difficulty suggests that solutions may not be readily devised. Yet the development of solutions is of such importance, particularly in a large, technically complex society, that further effort and analysis than it has been possible to undertake here would seem warranted.

Notes

Chapter 1
Introduction

-1. Edward C. Banfield, *Political Influence* (New York: Free Press, 1962), p. 336.

2. Amitai Etzioni, *The Active Society: A Theory of Societal and Political Processes* (New York: Free Press, 1968), p. 176.

3. Paul Davidoff, "Advocacy and Pluralism in Planning," *Journal of the American Institute of Planners* 31 (November 1965): 331–38.

4. Charles E. Lindblom, *The Intelligence of Democracy* (New York: Free Press, 1965), p. 151.

5. Norbert Wiener, *The Human Use of Human Beings* (Garden City, New York: Doubleday, 1954), p. 18.

6. This study can be distinguished by its analytical orientation from the macro-scale analyses of the same phenomenon undertaken by Easton, Deutsch, and Etzioni. See David Easton, *A Systems Analysis of Political Life* (New York: John Wiley and Sons, 1967); Karl W. Deutsch, *The Nerves of Government* (New York: Free Press, 1966); and Etzioni, *op. cit.*

7. Volumes have been written in this research area. Important works include the following: Robert E. Agger, Daniel Goldrich, and Bert E. Swanson, *The Rulers and the Ruled* (New York: John Wiley and Sons, 1964); Peter Bachrach and Morton Baratz, *Power and Poverty* (New York: Oxford University Press, 1970); Terry N. Clark, ed., *Community Structure and Decision Making: Comparative Analyses* (San Francisco: Chandler Publishing Co., 1968); Robert A. Dahl, *Who Governs?* (New Haven: Yale University Press, 1961); and Nelson W. Polsby, *Community Power and Political Theory* (New Haven: Yale University Press, 1963).

8. Another, more compact discussion of the school decentralization debate in the context of advocacy planning can be found in Stephen S. Skjei, "Urban Systems Advocacy," *Journal of the American Institute of Planners* 38 (January 1972), 11–24. The editor of the Journal has kindly given the author permission to use material from that study in the present work.

9. Francois S. Cillié, *Centralization or Decentralization?*, Contributions to Education No. 789 (New York: Teachers College Press, copyright 1940 by Francois S. Cillié).

10. *Ibid.*, p. 102.

11. Cleve O. Westby, *Local Autonomy for School-Communities in Cities* (New York: Bureau of Publications, Teachers College, Columbia University, 1947).

12. Norton L. Beach, "Public Action for Powerful Schools," Ed.D. dissertation, Teachers College, Columbia University, 1948.

13. *Ibid.*, p. 74.

14. Earlier an extensive study of the New York City power structure by Sayre and Kaufman reviewed the educational system descriptively, but it did not evaluate its organizational form. See Wallace S. Sayre and Herbert Kaufman, *Governing New York City* (New York: Russell Sage Foundation, 1960).

15. New York, N.Y., Temporary Commission on City Finances, *Better Financing of New York City*, Final Report (New York: The Commission, August, 1966), p. 173.

16. *Ibid.*, p. 177.

17. *New York Times*, March 19, 1967, p. 3.

18. New York, *Laws of the State of New York* (1967), c. 484.

19. *New York Times*, March 31, 1967, p. 1; *ibid.*, April 1, 1967, p. 14; *ibid.*, April 3, 1967, p. 1.

20. New York, N.Y., Board of Education, News Release N 284–66/67, April 3, 1967, p. 5. (Mimeographed).

21. *New York Times*, July 6, 1967, p. 1.

22. New York, Bill No. S. 5690; A. 7175, April 30, 1969.

Chapter 2
Information

1. Herbert Simon was one of the first to explore this distinction. See Herbert A. Simon, *Administrative Behavior* (2nd ed. revised; New York: Macmillan, 1961). See also Charles E. Lindblom, *The Intelligence of Democracy* (New York: Free Press, 1965).

2. For an example see Edward C. Banfield, *Political Influence* (New York: Free Press, 1961), p. 23.

3. Simon, *op. cit.*, pp. 53–60; Lindblom, *op. cit.*, pp. 141–45.

4. Diesing defines political rationality in terms of the objective of preserving a decision structure. See Paul Diesing, *Reason in Society* (Urbana: University of Illinois Press, 1962), pp. 231–32.

5. Simon, *op. cit.*, pp. 75–79 distinguishes among several different types of rationality. For Simon a decision is (a) objectively rational if it in fact makes maximal contributions to objectives, (b) consciously rational if it was made by a conscious process, (c) deliberately rational if the action taken in accordance with the decision is deliberate, (d) subjectively rational if given the information available it is the decision most likely to make the greatest contributions to ends. As used here the term rational decision is consistent with his concepts of objective, conscious, and deliberate rationality. The idea of a rational decision-making process reflects the intent of his notion of subjective rationality.

6. Standardized procedures also inhibit change. They can become obsolescent. One way of interpreting reluctance to change them is in terms of the costs of doing so. That is, the decision to change an existing set of rules and procedures is fraught with uncertainty. Reluctance to do so may reflect implicit recognition that the costs associated with no change or the benefits from change are much less than the costs associated with making the decision to change.

7. Frederick Mosteller and Daniel P. Moynihan, "A Pathbreaking Report," in Frederick Mosteller and Daniel P. Moynihan, ed., *On Equality of Educational Opportunity* (New York: Random House, 1972), pp. 3–66. In some cases a

negative relationship has been found. See Martin T. Katzman, "Distribution and Production in a Big City Elementary School System," *Yale Economic Essays* 8 (Spring, 1968): 219.

8. James S. Coleman et al., *Equality of Educational Opportunity* (Washington, D.C.: U.S. Department of Health, Education and Welfare, U.S. Government Printing Office, 1966).

9. In other words, only relevant information eliminates uncertainty. The point is that not just any information is useful in decision making. In planning a journey from A to B, information about the distance to C is of little value. It eliminates no uncertainty about the logistics of the trip being planned.

10. Christopher S. Jencks, "The Coleman Report and the Conventional Wisdom," in Mosteller and Moynihan, ed., *op. cit.*, p. 105. Also see Christopher Jencks, "A Reappraisal of the Most Controversial Educational Document of Our Times," *New York Times Magazine* (August 10, 1969), 42–43ff.

11. Answers to these questions are facts, refutable through observation and meaningless unless interpreted in terms of a set of values which recognizes the importance of universal education and the needs of an industrial society.

12. The process described here is based upon Hufschmidt's discussion of the field level process used in planning water resource systems. See Maynard M. Hufschmidt, "Field Level Planning of Water Resource Systems," *Water Resources Research* 1 (Second Quarter, 1965): 147–63.

13. The ideal model is not a good description of reality. See Paul Davidoff, "Advocacy and Pluralism in Planning," *Journal of the American Institute of Planners* 31 (November 1965): 331–38. Its use at this stage in the argument is not encumbered by this deficiency, however. Plural decision making is the antithesis of the close relation that the ideal model assumes between officials and technicians. And in concept it prevents any one group from imposing its values unilaterally on the others.

14. David E. Boyce and Norman D. Day, *Metropolitan Plan Evaluation Methodology*, a Report Prepared for the Bureau of Public Roads, Federal Highway Administration, U.S. Department of Transportation (Philadelphia: Institute for Environmental Studies, University of Pennsylvania, 1969).

15. See Joseph Horowitz, *Critical Path Scheduling* (New York: Ronald Press, 1967), and L.N. Morris, *Critical Path* (Oxford: Pergamon Press, 1967).

16. See H.S. Woodgate, *Planning by Network* (London: Business Publications Limited, 1964), pp. 188–89.

17. See Harold F. Dorn, "Pitfalls in Population Forecasts and Projections," *Journal of the American Statistical Association* 45 (September 1950): 311–34.

18. Several measures of information exist. Ackoff has proposed a measure which is related to the number of choices that exist in a state. See Russell L. Ackoff, *Scientific Method* (New York: John Wiley and Sons, 1962), pp. 164–70. A more conventional and manipulatable measure is provided by information theory. This measure assumes that uncertainty (about objectives, a state of the environment, or the consequences of action, for example) can be characterized by a probability distribution over the entities which are uncertain. Thus with respect to objectives uncertainty about the appropriateness of the efficiency objective might be characterized by two probabilities whose sum is 1, i.e., the probability that the objective is and the probability that it is not appropriate. For maximal uncertainty, these

probabilities are equal and have value ½. In the absence of uncertainty, one would have a value of 0 and the other a value of 1. Information is produced by revising an initial set of probabilities p, p' to q, q', and is measured by the formula $H = q \log q/p + q' \log q'/p'$ where the logarithms are to the base 2. A more detailed discussion of the versatility and characteristics of this measure of information may be found in Henri Theil, *Economics and Information Theory* (Amsterdam: North-Holland Publishing Company, 1967), pp. 1–49.

Most but not all uncertainty can be characterized by a probability distribution. The undefined (as opposed to that defined by a probability distribution) uncertainty explored by game theory is the major exception. The undefined uncertainty of game theory differs from the defined uncertainty associated with the flip of a fair coin. No probabilities may be associated with the alternatives normally analyzed in game theory, e.g., the responses an enemy may make to various strategies. On the other hand the probability ½ clearly defines the uncertainty associated with the flip of a fair coin. Once the optimal strategies of an enemy have been clearly defined, military tacticians will not be able to diminish their undefined uncertainty by acquiring better data, just as once the probabilities of heads or tails have been established the outcome of a coin flip is uncertain. But information may be acquired about the enemy's strategies and the probabilities governing the coin flip (the coin need not be fair).

From the standpoint of developing information for decision making needs, a further distinction may be made between ignorance and true uncertainty. In concept, at least, ignorance may be eliminated by pre-decision data. It corresponds to imperfect information about the alternative forms in which nature might manifest her caprice, about the parameters of a probability distribution (e.g., the fairness of a coin), about the appropriate objectives, and about the range and consequences of alternatives. In contrast, true uncertainty, which corresponds to the caprice of nature and the outcome of a random event when the parameters of the governing probability distribution are known (e.g., the flip of a fair coin), cannot be eliminated by pre-decision information. This is most clearly the case with problem environment data. Only when an event which is truly uncertain has occurred can problem environment information be complete. As a consequence, when true uncertainty exists, pre-decision data cannot be perfect.

19. The Chesapeake Bay Bridge-Tunnel spanning the Chesapeake Bay from outside Norfolk to Virginia's Eastern Shore is an example. Optimism abounded about the link. It was seen as critical to the development of a coastal route to the south. Ignored was the development of Interstate 95 several miles inland and connecting major cities along the east coast. Also ignored was the relatively small economic base of most communities along the coastal route. Commercial trucking operations would not be attracted to these communities with any great frequency and with the development of the interstate system these communities could be served more economically from warehouses in major cities. The traffic predicted for the Bay Bridge-Tunnel failed to materialize from the start. It has rarely been used to its full potential.

20. In an expanding economy or a growing society the probability of underestimating the magnitude of a problem is likely to be greater than the probability of overestimation. The latter, when it occurs, may reflect error, misinterpretation, or difficulty in obtaining any evidence about the problem.

21. New York, N.Y., Temporary Commission on City Finances, *Better Financing of New York City,* Final Report (New York: The Commission, August, 1966), p. 175.

22. New York, *Laws of the State of New York* (1967), c. 484, sec. 1.

23. *Ibid.*

24. Formally, expected value, EV, may be defined as $EV = \Sigma P_i V_i$ where P_i is the probability of the occurrence of value V_i. If V_i is interpreted as the net benefits of a given alternative under different environmental conditions i and P_i is the probability that the ith environmental condition will occur, the formula yields the expected net benefits of action to implement this alternative. Information is created when after the application of analytical techniques it is possible to revise an initial set of probabilities about the different environmental conditions. At the maximum, analysis may suggest that all but one environmental condition will not occur; the probability of this condition will be raised to 1 and the probabilities of the others reduced to 0. Such information would lead to a new estimate of the expected value of action.

The probability P_i may also be interpreted as the likelihood of a particular consequence of any alternative and V_i as the value of that consequence. Again information is created by analyses which permit revision of an initial set of probabilities, setting at the maximum one probability at a value of 1 and the others at a value of 0. Or the P_i may represent the likelihoods that different sets of objectives are relevant and the V_i the net benefits of any course of action in terms of objective set i. Again analysis, introspection, evaluation create data by revising a set of probabilities and thus lead to changed expectations about the value of action.

Finally, the V_i may be present values of a time stream. Present value is a summary measure which reveals the present worth of a stream of benefits and costs. It is obtained by first discounting the nth element of a stream by the quantity $(1 + i)^n$ where i is the interest rate. Once discounted all elements in the stream are commensurable and may be summed to provide a single index.

The terms "benefits" and "expected benefits," "costs" and "expected costs" will be used interchangeably and as synonyms respectively for "present value of expected benefits" and "present value of expected costs."

This approach to the value of information is based on the philosophy and approach of statistical decision theory. Good introductions to this field are provided by Howard Raiffa, *Decision Analysis* (Reading, Mass,: Addison-Wesley, 1968), and Samuel A. Schmitt, *Measuring Uncertainty* (Reading, Mass,: Addison-Wesley, 1969).

25. From an information theoretic viewpoint (see Theil, *op. cit.*) the findings of planning will occur in the form of a revision of the preplanning probabilities P_i which indicate initial expectations about the relevance of any objective, the likelihood of any environmental condition, or the likelihood of any given consequence of any alternative. Prior to planning, several different revisions of these probabilities may be anticipated but that which will actually emerge is unknown. If all revisions dictate the same course of action, there is no need to plan.

26. Banfield reports that Mayor Daley of Chicago used his planning staff for this purpose. See Edward C. Banfield, *Political Influence* (New York: Free Press, 1961), p. 271.

27. Lindblom, *op. cit.*

28. Simon, *op. cit.*, and James G. March and Herbert A. Simon, *Organizations* (New York: John Wiley and Sons, 1958).

29. Melville C. Branch, Jr., "Comprehensive Planning: A New Field of Study," *Journal of the American Institute of Planners* 25 (September 1959): 115–20; Donald N. Michael, "Urban Policy in a Rationalized Socity," *Journal of the American Institute of Planners* 31 (November 1965): 283–88; and Darwin G. Stuart, "Rational Urban Planning: Problems and Prospects," *Urban Affairs Quarterly* 5 (December 1969): 151–82.

30. Amitai Etzioni, *The Active Society* (New York: Free Press, 1968), pp. 282–309; and Amitai Etzioni, "Mixed Scanning: A 'Third' Approach to Decision-Making," *Public Administration Review* 27 (December 1967): 385–92.

31. There are several others; these are the most important. See Lindblom, *op. cit.*, pp. 152-65.

32. March and Simon, *op. cit.*, p. 151.

33. *Ibid.*, p. 140.

34. *Ibid.*, p. 169.

35. *Ibid.*, p. 140.

Chapter 3
Public Decision Systems

1. Wallace S. Sayre and Herbert Kaufman, *Governing New York City* (New York: Russell Sage Foundation, 1960), p. 710. The term "decision center" was suggested from this source, although it is used there in a different manner.

2. Sayre and Kaufman find this to be the case in New York. *Ibid.*, p. 711.

3. Groups are not normally part of an organizational chart. They have been added here for expositional purposes. An individual can, for purposes of analysis, be considered a group of one.

4. Strictly speaking Sayre and Kaufman do not permit the top officials of semi-independent and operating agencies to become members of their core groups, or the decision centers of decision systems. *Op. cit.*, p. 712.

5. Sayre and Kaufman, *op. cit.*, pp. 710-12.

6. Banfield found this form of decision system to predominate in Chicago. See Edward C. Banfield, *Political Influence* (New York: Free Press, 1961). The mayor of Chicago completely controlled the city council; his opinions, plans and policies were always adopted by it.

7. The example of voters as a decision center is used by Sayre and Kaufman, *op. cit.*, p. 711.

8. *Ibid.*, pp. 258-61.

9. The courts also may become decision centers. The decisions they make are often more strongly determined by the legal aspects of an issue than by its normative and factual aspects. Thus the courts may have limited use for problem and alternatives data and may be concerned with problem environment data to the extent that it reflects on issues at law.

10. Banfield, *op. cit.*, pp. 57-90.

11. *Ibid.*, p. 81.

12. *Ibid.*, p. 84.

13. *Ibid.*, p. 251.

14. Oliver P. Williams and Charles R. Adrian, *Four Cities* (Philadelphia: University of Pennsylvania Press, 1963), pp. 251–65.

15. *Ibid.*, p. 267.

16. *Ibid.*, p. 243.

17. Banfield, *op. cit.*

18. Robert A. Dahl, *Who Governs?* (New Haven: Yale University Press, 1961).

19. Roscoe C. Martin et. al., *Decisions in Syracuse* (Bloomington: Indiana University Press, 1961).

20. The origins and success of many groups may be attributed more to their ability to provide members with a private good than to their ability to protect or foster a common interest. Individuals may seek membership in a group solely in order to consume the good that it provides its members. See Mancur Olson, Jr., *The Logic of Collective Action* (New York: Schocken Books, 1968).

21. This definition owes something to both Downs and Gross. Its shortcomings reflect on the works of neither, however. See Anthony Downs, *Inside Bureaucracy* (Boston: Little, Brown and Co., 1967) and Bertram M. Gross, *The Managing of Organizations* (2 vols.; London: Free Press of Glencoe, 1964).

22. Sayre and Kaufman, *op. cit.*, p. 258; also see Gross, *op. cit.*, I, pp. 410–32 for a broader discussion of the groups forming about an organization.

23. Downs, *op. cit.*, pp. 7 and 16; Gross, *op. cit.*, II, pp. 486–93, 657–93.

24. Banfield, *op. cit.*, p. 251.

25. *Ibid.*, pp. 275–76.

26. Organizations develop information for their own control purposes. Discussions of their need for this data and the difficulties encountered in producing it may be found in Downs, *op. cit.*, pp. 112–32 and in Harold L. Wilensky, *Organizational Intelligence* (New York: Basic Books, 1967), pp. 161–72. This problem would be of concern here only to the extent that it affected organizational participation. Since its primary impact would be to inhibit or impede the production of information by an organization, its impact on the control capability of plural decision making could not be positive. Thus it is like other factors such as distortion which have been set aside on the grounds (a) that their implications were obvious and (b) that analytical clarity might be improved by so doing.

27. These examples may also be interpreted as being illustrative of either type of ambivalent behavior. Whatever might lead a myopic participant to consider only a fraction of the expected benefits from information might also influence an ambivalent participant to do so. Equally, whatever would induce a myopic participant to consider only a fraction of the expected resource savings from information might also induce an ambivalent participant to do so.

28. The seminal discussion is Paul A. Samuelson, "The Pure Theory of Public Expenditure," *The Review of Economics and Statistics* 36 (November 1954): 387–89.

29. The terminology used here is that used by Terry N. Clark, "Social Stratification," in *Community Structure and Decision Making: Comparative Analyses*, ed. by Terry N. Clark (San Francisco: Chandler Publishing Co., 1968), pp. 37–39.

30. Wilensky, *op. cit.*, p. 163.

31. Nuttall et al. describe a decision system in which a number of participants were without any power or influence and in which the power of some participants was nullified. See Ronald L. Nuttall, Erwin K. Scheuch, and Chad Gordon,

"On the Structure of Influence," in *Community Structure and Decision Making: Comparative Analyses, loc. cit.*, pp. 367–75. Dahl describes an apparently similar situation in his example of the "metal houses," *op. cit.*, pp. 192–99.

32. Aaron Wildavsky, *Leadership in a Small Town* (Totowa, N.J.: Bedminster Press, 1964), pp. 341–44.

33. Some of Dahl's integrative mechanisms are also examples. His coalition of chieftans and to some degree his executive centered coalition and rival sovereignties constructs can imply polylithic power structures coordinated by bargaining and negotiation among leaders or leadership groups. See Dahl, *op. cit.*, pp. 184–220.

34. An extensive discussion of bargaining and negotiation can be found in Charles E. Lindblom, *The Intelligence of Democracy* (New York: Free Press, 1965), pp. 54–84.

35. Members of the Oberlin city council were frequently susceptible to persuasive reasoning. See Wildavsky, *op. cit.*, pp. 258–60.

36. Wildavsky, *op. cit.*, pp. 81–99.

37. Williams and Adrian, *op. cit.*, p. 293.

38. Banfield, *op. cit.*, pp. 270–71.

Chapter 4
The Control of Collective Action

1. A social welfare function is a theoretical concept used by welfare economists to analyze alternative social states. To assume that decision makers employ such a tool or some broad notion of the general interest in the evaluation of public programs and policy would beg the question of how the ends of collective action are set. For a discussion of the economist's social welfare function see Jerome Rothenberg, *The Measurement of Social Welfare* (Englewood Cliffs, N.J.: Prentice-Hall, Inc., 1961).

2. This number is the product 2·3·3·3, where 2 represents the number of subcomponents in the first major component and so on.

3. For each category of decision system, eighteen possible combinations of the remaining three components are possible. After eliminating two of the possible objectives configurations, only six of these combinations remain. Twelve of the eighteen can therefore be neglected.

4. The criticism may be made that individuals do not make decisions rationally. This is a thorny methodological criticism, for it amounts to condemning an analysis on the basis of its assumptions when in fact the validity of that analysis should be judged by the degree to which its predictions correspond to reality. While in practice individuals may not make decisions rationally, if they act as if they do so the conclusions may hold.

5. What society seeks is, of course, determined by a decision center. When objectives are mutual a decision center can and is assumed to advance the ends of several participants simultaneously. In a democracy decision centers have the responsibility for determining the ends of collective action and have the formal authority to do so. Thus the uncertainty confronting society in any problem situation is a function of the conclusion a decision center reaches about the ends of collective action. It is not dependent upon a mythical welfare function or some generalized notion of the public interest but upon the priorities and goals asserted as relevant by a decision center.

6. Edward C. Banfield, *Political Influence* (New York: Free Press, 1961), p. 336.

7. This assumes that the welfare of one participant is not of concern to another. When the objectives of one participant are of concern to another, he is analytically indistinguishable from this participant. The analysis assumes participants with distinct objectives.

8. The benefit changes $\bar{B}_x$ and $\bar{B}_h$ are assumed to be expressed in the same units of measurement as the benefit changes B_x and B_h.

9. Martin Meyerson and Edward C. Banfield, *Politics, Planning, and the Public Interest* (New York: Free Press, 1955).

10. *Ibid.*, pp. 189–267, esp. p. 239.

11. *Ibid.*, p. 275.

12. While $\bar{B}_x$ will be interpreted for expositional convenience as a change in social costs, the conclusions hold for those situations, such as compromise, in which it reflects the benefit losses sustained by members of $\bar{m}$ in order that increased contributions might be made to the objectives of the members of m.

13. Strictly speaking a closed decision system is not an example of plural or participatory decision making. It is included in the analysis because it is an extreme type of decision system in which those whose interests will be served by collective action are assured that their plans and proposals will be adopted. Even here the plans and proposals of participants may not provide an adequate basis for controlling collective action.

14. Banfield contends that one advantage of plural decision making is that it induces participants to examine "each other's positions with great care" (*op. cit.*, p. 334). In a large decision system this may of course be impossible; the number of planning field members may preclude any attempt at analysis or synthesis of the alternative proposals by one participant. Moreover, as the analysis here suggests, criticism of another participant's proposals may not be the most socially useful form of information. Where the objectives configuration is inconsistent, a participant may better advance control capability by producing separable data demonstrating how the social costs imposed on him may be reduced without decreasing the contributions made to the objectives of the beneficiaries of collective action.

15. Charles E. Lindblom, *The Intelligence of Democracy* (New York: Free Press, 1965), pp. 66–84.

16. This may also occur in open systems and will surely occur in systems perceived to be closed. What often is criticized as apathy may be a rational response to the uncertainties (advisory and open systems) or the certainties (closed system) of a decision system.

17. From a societal perspective the feedback produced by participants may, like pre-decision data, be inadequate or it may be developed only long after collective action has been implemented. On the other hand, feedback may be premature. The initial success of innovative educational programs is often not lasting and may depend on factors which are wholly noneducational. See Desmond L. Cook, "The Hawthorne Effect in Educational Research," *Phi Delta Kappan* 44 (December 1962): 116–22; and Miriam L. Goldberg, "Problems in the Evaluation of Compensatory Programs," in *Developing Programs for the Educationally Disadvantaged*, ed. by A. Harry Passow (New York: Teachers College Press, Columbia University, 1968), p. 50. In these cases it might be argued, however, that uncertainties surrounding the response to a problem were not correctly perceived.

18. Banfield, *op. cit.,* p. 332.

19. Lindblom, *op. cit.,* p. 151.

20. Michael Lipsky, *Protest in City Politics* (Chicago: Rand McNally & Co., 1970), p. 168.

21. Meyerson and Banfield, *op. cit.,* p. 250.

Chapter 5
An Empirical Investigation of Plural Decision Making

1. For a comprehensive discussion of these proposals see New York State Bureau of School and Cultural Research, *Historical Review of Studies and Proposals Relative to Decentralization of Administration in the New York City Public School System* (Albany: University of the State of New York, June, 1967).

2. See, for example, Preston R. Wilcox, "The Controversy over I.S. 201: One View and a Proposal," *The Urban Review* 1 (July 1966): 12–16, esp. p. 14; and Marilyn Gittell, "Problems of School Decentralization in New York City," *The Urban Review* 2 (February 1967): 4 and 27–28.

3. The assertion "*p* implies *q*" logically is equivalent to "non-*q* implies non-*p*." In the argument made by many advocates of decentralization, the initial assertion is that centralization (*p*) implies low quality education (*q*).

4. Kristol has argued that it was not even correct to say that the centralized system did not work. In his view it was only proper to assert that in the late 1960s the centralized school system worked "no less well than it ever did" (p. 21) but that the problem it faced had changed. See Irving Kristol, "Decentralization for What?" *The Public Interest* 11 (Spring 1968): 17–25.

5. Women's City Club of New York, *Performance and Promise: New York City's Local School Boards Revisited* (New York: The Club, 1966). This study also contained specific recommendations for improving the effectiveness of local school boards.

6. *New York Times,* February 22, 1967, p. 38; *ibid.,* March 23, 1967, p. 1.

7. *New York Times,* March 23, 1967, p. 1.

8. *New York Times,* March 30, 1967, p. 1.

9. New York, *Laws of the State of New York* (1967), c. 484, sec. 2.

10. *New York Times,* March 31, 1967, p. 1; *ibid.,* April 1, 1967, p. 14; *ibid.,* April 3, 1967, p. 1.

11. New York, N.Y., Board of Education, News Release N 284-66/67, April 3, 1967, p. 5. (Mimeographed).

12. *New York Times,* July 6, 1967, p. 1.

13. Mayor's Advisory Panel on Decentralization of the New York City Schools, *Reconnection for Learning* (New York: The Panel, 1967).

14. *Ibid.,* p. 14.

15. *Ibid.*

16. *Ibid.,* p. 6.

17. *Ibid.,* p. 15.

18. *Ibid.,* p. 43.

19. *Ibid.,* cover letter.

20. *Ibid.,* p. 11.

21. *Ibid.,* p. 15.

22. *Ibid.,* pp. 72–76.

23. *Ibid.,* p. 43.

24. *Ibid.,* cover letter.

25. In an interview on December 3, 1969, Mario D. Fantini, the panel's executive secretary, affirmed that quality education and community involvement were equally important and that efficiency was not a panel concern.

26. Mayor's Advisory Panel, *op. cit.,* pp. 4–5.

27. *Ibid.,* p. 5.

28. *Ibid.,* p. 74.

29. *Ibid.,* pp. 27, 45–48.

30. *Ibid.,* cover letter.

31. *Ibid.,* p. 3.

32. *Ibid.,* p. 8.

33. New York, N.Y., Temporary Commission on City Finances, *Better Financing of New York City,* Final Report (The Commission, August, 1966), p. 175.

34. Public Education Association, "Decentralization of Authority to Select and Assign Local School District Personnel" (New York: The Association, Feburary 1, 1967). (Mimeographed.)

35. New York, N.Y., Board of Education, *Decentralization: Statement of Policy* (The Board, April 19, 1967).

36. Luvern L. Cunningham et al., *Report on the Merger Issue* (Louisville, Ky.: Louisville Board of Education and Jefferson County Board of Education, 1966).

37. Mayor's Advisory Panel, *op. cit.,* pp. 17 and 78–88.

38. *Ibid.,* p. 23.

39. *Ibid.,* p. 20.

40. *Ibid.,* pp. 41–42, 77–78 and 87.

41. *New York Times,* November 29, 1967, p. 41; and Marcia Marker Feld, "Planning for the School System," *Journal of the American Institute of Planners* 35 (July 1969): 281–83.

42. Letter from Mayor John V. Lindsay to Hon. Nelson A. Rockefeller, Governor, Members of the State Legislature and Members of the Board of Regents, January 2, 1968. (In the files of the Mayor's office, New York, N.Y.); "Memorandum: Background and Summary of New York City School Decentralization Plan" (Mayor's Office, New York, N.Y., February 26, 1968). (Mimeographed.); and "Analysis of Proposed Legislation for the Decentralization of the New York City School System" (Mayor's Office, New York, N.Y., n.d.). (Mimeographed.)

43. Letter from Mayor John V. Lindsay, *op. cit.,* p. 6.

44. *Ibid.,* p. 12.

45. The panel sought to involve all groups with an interest in the school system, drawing on their views to guide its own efforts. Advice and opinions were sought from teachers, parents, educators, the union, administrators, supervisors, and various city interest groups. In general their advice was found to be more valuable and pertinent when in the form of a reaction to a panel proposal than as an unstructured comment or observation. Consequently the panel employed a sequential

planning process; plans were prepared and presented, reactions were obtained and modifications were made, and then the plans were presented again.

46. Interview with Mario D. Fantini, executive secretary to the panel, December 3, 1969; and interview with David S. Seeley, Mayor's Education Liaison Officer 1967–69, January 30, 1970.

47. *New York Times*, Feburary 15, 1970, p. 37; *ibid.*, April 23, 1970, p. 41.

48. See *New York Times*, July 3, 1970, p. 31 for "Text of Hayes Memorandum on Consultant Contracts."

49. United Federation of Teachers, *The United Federation of Teachers Looks at School Decentralization* (New York: United Federation of Teachers, 1967), p. 2.

50. *Ibid.*, pp. 8–10.

51. *New York Times*, December 4, 1967, p. 32; *ibid.*, September 20, 1968, p. 36.

52. For example, Albert Shanker, *Some Comments on 'Community Control'* (New York: United Federation of Teachers, n.d.) and United Federation of Teachers, *The United Federation of Teachers Supports the Decentralization of the New York City School System* (New York: United Federation of Teachers, March, 1969) contain ideas presented in the 1967 and 1969 plans.

53. New York, Bill No. S. 4893, February 25, 1969 and New York, Bill No. A. 4892-A, February 25, 1969.

54. United Federation of Teachers, *The Federation Supports,* p. 1.

55. *Ibid.* In a separate statement union president Shanker said that decentralization would foster the "militant parent-teacher alliance that the UFT has always advocated as a means to improve the schools." The union viewed increased community involvement as a means of supplementing its power in the pursuit of educational reform. See Albert Shanker, "Quality and Equality in Education," *The American Federationist* 76 (March 1969): 3.

56. Interview with Mrs. Sandra Feldman, United Federation of Teachers Special Assistant, April 21, 1970.

57. Three of the more accessible studies are Maurice R. Berube and Marilyn Gittell, eds., *Confrontation at Ocean Hill-Brownsville* (New York: Frederick A. Praeger, 1969); Martin Mayer, *The Teachers Strike: New York, 1968* (New York: Harper and Row, Publishers, 1968); and Naomi Levine, *Ocean Hill-Brownsville: Schools in Crisis* (New York: Popular Library, 1969).

58. Harlem Parents Committee, "Operation Excellence" (New York: The Committee, March, 1967), p. 2. (Mimeographed.)

59. Ocean Hill-Brownsville Demonstration School District, "A Plan for an Experimental School District: Ocean Hill-Brownsville" (New York: The District, [1967]), p. 1. (Mimeographed.)

60. Ocean Hill-Brownsville Demonstration Project Governing Board, Statement of Objectives, October, 1967. (In the files of the Ocean Hill-Brownsville Demonstration School District, New York, N.Y.). p. 2. (Mimeographed.)

61. Ocean Hill-Brownsville Demonstration School District, "News Release" (New York: The District, March 5, 1968). (Mimeographed.)

62. Interview with Rhody McCoy, Unit Administrator, Ocean Hill-Brownsville Demonstration School District, April 29, 1970.

63. The success of any of these efforts is difficult to assess, however. No explicit criteria for judging them have been promulgated. In an interview on March 4, 1970, Walter G. Lynch, Community Liaison Officer, indicated that involvement in the educational process had improved but was not what it should be. The Unit Administrator, Rhody McCoy, on the other hand, in an interview on April 29, 1970, expressed satisfaction with community interest in schools. Moreover, the miscellaneous raw data which might reflect the extent of participation is ambiguous. According to the governing board, about 25 percent of the community voted in board sponsored elections. But this is neither particularly impressive nor particularly reflective of involvement in educational policy making. From time to time some community members have vociferously objected to board actions. This again is not significant. Opposition to local board policies implies nonparticipation no more than opposition to Board of Education policies indicated nonparticipation. Participation does not imply consensus.

64. Board of Education, *Decentralization: Statement.*

65. Tape recording of the April 19, 1967 meeting of the Board of Education of the City of New York. (In the files of the board).

66. Board of Education, *Decentralization: Statement,* p. 5.

67. New York, N.Y., Board of Education, *A Plan for Educational Policy and Administrative Units* (The Board, March 7, 1968).

68. *Ibid.,* p. 2.

69. Mayor's Advisory Panel, *op. cit.,* pp. 7–8.

70. David Rogers, *110 Livingston Street* (New York: Vintage Books, 1969), p. 326.

71. See Memorandum to The Members of the Board of Education from the Superintendent of Schools, July 24, 1968. (In the files of the New York City Board of Education.) An account of the public hearings is described in *New York Times,* August 29, 1968, p. 41. The board's proposal for school decentralization is found in The Public Schools of New York City, "Decentralization for the School Year 1968–69," *Staff Bulletin,* a supplement to the October 28, 1968 issue.

72. New York, N.Y., Board of Education, *Guidelines to Decentralization: For the Period Ending June 30, 1969* (The Board, December 1968).

73. New York, N.Y., Board of Education, *Plan for Development of a Community School District System for the City of New York* (The Board, January 29, 1969).

74. *Ibid.,* Minority Report by Mrs. Shapiro, Mr. Barkan, and Mr. Iushewitz, pp. 37–41.

75. *Ibid.,* pp. 12–13.

76. *Ibid.,* p. 2.

77. Public Education Association, "Decentralization of Authority to Select and Assign Local School District Personnel" (New York: The Association, February 1, 1967), p. 2. (Mimeographed.)

78. Public Education Association, "Statement of the Public Education Association on Fiscal Aspects of School Decentralization," in Transcript of Minutes of a Public Hearing of the Senate Standing Committee on the City of New York, February 7, 1968, p. 177.

79. United Parents Associations, "UPA Policy and Proposals for Decentralization as Approved by the Delegate Assembly" (New York: The Associations, January 8, 1968), p. 2. (Mimeographed.)

80. *Ibid.,* p. 5.

81. United Parents Associations, "Memo to Board of Education Re: Proposed Decentralization Plan" (New York: The Associations, January 16, 1969), pp. 3–4.

82. Liberal Party, "Statement of the Liberal Party on Education and School Decentralization" (New York: Liberal Party, n.d.), p. 1. (Mimeographed.)

83. African-American Teachers Association, "Mandate for Community Action in School Crisis" (New York: The Association, November 19, 1968), p. 1. (Mimeographed.)

84. *Ibid.*

85. Teachers for Community Control, "Primer on Community Control" (New York: The Teachers, n.d.); and City-Wide Coalition for Community Control of Public Schools, Proposals for Decentralization Legislation (New York: The Coalition, n.d.). (Mimeographed.)

86. These were The New York City People's Board of Education, the United Bronx Parents, the governing boards of the I.S. 201 and the Ocean Hill-Brownsville Demonstration School Districts, the members of EQUAL (a militant white middle-class parents organization) and the Grand Parent Community Association.

87. Teachers for Community Control, *op. cit.,* p. 3.

88. New York Board of the Anti-Defamation League of B'nai B'rith, Statement Presented at a Public Hearing of the City Commission on Human Rights on Proposals for School Decentralization, Teacher Training and Curriculum (New York: The League, December 24, 1968), p. 2. (Mimeographed.)

89. New York Board of the Anti-Defamation League of B'nai B'rith, "Position Paper on Decentralization of the New York City Public School System" (New York: The League, March 27, 1968), (Mimeographed.)

90. Mayor's Advisory Panel, *op. cit.,* p. 8.

91. Council of Supervisory Associations, "The Program of the Council of Supervisory Associations" (New York: The Council, January 5, 1968), p. 2. (Mimeographed.)

92. *Ibid.,* p. 4.

93. *Ibid.,* p. 5.

94. High School Principals Association, "Plan for the Decentralization of New York City Schools" (New York: The Association, November, 1968), p. 1. (Mimeographed.)

95. *Ibid.,* p. 2.

96. Arnold W. Webb, Position Paper for the New York Association of Black School Supervisors and Administrators (New York: The Association, December 12, 1968). (Mimeographed.)

97. *Ibid.,* p. 6.

98. Statement of Testimony of Murray Rockowitz, Examiner in Charge of Research and Development, to the New York City Commission on Human Rights, December 4, 1968.

99. New York State Education Department, *Recommendations of the Commissioner of Education to the Board of Regents Concerning Decentralization of the City School District of the City of New York* (Albany, March 27, 1968).

100. *Ibid.,* p. 2.

101. New York State Education Department, *Recommendations of the Board of Regents Concerning A Plan for the Development of a Community School District System for the City of New York* (Albany, February 1969).

102. Transcript of Minutes of a Public Hearing of the Senate Standing Committee on the City of New York (Albany, February 28, 1968), p. 215.

103. *Ibid.,* p. 213.

104. Transcript of Minutes of a Public Hearing of the Senate Standing Committee on the City of New York (Albany, February 21, 1968), p. 85.

105. Letter from New York Assemblywoman Constance E. Cook, December 8, 1969.

106. New York, *Laws of the State of New York* (1968), c. 568, sec. 1. The bill adopted by the legislature is actually a revised version of two similar bills Senator Marchi introduced. See *New York Times,* May 23, 1968, p. 1; *ibid.,* May 26, 1968, p. 1.

107. New York, *Laws of the State of New York* (1968), c. 568, sec. 1.

108. *Ibid.*

109. New York, Bill No. S. 5690; A. 7175, April 30, 1969.

110. Francis Keppel, *The Necessary Revolution in American Education* (New York: Harper and Row, 1966), p. 118.

111. This claim was challenged by the mayor's office in 1968. See Transcript of Minutes of a Public Hearing of the Senate Standing Committee on the City of New York (Albany, February 7, 1968), p. 76.

112. United Federation of Teachers, "UFT Statement on Decentralization" (New York: The Union, November 28, 1967), p. 4. (Mimeographed.)

113. Board of Education, *A Plan for Educational Policy,* p. 2.

114. Mayor's Advisory Panel, *op. cit.,* p. 2.

115. Higher Horizons was a program which was developed by the board to direct intensive compensatory education at ghetto schools. The initial successes with it in a single school were not duplicated when the program was expanded.

116. This program was developed by the teachers' union.

117. Mayor's Advisory Panel, *op. cit.,* pp. 3 and 7–8.

118. Rogers, *op. cit.,* p. 267.

119. Princeton University Conference, April 10 and April 11, 1969, *Urban Schools and Urban Form* (Princeton, N.J.: Princeton University School of Architecture and Urban Planning, 1969), p. 40.

120. *Ibid.,* pp. 88–89.

121. *Ibid.,* p. 88.

122. Mayor's Advisory Panel, *op. cit.,* p. 3.

123. Robert J. Havighurst, *Education in Metropolitan Areas* (Boston: Allyn and Bacon, Inc., 1966), pp. 74–78, 85–124, 187–88.

124. Fred L. Strodtbeck, "The Hidden Curriculum of the Middle Class Home," in *Urban Education and Cultural Deprivation,* ed. by C.W. Hunnicutt (Syracuse, N.Y.: University Division of Summer Sessions, Syracuse University, 1964), pp. 15–33. See also Edith H. Grotberg, "Role of the Parent in Fostering Early Learning," *Education* 89 (September 1968): 35–39, and Maya Pines, "Why Some 3-Year-Olds Get A's—and Some Get C's," *New York Times Magazine,* July 6, 1969, pp. 4–5, 10, 12–17.

125. James S. Coleman et al., *Equality of Educational Opportunity* (Washington, D.C.: U.S. Department of Health, Education and Welfare, U.S. Government Printing Office, 1966), pp. 325 and 21.

126. Rogers, *op. cit.,* p. 59.

127. Coleman et al., *op. cit.,* p. 319; and Mayor's Advisory Panel, *op. cit.,* p. 12.

128. Coleman et al., *op. cit.,* p. 319.

129. *Ibid.,* pp. 288–89.

130. Mayor's Advisory Panel, *op. cit.,* p. 18.

131. *Ibid.,* p. 67.

132. Roscoe C. Martin, *Government and the Suburban School* (Syracuse, N.Y.: Syracuse University Press, 1962), pp. 46–47.

133. Robert F. Lyke, "Representation and Urban School Boards," in *Community Control of Schools,* ed. by Henry M. Levin (Washington, D.C.: The Brookings Institution, 1970), p. 156.

134. Martin, *op. cit.,* pp. 51–58; and Richard F. Carter, *Voters and Their Schools* (Stanford, Calif.: Institute for Communication Research, Stanford University, Cooperative Research Project no. 308, 1960), pp. 7–25.

135. Lester W. Milbrath, *Political Participation* (Chicago: Rand McNally, 1965), p. 127.

136. *Ibid.,* p. 133.

137. William S. Vincent, *The Influence of Statutory Controls on the Fiscal Capability of School Boards* (New York: Institute of Administrative Research, Teachers College, Columbia University, 1967).

138. Kenneth B. Clark, "Background Statement," in Metropolitan Applied Research Center, Inc., *An Intensive Program for the Attainment of Educational Achievement* (New York: Metropolitan Applied Research Center, Inc., 1968), p. 3.

139. Ocean Hill-Brownsville Demonstration School District, "A Plan," p. 2.

140. Interviews with Mrs. Beatrice Steinberg, Special Assistant to the Secretary of the Board of Education, November 1969 and April 1970; and Walter G. Lynch, Community Liaison Officer, Ocean Hill-Brownsville Demonstration School District, April 29, 1970.

141. Martin, *op. cit.,* pp. 46–57; Carter, *op. cit.,* pp. 7–16.

142. Mayor's Advisory Panel, *op. cit.,* p. 67.

143. Lyke, *op. cit.,* pp. 154–58 and 166–68.

144. Herbert A. Simon, *Administrative Behavior* (2nd ed. revised; New York: Macmillan, 1961), p. xxiv.

145. Charles E. Lindblom, *The Intelligence of Democracy* (New York: Free Press, 1965), p. 145. One of the tenets of incrementalism is that decision makers do not decide about values separately from their decision about an appropriate course of action. Instead, when after viewing several alternative responses to a problem they select a preferred response, they establish the objectives and priorities of action. This, however, assumes that a decision maker can perceive the values actually imbedded in alternative choices. With the exception of the redistribution of authority and power in educational decision making, neither the legislature nor any participant was able to identify the values inherent in any course of action.

146. Transcript of Minutes of Senate Standing Committee, February 28, 1968, p. 268.

147. Joseph Pois, *The School Board Crisis* (Chicago: Educational Methods, Inc., 1964), p. 198.

148. Martin Deutsch, "The Role of Social Class in Language Development and Cognition," in *The Disadvantaged Child*, ed. by Martin Deutsch (New York: Basic Books, 1967), pp. 357–69; and R.T. Osborne, "Racial Differences in Mental Growth and School Achievement: A Longitudinal Study," *Psychological Reports* 7 (October 1960): 233–39.

149. Transcript of Minutes of Senate Standing Committee, February 21, 1968, pp. 430–33.

150. Leonard Buder, "Less for Those Who Need More," *New York Times,* December 10, 1972, sec. 4, p. 9.

151. *New York Times,* December 2, 1972, p. 42.

152. Mayor's Advisory Panel, *op. cit.,* pp. 7–8.

153. Interview with Mrs. Beatrice Steinberg, Special Assistant to the Secretary of the Board of Education, New York City, November 1969. The original concept of demonstration school districts apparently called for seven experiments. See Public Schools of New York City, *Staff Bulletin,* May 15, 1967, pp. 3 and 15. Only three were implemented, however—one in Harlem, called the I.S. 201 district, the Ocean Hill-Brownsville district, and the Two Bridges district in lower Manhattan. Of these three, only the first two appear to have become involved in the decentralization debate.

154. Wallace S. Sayre and Herbert Kaufman, *Governing New York City* (New York: Russell Sage Foundation, 1960), p. 712.

155. New York, *Laws of the State of New York* (1967), c. 484, sec. 2.

156. United Federation of Teachers, *The Federation Supports,* p. 1.

157. James A. Robinson and R. Roger Majak, "The Theory of Decision Making," in *Contemporary Political Analysis,* ed. by James C. Charlesworth (New York: Free Press, 1967), pp. 177–79.

158. Amitai Etzioni, *The Active Society* (New York: Free Press, 1968), p. 283.

159. Paul Diesing, *Reason in Society* (Urbana: University of Illinois Press, 1962), p. 184.

160. *New York Times,* November 19, 1972, p. 1.

161. *New York Times,* November 19, 1972, p. 76.

162. *New York Times,* November 30, 1972, p. 1.

163. Leonard Buder, "The Boycott of Schools in East Harlem," *New York Times,* December 2, 1972, p. 42; and Leonard Buder, "Rezoning Schools in Brooklyn District 18," *New York Times,* December 19, 1972, p. 86.

164. Boulton H. Demas, *The School Elections: A Critique of the 1969 New York City School Decentralization,* A Report of the Institute for Community Studies, Queens College, C.U.N.Y. (New York: Institute for Community Studies, March 1971).

165. Edward Banzal, "Misuse of Funds Laid to Schools," *New York Times,* February 8, 1973, p. 48; and Murray Schumach, "Council Acts on Hiring School Guards," *New York Times,* March 1, 1973, p. 1.

Chapter 6
Conclusions

1. For an analysis which challenges the traditional market analysis, to some degree, on the basis of its assumptions about self-interest see Harvey Leibenstein "Allocative Efficiency vs X-Efficiency," *American Economic Review,* 56 (1966), 392–415.

2. Michael P. Brooks and Michael A. Stegman, "Urban Social Policy, Race, and the Education of Planners," *Journal of the American Institute of Planners* 34 (September 1968): 280.

3. Alan A. Altschuler, *The City Planning Process* (Ithaca, N.Y.: Cornell University Press, 1965), p. 398.

4. John T. Howard, "Planning as a Profession," *Journal of the American Institute of Planners* 20 (Spring 1954): 58–59; and John T. Howard, "In Defense of Planning Commissions," *Journal of the American Institute of Planners* 17 (Spring 1951): 89–94.

5. Melville C. Branch, Jr., "Planning and Operations Research," *Journal of the American Institute of Planners* 23 (1957): 168–75.

6. John Freidmann, "Regional Planning as a Field of Study," *Journal of the American Institute of Planners* 29 (August 1963): 168–75.

7. Willard B. Hansen, "Metropolitan Planning and the New Comprehensiveness," *Journal of the American Institute of Planners* 34 (September 1968): 295–302.

8. Paul Davidoff, "Advocacy and Pluralism in Planning," *Journal of the American Institute of Planners* 31 (November 1965): 331–37.

9. Harvey S. Perloff, "New Directions in Social Planning," *Journal of the American Institute of Planners* 31 (November 1965): 297–304.

Index

Advisory decision systems, 68, 103ff.
African-American Teachers Association, 133
Alternatives information, 14, 22; in school decentralization debate, 145–50
Altruistic participation, 58–60, 76, 83, 85, 86, 93ff., 102
Altschuler, A. A., 164
Ambivalent participation, 60–62, 76–80, 87–89, 93ff.
Anti-Defamation League, 133
Association of Black School Supervisors and Administrators, 135

Banfield, E. C., 1, 51, 52, 53, 57, 68, 112, 177
Bargaining and negotiation, 67, 105–07

Citizen participation, 1; in New York City, 115–16
City-Wide Coalition for Community Control of Public Schools, 133
Closed decision systems, 65, 66, 102
Conflicting objectives, 73ff., 102, 103
Control, 2, 3, 26, 110–13, 161ff.
Council of Supervisory Associations, 134

Dahl, R. A., 53, 176
Decision centers, 47–53, 176

Etzioni, A., 1, 45, 157
Evaluation, 14
Expectations about the value of information, 32, 33, 74, 75; in school decentralization debate, 150–53
Expected value of action, 27, 28, 32, 173

Facts and values, 9, 10
Feedback, 15, 23, 177

Groups, 53; motivations of, 54–57

High School Principals Association, 135

Ideal planning process, 16–18
Imperfect control, 37–40, 45, 73, 76; in school decentralization debate, 136ff.
Inconsistent objectives, 91ff., 103–107
Incrementalism, 42

Influence, 64–65, 107ff.; in school decentralization debate, 155–58
Information: decision to collect, 2, 3; definitions, 171–72; quality and quantity, 20; school decentralization debate, 139ff.; types, 12; value of, 20, 21, 24–26

Liberal party, 132
Lindblom, C. E., 1, 42, 112, 145, 151
Lipsky, M., 112

Martin, R. C., 53, 144
Maximal control, 34–37
Mayor's Advisory Panel, 5, 117ff.
Milbrath, L. W., 145
Mixed scanning, 45
Mutually consistent objectives, 82ff., 103–05
Myopic participation, 62–63, 80–81, 87, 89–90, 93ff.

New York City Board of Education, 6, 7, 69, 117, 127–30; Board of Examiners, 135
New York City, mayor, 6, 26, 121–23
New York City school system, 5
New York State Board of Regents, 69, 136
New York State Legislature, 6, 7, 27, 116, 136–39

Objectives configurations, 71–72
Ocean Hill-Brownsville Demonstration School District, 5, 125–27
Open decision systems, 66–68, 103ff.
Organizations, 53; motivations of, 54–57

Participant: motivations of in school decentralization debate, 154–58; resources of in school decentralization debate, 153; types, 57–63
Participatory decision making, 1, 110–13, 161ff.
Planning: consequences of, 27–31; expected findings from, 32, 173
Planning fields, 47–50; members of, 53, 54
Planning process: alternatives to ideal, 18–20; and control, 26; ideal, 16–18
Power, 3, 64–65, 107ff.; in school decentralization debate, 155–58
Preplanning assessments, 26, 27

Problem environment information, 13, 22; in school decentralization debate, 141–45
Problem information, 12, 21; in school decentralization debate, 140
Public decision system, 47–50; types, 65
Public Education Association, 130, 131

Rational decision making, 10–12, 72, 73, 76
Rational decisions, 10
Rational planning, 44

Satisficing, 43
Sayre, W. S. and Kaufman, H., 45, 49
School decentralization, New York City, 5, 26, 27, 69, 70, 107, 109, 115–16

Simon, H. A., 43, 151

Teachers for Community Control, 133
Teachers strikes, 125, 158–59
Time, 40

Uncertainty, 2, 3, 20, 82–84, 91–93, 98–104, 108ff., 172; in school decentralization debate, 136ff., 155–58
United Federation of Teachers, 123-25
United Parents Associations, 131–32

Wiener, N., 1
Wildavsky, A., 67
Wilensky, H. L., 66, 175
Williams, O. P. and Adrian, C. R., 52, 68

About the Author

Stephen S. Skjei holds the B.A. degree from the College of William and Mary, the M.A. from Cambridge University, and the M.R.P. and Ph.D. in City and Regional Planning from the University of North Carolina. In addition to public decision making procedures, his research interests include quantitative approaches to land use planning and the implications of environmental considerations for urban development.